ABOLITION AND SOCIAL WORK

"*Abolition and Social Work* provides a frank and detailed analysis of how social work is shaped by and executes the work of the carceral state, and how social workers committed to abolition are struggling to dismantle criminalization within institutions designed to contain and control people. This book should be required reading for all social work students and everyone else who works closely with social workers—lawyers, nurses, teachers, mental health providers of all kinds. This book breaks the humanitarian illusion of social work and raises the real questions about if and how we can infiltrate its systems to redistribute, disrupt, and support liberation."

—DEAN SPADE, author of *Mutual Aid: Building Solidarity During This Crisis (and the Next)*

"The contributors to this visionary book have offered a timely gift to social workers and other comrades working for freedom. It is both a call to remember the radical origins of social work practice and an invitation to redirect our current and future work—unapologetically—toward justice. We need this guidance more than ever; *Abolition and Social Work* serves as a compelling and timely resource for scholars, activists, and practitioners alike."

—BETH E. RICHIE, author of *Arrested Justice: Black Women, Violence, and America's Prison Nation*

"If you are working to limit or end the violence of policing and prisons, this book is required reading. Gathering the fruits of decades of experience from a wide range of perspectives, editors and contributors illuminate the traps, pitfalls, and dead ends of simply substituting counselors and caseworkers for cops and cages—most important, that caseworkers often act as or collude with cops, policing people instead of supporting them, producing similar and expanded forms of harm. This critical collection invites everyone in a 'caring profession' into a critical assessment of their collusion with the carceral state, points to the promise of an abolitionist approach to care work, and challenges all of us to reach beyond

policing in new forms to radically reimagine how we care for each other. A necessary and critical intervention, right on time."
—ANDREA J. RITCHIE, cofounder of Interrupting Criminalization and coauthor of *No More Police: A Case for Abolition*

"Timely and powerful, this collection is required, transformative reading not just for social workers but for all of us who engage in the daily radical labor to build a more free and flourishing world. Full of key tools to engage in abolitionist practices, *Abolition and Social Work* is a book to study and struggle with now."
—ERICA R. MEINERS, coauthor of *Abolition. Feminism. Now.*

ABOLITION AND SOCIAL WORK

POSSIBILITIES, PARADOXES, AND THE PRACTICE OF COMMUNITY CARE

Edited by
Mimi E. Kim,
Cameron W. Rasmussen,
and Durrell M. Washington Sr.

Haymarket Books
Chicago, Illinois

© 2024 Mimi E. Kim, Cameron W. Rasmussen, and Durrell M. Washington Sr.

Published in 2024 by
Haymarket Books
P.O. Box 180165
Chicago, IL 60618
773-583-7884
www.haymarketbooks.org
info@haymarketbooks.org

ISBN: 979-8-88890-136-6

Distributed to the trade in the US through Consortium Book Sales and Distribution (www.cbsd.com) and internationally through Ingram Publisher Services International (www.ingramcontent.com).

This book was published with the generous support of Lannan Foundation, Wallace Action Fund, and the Marguerite Casey Foundation.

Special discounts are available for bulk purchases by organizations and institutions. Please email info@haymarketbooks.org for more information.

Cover artwork and design by Kill Joy, La Onda Gráfica. Visit joyland.space for more information.

Library of Congress Cataloging-in-Publication data is available.

Contents

	FOREWORD *Mariame Kaba*	vii
	INTRODUCTION *Mimi E. Kim, Cameron W. Rasmussen, and Durrell M. Washington Sr.*	I
1	Society for Social Work and Research Keynote *Angela Y. Davis*	7

Section 1: Possibilities

2	Conceptualizing Abolitionist Social Work *The Network to Advance Abolitionist Social Work*	21
3	Abolitionist Reform for Social Workers *Sam Harrell*	33
4	Indigenist Abolition: A Talk Story on Ideas and Strategies for Social Work Practice *Ramona Beltran, Danica Brown, Annie Zean Dunbar, Katie Schultz, and Angela Fernandez*	46
5	Abolition: The Missing Link in Historical Efforts to Address Racism and Colonialism within the Profession of Social Work *Justin S. Harty, Autumn Asher BlackDeer, María Gandarilla Ocampo, Claudette L. Grinnell-Davis*	65

Section 2: Paradoxes

6	Is Social Work Obsolete? *Kassandra Frederique*	79
7	Abolition and the Welfare State *Mimi E. Kim and Cameron W. Rasmussen*	92
8	Ending Carceral Social Work *Alan Dettlaff*	109
9	Social Work and Family Policing: A Conversation between Joyce McMillan and Dorothy Roberts *Joyce McMillan and Dorothy Roberts*	116
10	Reaching for an Abolitionist Horizon within Professionalized Social-Change Work *Sophia Sarantakos*	130

Section 3: Praxis

11 Staying in Love with Each Other's Survival:
   Practicing at the Intersection of Liberatory Harm Reduction
   and Transformative Justice   143
   Shira Hassan

12 A Conversation with Charlene A. Carruthers
   about Social Work and Abolition   158
   Charlene A. Carruthers and Mimi E. Kim

13 No Restorative Justice Utopia: Abolition and Working with the State 171
   Tanisha "Wakumi" Douglas

14 Boycott, Divestment, Sanctions as Abolitionist Praxis for Social Work 184
   Stéphanie Wahab

15 Abolitionist and Harm Reduction Praxis for Public Sector Mental
   Health Services: An Application to Involuntary Hospitalization   196
   Nev Jones and Leah A. Jacobs

ACKNOWLEDGMENTS   216

NOTES   218

INDEX   235

Foreword

Mariame Kaba

In their contribution to this volume, Sam Harrell discusses a controversy over lynching in the South in 1901 between two social work pioneers, Jane Addams and Ida B. Wells-Barnett.

Both Addams and Wells-Barnett opposed lynching. Addams, though, believed the myths that said that victims of lynching were in fact criminals who had attacked white women. Addams thought lynching was wrong only because it failed to control "the bestial in man," by which she meant that it failed to prevent Black criminality. She argued that Black men in the South should be incarcerated through rule of law.

Wells-Barnett, in contrast, saw clearly that lynching was not a misguided effort to restrain Black violence, but was instead a vicious, violent effort to impose white supremacy through murder and terror. Addams, Wells-Barnett said, was effectively making a "plea for the lyncher," and in doing so was excusing "America's national crime."

Wells-Barnett has been a touchstone of mine for years. I helped to raise tens of thousands of dollars to build a monument to her legacy in Chicago. Her courageous work against lynching made her a target for the violence she decried. Her newspaper in Memphis was firebombed in 1892, and the threat of violence forced her to leave the south for three decades.[1] After she moved to Chicago, she became a probation officer for Cook County. The salary helped cover the costs of the Negro Fellowship League (NFL), which she founded in 1910, and which found thousands of Black people employment and housing.[2]

Wells-Barnett, then, worked as a social worker both inside and outside the state to help those in her community confront racism, violence, and enforced poverty. Yet, despite her example—and in some ways because of it—I find myself deeply ambivalent and even conflicted about social work as a profession.

Social work has the potential to attend to the material needs of people and their communities. And yet, as Addams' ambivalent statements on lynching show, social work has also been a conservative and sometimes harmful profession, which has embraced carceral violence and racism rather than liberation.

Soft Policing

In our book *No More Police: A Case for Abolition*, Andrea Ritchie and I discuss what we call "soft policing."[3] Soft policing is surveillance, hostile regulation, and incarceration done by an official who is not a cop. You may encounter soft policing in schools, in hospitals, and in offices, where the soft police may be teachers, doctors, nurses, bureaucrats—or social workers.

This volume includes numerous examples of ways in which social workers may find themselves acting as a supposedly kinder, supposedly gentler police force, whose purpose is not to replace cops but to expand their reach.

In their conversation on "Social Work and Family Policing," for example, Joyce McMillan and Dorothy Roberts discuss the brutality of the child "welfare" system. "So-called residential therapeutic centers are like prisons. They are violent places where no child should be," Roberts says. But because the centers are not *called* prisons, people are OK with, or even eager to, incarcerate children inside them.

Mimi E. Kim and Cameron W. Rasmussen write about the way that the welfare state, administered by social workers, and the prison industrial complex have become interwoven, "integrating social and penal regulations toward a cumulative punishment of individuals who are poor and disproportionately Black." Social workers are in prisons to supposedly provide care; police officers are in shelters and schools and offices to supposedly provide safety. The result is a seamless web of surveillance, which demands obedience to a regime of paternalistic kindness under threat of violent coercion.

Again, the problem is not just that soft policing reproduces a milder form of policing. The problem is that soft policing, like social work, can make policing seem more palatable or can prevent us from imagining abolitionist possibilities.

For example, some organizations, attempting to propose alternatives to policing, use slogans such as "Counselors, Not Cops" or "Treatment, Not Punishment." These may sound, on the surface, like abolitionist sentiments. But in fact they imagine that soft police—school counselors, treatment facility staff—will continue to regulate and control marginalized and targeted populations.

Abolitionist slogans, in contrast, would call for "Care, Not Cops" and "Books, Not Bars." A world without police is one in which individuals have the ability to care for themselves and each other—to determine both the help they can ask for and the help they can offer. It's a vision of mutual aid, rather than a vision of top-down control imposed, magically, with fewer uniforms and fewer guns.

Andrea Ritchie and I emphasized that "imagining a future *without policing* is not the same as a future without *police*."[4] As abolitionists, we seek a society of mutual care, not punishment, in which access to resources is equitable and abundant rather than regimented and restricted to the powerful through hierarchical surveillance.

Social workers have many incentives to work with police, or to model themselves on police. Institutional connections to the police can give social workers access to funds, prestige, and influence. Social workers who embrace soft policing are granted authority over others and told by institutions, donors, and politicians that they are benevolent saviors dispensing tough love.

It's not a surprise, then, that social workers are too often tempted to collaborate, treating those they work with as "perfect, passive, submissive victims needing help from the state," as Shira Hassan in this volume describes the approach of one shelter. "Keeping the institutions lawsuit free and the system intact, is the primary purpose of hospital administrators and the vast majority of mainstream nonprofits," Hassan adds. The carceral state calls social workers to soft policing, and it's a difficult call to ignore.

Ida B. Wells-Barnett and Abolitionist Social Work

Social work has been so entangled in the carceral state, and so involved in soft policing, that it sometimes feels like "abolitionist social work" must be an oxymoron. Ida B. Wells-Barnett's life and work, though, provide a blueprint for how social work and abolitionist practice can inspire and build on one another.

Wells-Barnett was born enslaved in 1862. She became a teacher, a journalist, and an activist. And, as I've mentioned, she was also a social worker. She founded the Negro Fellowship League (NFL) in 1908 in Chicago with a group of the Bible study class students.

The NFL offered many services associated with social work. But it did so in the context of mutual aid and outreach, rather than as a punitive arm of the state. It had a reading room and a quiet place to study and write letters—no small thing at a time when Black people were barred from most public establishments and would not have had access to many libraries. It offered lectures from white and Black public intellectuals like Jane Addams and William Monroe Trotter.

More, the NFL provided housing. The Great Migration was underway, as Black people fled the Jim Crow south in hopes of a better life up north. In the NFL, young Black men could get a bed at 50 cents a night and/or meals. The organization also helped people find employment; the NFL placed 115 men in jobs during its first year of operation.[5]

The NFL didn't just work in accordance with proto-abolitionist principles, though. It directly worked to support prisoners and to protect Black men in particular from injustice. Wells-Barnett and her husband Ferdinand Lee Barnett worked through the NFL to provide representation to men who were falsely accused of crimes and to secure the release of convicted individuals.

One example is Wells-Barnett's involvement in the case of Chicken Joe Campbell, a Black man imprisoned in Joliet Prison. In 1915, the warden's wife was killed in a fire, and Campbell was accused of murdering her. The evidence was weak, but after being "confined to solitary in complete darkness for fifty hours on bread and water"[6] and then subjected to forty hours of questioning, Campbell broke down and signed a confession.

Wells-Barnett took up the call immediately. She wrote a letter to local papers in which she demanded, "Is this justice? Is this humanity? Can we stand to see a dog treated in such a fashion without protest?"[7] She also had her husband Ferdinand, a lawyer, volunteer to defend Campbell. After Campbell was convicted in 1916, Wells-Barnett and Ferdinand supported him through three appeals, and finally helped convince the governor to commute his death sentence to life in prison.

When I am feeling run down and exhausted from working to dismantle this criminal injustice system, I think of Ida B. Wells-Barnett. She was able to secure individual contributions and some grant funding for the first couple of years of the NFL's existence. But her politics were too radical for most funders. From 1913 to 1916, she had to sustain the organization on her $150 monthly salary from her work as a probation officer. In 1920, the NFL had to close when the money ran out.

Many in the abolitionist community, including me, can relate to that; we all know what it means to try to sustain organizations without much funding, subsidizing our activism with our own funds. What I respect most about Ida is her integrity and her uncompromising dedication to supporting the most marginalized people by any means necessary.

Wells-Barnett's Legacy

For social workers in our day as in Wells-Barnett's, you can choose to receive adequate private and state funding or you can do abolitionist work. To do both is rarely an option.

Despite the barriers, though, many social workers do try to follow in Ida's footsteps, offering mutual aid and assistance to those most in need without coercion or state surveillance and standing with incarcerated and oppressed people rather than over them, or between them and access to resources. This book offers a number of examples of abolition-informed social work initiatives.

Nev Jones and Leah A. Jacobs, for example, talk about ways in which social workers can work against or reduce the harm done by involuntary hospitalizations. One recommendation is simply to provide debriefings in which the harm of involuntary incarceration is acknowledged—a seemingly commonsense intervention that is almost never implemented because it would mean admitting that social workers and the mental health infrastructure can themselves cause harm. Stéphanie Wahab writes about the importance for social workers of standing in solidarity with the Palestinian BDS movement, arguing that—as for Wells-Barnett—a social work committed to equality and justice can't shy away from activism or from unpopular causes.

The promise of social work is often a carceral promise. The state and its representatives look to social workers when cops seem too violent or too expensive—when they need "someone else" to call or "somewhere else" to incarcerate people. Ida Wells-Barnett, though, and the contributors to this book, show that social work can do more than just tape some cushions to the bars. It can work to pull them down.

Introduction

Mimi E. Kim, Cameron W. Rasmussen, and Durrell M. Washington Sr.

Defund the Police: Fund Social Workers?

In the summer of 2020, mass outrage over the police murders of George Floyd, Breonna Taylor, Tony McDade, and so many other Black and Brown victims of police violence reverberated from urban centers to rural outposts across the United States and the globe. As many as twenty-five million people, many of whom had never joined a protest, went to the streets to name police brutality and white supremacy not as aberrations, but as enduring US institutions. Demands to dismantle and defund were met with urgent imaginings of what could take their place.

During this time, social work was touted as an alternative that could ameliorate the violence of the police. But just as placards were raised to champion social work as a solution, the profession was called out for its own traditions of police collaboration and role in the surveillance and discipline of this country's dispossessed, shaped along the contours of race, class, gender, sexuality, migration status, ability, and age. Social work, its many critics claimed, was not an alternative but rather a representative of *soft police*,[1] rooted in its historical stance as defender of white supremacist notions of the good citizen versus the unruly immigrant, the undeserving welfare queen, the bad mother, the absent father, the uncivilized, the traitorous, the sinful, the criminal, the mad. Social work, in its role as the soft police, collaborated in the identification of those who had been literally named as *deviant* and offered a promise to discipline, care for, save, and, if necessary, rid society of those who do not conform to white middle-class heteropatriarchal standards of citizenship.

Some of social work's harshest critics have come from its own ranks. Their intimate knowledge of the mechanisms of discipline from their own roles as social workers (degreed or not), social work scholars and academics, policy makers, and, in many cases, service users informed both critique and vision of what could be. The summer of 2020 captured these imaginations, outrage, despair, and collective demands for radical change, just as it had for the other twenty-five million who joined the protests. However, a discipline and profession short on self-criticism and easily satisfied with its ill-defined tenet of *social justice*[2] faced deepening fractures over its own failures to deliver this mission.

It is in this context that social workers, many of whom were located at the subversive margins of the field, found each other on the signature rosters of public pronouncements condemning social work's long-time collusion with law enforcement. Deep critics of the child welfare system, resonating with the sentiments of critical scholars such as Dorothy Roberts, began to organize public forums and echo Joyce McMillan's demands for "mandated support" rather than mandates to report. Challenges to the very pillars of social work, once silenced, began to gain ground. What was once incomprehensible began to seem logical—even common sense.

The Emergence of Abolitionist Social Work

For the anti-carceral or abolitionist within and at the margins of social work,[3] the protests of 2020 and the moment of public acclaim, derision, and takedown of social work as an alternative to policing offered an opportunity for the naming and definition of *abolitionist social work*. That summer of 2020, we as coeditors came together with others in our social work community to form the Network to Advance Abolitionist Social Work (NAASW), echoing and subverting the acronym of the National Association of Social Work (NASW), which had long represented the vexed tenets of the profession. In June 2020, the president of NASW had publicly responded to the call for social work by reaffirming the role of the field in its historic position flanking the police, adding social work's attention to *care* to soften and ameliorate the harsher functions of the police. A rapid-fire critique of the NASW position resulted in

1,140 signatures by social workers protesting the soft policing role of the profession.[4] These positions and the further critiques and defenses that ensued mapped the lines of contention and contradiction that animated an unprecedented demand for and by social workers to name, imagine, and manifest what some were beginning to call *abolitionist social work*.

The coeditors of this book similarly found each other, connecting through the sinewy networks of what is now known as abolition. We represent subversive practitioners of transformative justice or nonpolice interventions to domestic and sexual violence, those whose personal ties to and professional work with people inside the carceral system fueled a commitment to the abolition of cages altogether, and wayward social work academics committed to radical questioning and the possibility of transformative change. In 2020, NAASW provided a collective platform for what some of us had long ago prefigured as an abolitionist social work, sometimes articulated as *anti-carceral*, especially during a time when abolition as a concept was less familiar or prompted anxieties that distracted from the content. This historical moment opened up opportunities for a more overt abolitionist stance. Later in the summer of 2020, NAASW presented our first public presentation on abolitionist social work in the form of a Haymarket Books webinar. The webinar offered the title that inspired this book, further informing its content and organization. Through the introduction of the words *abolitionist social work* to the public domain, we joined with others to shape a still-emergent political location of possibilities, paradoxes, and praxis.

Abolition and Social Work versus Abolitionist Social Work

Through our journey from that first webinar toward the publication of this book, energetic debates[5] in the intersecting space of abolition and social work raised questions about whether the establishment of an *abolitionist social work* is even a meaningful or worthy goal. Rather, politically aligned critics asked if the compounding of those words might distract us from more important struggles and priorities of our work as abolitionists *through*, *despite*, or *around* the project of social work. The book's title reflects these debates and the wisdom that these questions raise. As scholars, organizers, and editors of this book, we are less concerned with the formalization of an *abolitionist social work*, or the drawing of boundaries of what does and does not fit into a more rigid formulation. We are instead focused on the examination of whether and how we can bring abolitionist principles and politics into social work and the possibilities, paradoxes, and praxis that come from this exploration.

Organization of the Book

Abolition and Social Work: Possibilities, Paradoxes, and the Practice of Community Care centers, probes, and problematizes the relationship between abolition and social work, more productively examining the intersection of abolition in engagement with the project of social work without presuming nor preempting the merging of the two. The book asks: (1) Does social work indeed hold any promise in bolstering the work of abolition? (2) In the context of abolition, what are the paradoxes of and tensions within social work given the roots, traditions, and trajectories of the profession? (3) Are there examples of social work praxis rooted in abolitionist principles that can ground and inform further praxis? Could these examples demonstrate the possibilities of a future *abolitionist social work*?

Possibilities

The possibilities of bringing abolitionist politics and principles to social work lie not only in a developing solidarity against the prison industrial complex, but in the remaking of a social work committed to ending racial capitalism and settler colonialism and to a social work praxis rooted in the realization of self-determination, collective care, and mass well-being. This book, in part, aims to offer a place to envision the possibilities of making social work the work of abolition and to articulate why and how those possibilities are compelling and feasible. This portion of the book brings together abolitionist and social work thinkers and organizers to offer scaffolding toward bringing these two worlds together, in ways that address the harms of social work while strengthening the liberatory visions and praxis of abolition.

Paradoxes

Considering the possibilities of abolition and social work reveals many tensions and contradictions. At its core, abolition is anti-carceral and built on solidarity and the liberation of all people, especially those most marginalized. However, social workers and the profession itself have been deeply entrenched in the very systems that abolitionists are fighting to dismantle. Social work has a long history of reinforcing domination and separation, starting with the racially divided settlement houses created by those who are recognized as venerable founders of the profession. As a central feature of the welfare state, social work has continued to cloak its disciplining function under the cover of care, further strengthened by claims to the ill-defined NASW tenet of *social justice*. The rise of social work's professionalization has brought an increased perception of its legitimacy, but its quest for recognition as a "serious" profession comes with a cost. The drive to legitimization requires submission to dominant ideologies and existing power structures. Even explicit commitments to social change are bereft of meaning if the mechanisms are to be subsumed under those acceptable to the status quo. Such collusions have limited any force that social work might have at challenging and transforming the structural conditions at the root of white heteropatriarchal supremacy that continue to generate gaping inequalities and profound, systemic human suffering. Very few spaces in professional social work remain immune to these realities. This section of the book explores the contradictions and tensions embedded in social work's complicity in carceral systems and examines the deep ties to racial capitalism and neoliberalism that have long captured the profession.

Praxis

The pervasiveness of the disciplining and regulating role of social work can often obscure and muddy the quotidian examples of abolitionist praxis that exist in the social work community. Many in social work are yearning for more examples of abolitionist praxis. This final portion of the book provides concrete illustrations of efforts that are aligned with the bridging of abolition and social work. These chapters reveal hidden treasures of abolitionist praxis—slow experiments; collective life-in-action of those with lived experiences of oppression, trauma, and brilliance;

and abolitionist-inspired programs subversively crafted from conditions of regulation and domination. From the creation of mutual aid and transformative justice practices outside of the state, to abolitionist aligned international solidarity with Palestine, to liberatory forms of social work led by those with lived experience—these works demonstrate the various ways that we can escape from, wrestle with, and directly challenge the fraught and compromising relationships of organized care within regulatory and punitive state institutions. We end our book with these brilliant examples to bring to life the intersections of abolition and social work, or perhaps of an emergent *abolitionist social work*, and to honor those who have already been moving the work of abolition from theory to praxis.

Society for Social Work and Research Keynote

Angela Y. Davis

We begin our book with a speech made by Dr. Angela Y. Davis at the Society for Social Work and Research (SSWR) annual conference on January 17, 2019. In this historic talk, Dr. Davis highlights the prominence of Black feminists—Black women, Black trans women—in the struggles to end sexual violence and create collective, abolitionist responses to violence in all of its forms. This talk emphasizes the failures of white feminists to acknowledge the central location of Black women as survivors of pervasive, devastating, and systemic forms of gender-based violence and as oft-forgotten leaders in a broad and powerful antiviolence movement. In highlighting *abolition feminism*, Dr. Davis offers a guiding light for our work as abolitionists at the intersection of social work practice, scholarship, and radical organizing. We are honored to present these words for the first time in print and are forever grateful to Dr. Davis for her generosity as a racial justice, feminist, abolitionist, and anti-capitalist movement leader, scholar, and mentor.

Society for Social Work and Research—2019 Presidential Plenary Session with Dr. Angela Davis

Before I begin my presentation, I would like to acknowledge that we convene here this afternoon on Ohlone land and that we cannot afford to minimize the genocidal violence of settler colonialism that continues to affect the lives of Indigenous people. So the very least that we can do here in San Francisco this afternoon is to recognize our debt to the Ohlone and to express ongoing solidarity with the struggles of the first peoples of this continent.

I want to thank the Society for Social Work and Research for inviting me to participate in your 2019 conference, the theme of which is "Ending Gender-Based Family and Community Violence." Your contributions as faculty, as researchers, as students, and as activists are especially important during this extraordinarily difficult historical moment, both within the United States as well as in other parts of the world.

I had a wonderful meeting with the board of directors of this organization this afternoon, during which I had the opportunity to learn about the history and mission of your organization. So I want to tell you, first of all, that I especially appreciate your efforts to articulate together what are often considered to be very different modes of violence: gender violence, family violence, community violence. As a result of the academic training we receive, we are encouraged to treat each form of violence as discrete and unconnected from other expressions of violence. However, all of these modes of violence are linked to institutional and ideological structures that are responsible for their seeming permanence in our worlds. I really like the fact that your theme not only draws attention to the connections among these violences, but to the fact that they can be ended—that these violences can be ended. We do not have to assume that women, Black women, Indigenous women, disabled women, trans women, and all of the identities that may be embraced by the category women—we do not have to assume that they will forever be the targets of gender-based violence.

We do not have to assume that intimate violence, child abuse, incest will forever be associated with the form of collectivity we call the family. We do not have to assume that the proliferation of guns—well over three hundred million guns in the hands of civilian people in this country—along with police violence, gang violence, school shootings—will be forever defining features of our communities. And, of course, gender, family, and community violence are deeply connected to the violence of the state—repressive apparatuses such as institutions of policing and punishment and machineries of intelligence and war.

As someone who has had a very long history of radical social justice activism, I have always appreciated the insights, perspectives, and practices from the field of social work—especially critical, radical social work—that have helped to guide movements for social justice. I first became aware of the connections between social work and radical social transformation many, many years ago, when I learned from my own mother about her career aspirations as a young girl. My mother, Sallye Bell Davis, grew up as a foster child under extremely impoverished circumstances in the small Alabama town of Sylacauga—a town of less than thirteen thousand today, probably no more than three thousand people at the time, with a very small percentage of Black people. Education and every other aspect of society there were strictly segregated. I suppose she first learned about social work because she was in the foster system. Her foster parents, who were older, believed that her role after finishing elementary school was to seek work and help to support them. These were the expectations of that era. And as there were no nearby high schools for Black students, her chances of a further education were practically nil. But because one of her elementary school teachers had so emphasized the value of an education, at the age of thirteen or so, my mother left Sylacauga against the wishes of her foster parents and moved to Birmingham in order to attend high school. And when we were little, she used to tell us this story all the time. We heard it over and over again—so much that we failed to understand the extraordinary nature of a child, who could decide at age thirteen to basically run away from home in order to go to high school. So, as you might surmise, she held educators in great esteem, and eventually became a teacher herself. She finished high school and college in Birmingham and eventually earned a postgraduate degree at New York University.

When my siblings and I were young, my mother spoke a great deal about wanting to be a social worker—it was from her that I first learned about the field. When she attended the only Black high school, originally named Negro High School, it had been renamed Industrial High School, and later it became A.H. Parker High School, the high school I attended. My mother lived in a room at the YWCA [Young Women's Christian Association], and she paid for that room and her other expenses by doing domestic work. Her experience at the Y left such an impression on her that she spoke about it as a defining period of her life. There she probably came into contact with Black social workers who believed in social justice and whom she wanted to emulate. And, incidentally, I also spent a lot of my time as a young girl at the Y. And it was only later that I realized how radical the YWCA has been. As a matter of fact, when I was on trial, decades ago, facing three capital charges, the YWCA sent a representative, who was in the courtroom for the entire duration of my trial.

During the generations after slavery, Black women had few alternatives to agricultural work and domestic work. During the early decades of the twentieth century, so many Black women and their families deposited their dreams and aspirations into the fields of teaching and social work. Historically, these were also the fields that promised to provide a refuge from the threat of sexual violence that saturated domestic and agricultural work—a refuge both in terms of the economic security they represented and also in terms of the knowledges they could generate about the institutions and structures responsible for the production and reproduction of violence.

If I were asked what kind of world I would ultimately like to see, I think I could summarize my desire for race, gender, economic justice, equality, and freedom simply by saying, "I want a world without violence, without racist violence, without gender violence, without economic violence, without war." My earliest childhood memories are the explosive sounds of racist violence emanating from the bombings of a house across the street from my family's home. Later we discovered that the same KKK members who bombed that house would also bomb Black churches (including the church we attended), synagogues, and other homes in Birmingham and eventually bombed the 16th Street Baptist Church. We lived on the border of a neighborhood that was zoned for Black people; the neighborhood across the street being zoned as white—*officially* zoned as white. Whenever a Black family bought homes in the white area (assisted, of course by progressive white people), their house was either dynamited or burned.

I also remember a late-night knock on our front door by a woman who was fleeing a man whom I later found out had raped her. In elementary school I remember whispered conversations about a classmate and friend who had been the target of sexual assault. And I distinctly remember questioning in my own mind why she was assumed to be responsible for this act of violence against her. Around the same time, Emmett Till was lynched because of a putatively sexualized comment to a white woman in Money, Mississippi.

I make these autobiographical observations as a preface to a brief discussion about the way we periodize the antiviolence movement, the antirape movement, the movement against domestic violence. The US antirape movement is most frequently periodized in connection with the 1966 founding of the National Organization for Women and the later creation of a task force on rape. Without wanting to minimize the important work that has been done over the years and without undermining the eventual emergence of a very powerful antirape and antiviolence movement, I do want to trouble this genealogy.

Genealogies should always be questioned because there's always an unacknowledged reason for beginning at a certain moment in history as opposed to another. Looking at the genealogy of the antiviolence movement, one can question how the work against rape and sexual violence that occurred within the Southern Black Freedom Movement came to be so marginalized, so much so that it required many years of research and activism to recognize Rosa Parks for the role she played in antirape activism. So we are challenging the legendary misrepresentation of Rosa Parks as someone who refused to move to the back of the bus because she was a "tired old woman." She was definitely not "tired" in the way the story goes. She herself often pointed out she wasn't even old when she refused to move to the back of the bus. In fact, Rosa Parks was an organizer. She was a trained and experienced organizer. She and her husband were actively involved in the campaign to free the Scottsboro Nine. As many scholars and activists have pointed out, the struggle to defend Black men from fraudulent rape charges was directly linked to the defense of Black women who were the targets of rape. Rape and the racist use and manipulation of the rape charge were directly connected.

So in the 1930s—long before the 1955 Montgomery boycott—Rosa Parks was an active participant in the movement to free the Scottsboro Nine, who were facing fraudulent charges of raping a white woman. In 1944, when she was a leader of the NAACP [National Association for the Advancement of Colored People], she served as lead investigator of the gang rape by white boys of Recy Taylor in the town of Abbeville, Alabama. Rosa Parks then founded the Committee for Equal Justice for Mrs. Recy Taylor, which launched an international campaign, characterized by the *Chicago Defender* as the strongest campaign for equal justice in a decade. Interestingly, this has been completely erased from our historical memory. As a matter of fact, it has been pointed out that the Montgomery Improvement Association, of which Dr. Martin Luther King later became the head, emerged from this committee for Equal Justice for Mrs. Recy Taylor. In terms of genealogies, there's a direct line between this campaign against sexual violence and the emergence of a full-blown Civil Rights movement in connection with the Montgomery bus boycott.

But how could this happen? Why? And why did white women anti-rape activists fail to acknowledge that history and how important it might have been to cultivate a political consciousness that linked sexual violence to racism? In this context, I want to evoke the name of Anne Braden. Some of you may be aware of her work. She was an extraordinary Southern white woman antiracist leader. In 1972, Ann Braden (who, incidentally, was a friend of my mother and a political mentor for me) wrote an open letter addressed to white Southern women ["A Letter to White Southern Women" in *Anne Braden Speaks*, Ben Wilkins, ed., 2022].

At that moment, Anne was envisioning a strong and powerful multiracial women's movement. She wrote: "[W]e haven't had that kind of strength and don't now because of the deep chasm that divides white women from Black in our society. A chasm created by crimes committed in the name of white womanhood."

She went on to say: "[I]t may seem paradoxical, but in this racist society, we who are white will overcome our oppression as women only when we reject once and for all the privileges conferred on us by our white skin. For these privileges are not real. They are a device through which we are kept under control."

Moreover, "[W]e can make a beginning toward building a really strong women's movement as we openly reject and fight racist myths that have kept us divided. We can begin by joining with our Black Sisters in a campaign to free Thomas Walmsley and go on from there to free others and ourselves."

The case of Thomas Walmsley—you can look up at this important case of the early '70s involving a young Black man who, like so many others, was a target of the racist manipulation of the rape charge.

As many scholars and activists have pointed out, existing social hierarchies have determined who gets to be a legitimate survivor of gender violence, who gets to represent those who constitute legitimate victims. Beth Richie, in her wonderful book, *Arrested Justice, Black Women, Violence and America's Prison Nation* [NYU Press; 2012], has written about the *everywoman*, who populates our imaginaries regarding gender violence. As she has pointed out, the everywoman is actually a racialized construction—this *everywoman* is racialized as white. And so this leads us to the question, why is it so difficult to posit Black women and women of color as exemplary? Why cannot women of color stand in for all women?

This is the question that Tarana Burke asks. Black women's experiences are rich and generative, but why are they considered experiences that relate only to Black women or, at the most, women of color? Perhaps if it had not been assumed that we had to work with the most general of categories, and perhaps if racist hierarchies were not already internalized within that presumption of generality, we might have recognized the epistemological value of holding on to the specific and the particular.

This is the lesson, I think, that the Black Lives Matter movement has been trying to impart to us a century and a half after this insight should have animated our history. That is to say that there are those who assume that the call to make Black Lives Matter is only a call about Black people, whereas the logic actually goes something like this: if ever Black lives were to truly matter, that would mean that all lives matter. But white has always been the subject of generalization and universalization. Asian American, Black, Latinx, Indigenous always remained at the level of the particular, that which cannot be helpful in the production of the category "women."

Why also do we assume that disabled women are to be treated always as a marginalized category? Disabled women have a 40 percent greater risk of intimate violence, especially, as the American Psychological

Association has pointed out, with more severe consequences than their nondisabled sisters. Why are trans women, especially if they are Black trans women and trans women of color, why are they always dismissed and demeaned? Why can we not recognize that if we want to eradicate gender violence from our worlds, we have to address the conditions surrounding those who are most subject to violence, intimate violence, stranger violence, economic violence, state violence?

The Human Rights Campaign, which advocates for justice for LGBTQ [lesbian, gay, bisexual, transgender, queer] communities, recently released a report entitled *The National Epidemic: Fatal Anti-Transgender Violence in America* in 2018. And, of course, the overwhelming majority of trans women killed are women of color. Beth Richie's analysis in *Arrested Justice* points to the pitfalls of assuming that the figure of the middle class cis heterosexual white woman should stand in for all targets of gender violence. If, on the other hand, one looks at Black women, Black trans women, there are insights to be gleaned that would have been otherwise unavailable. I frequently emphasize the insights that emerge from work around trans prisoners—not only insights about physical and psychological violence, but also about ideological and epistemic violence. Moreover, in this context we have learned that as an institution, prison is not only a repressive apparatus, but rather also a gendering apparatus. It is not only an apparatus of punishment, but it ideologically reproduces the gender binary. This insight would not have been available had we not begun with the experiences of trans prisoners.

So how does our view of gender violence, family violence, community violence change if we look at it from the vantage point of Black women, Indigenous women, poor women? Because of the assumed privatization of the lives of middle-class white women and because the private sphere is supposed to be a haven of freedom, Catherine MacKinnon and other feminist scholars have examined these contradictions. If privacy is the sphere to be juridically protected, for example, in *Roe v. Wade*, it is necessary to acknowledge the limitations of this logic. One may have the abstract "right" to privacy, without having access to the privacy that allows one access to the right. In the case of *Roe v. Wade*, this privacy refers to the relationship between a woman and her doctor. So what happens to all of those women who enjoy no such privacy, who enter into no such relationships? While they may enjoy that right abstractly, abortion has become effectively illegal for women who cannot afford to pay for it, women who can't afford to have their own doctors. Moreover, constructing the sphere as a sphere that deserves protection invites the securing of that freedom through repressive apparatuses. This process simply does not work for those who are never acknowledged as subjects of freedom in the private sphere.

So what I'm suggesting is that an analysis that does not explore the structural basis of violence can easily rely on carceral methods to address gender violence. If it is assumed that gender violence is an individual problem, then the individual perpetrator, whose accountability is rendered through the juridical realm, can only be subjected to carceral violence. Thus the so-called solution ends up recapitulating and reproducing the problem of gender violence.

So this is a critique of what is often referred to as *carceral feminism*. The tendency to think about gender violence as a collection of individual problems attributable to individual perpetrators and primarily affecting specific individuals emanates from the failure to consider the social and economic conditions endemic to gender violence.

How many of you have seen Dream Hampton's documentary series *Surviving R. Kelly* [aired January 3 to January 5, 2019, on Lifetime]? Dream Hampton is a phenomenal documentarian. This is not only an exposé based on the testimony of many young women who were targeted by R. Kelly, but it is also a look at the complex forces that pushed him to systematically dehumanize and physically and psychologically assault so many young Black women. And this is what we often fail to do. We don't ask why, and we therefore tend to rely on criminalization as the only possible answer. But criminalization prevents us from exploring how we might actually begin to *end* to this violence. Criminalization assumes that the violence will recur repeatedly, and that the only solution is to send the perpetrators to prison.

But prisons are ideological apparatuses as well. They are not only punishment apparatuses and gendering apparatuses, but also sites into which we can deposit those problems about which we simply do not want to think. And so, by assuming that by sending perpetrators to prison, we have addressed the problem of gender violence, we absolve ourselves of the responsibility of attempting to figure out how to extricate our worlds from these horrendous forms of violence.

I haven't yet seen all of the episodes of *Surviving R. Kelly*. It's very hard to watch. It's especially hard to listen to the testimony of these young women who have been so deeply hurt by the actions of R. Kelly. Jim DeRogatis, a music journalist, who has been collecting interviews over the years—this goes way back—said that "[t]he saddest fact I've learned is nobody matters less to our society than young Black women. Nobody."

I will move toward a conclusion by suggesting an alternative to carceral feminism, which we have begun to call *abolition feminism*. W. E. B. Du Bois imagined that the best outcome of the abolition of slavery, which did not happen, of course, would have been to reframe the very democratic framework of US society at that time. It would not have been to simply end the discrete institution of slavery, but rather to ask what kind of society would we need in order to guarantee the incorporation of a formerly enslaved people into a new democracy? That is the question that should have been asked then. It was not about focusing so myopically on the people who had suffered under slavery as much as it was about changing the larger society. And if you think about, our tendency always to focus on the particular problematic without asking questions about the larger framework—how do we deal with racism, diversity, and inclusion? It doesn't matter that everything else remains the same. The society remains or the institution remains as racist as it was before the diversity, before the inclusion. Abolition feminism calls upon us to have a more capacious understanding of the changes that need to be made— not simply to focus on the instance of violence—not simply to focus on one institution. Abolition feminism urges us to understand the serious limitations of the concept of prison reform—the idea that you can create a better prison while leaving the society that gave rise to it intact. This is actually a contradiction in terms.

Finally, I want to remind us that we live in the world. We don't just live in a place called the United States of America. We live in the world, and gender violence is the most pandemic form of violence in the world. We need to remind ourselves that gender violence is linked to the so-called crisis at the border. There's no crisis at the border. And if there is a crisis, it has to do with femicide and other conditions that are forcing people to leave their home countries, conditions oftentimes produced by corporations located in the United States.

We live in the world, a world where Brazilian feminist Marielle Franco, who spoke out against gender violence, racist police violence, and against community violence, was assassinated in Rio de Janeiro for her activism. We live in a world where Leyla Güven, who is in prison in Turkey, has been on a hunger strike for the last two months for speaking out on behalf of the Kurdish people. She has spoken out against the isolation of Abdullah Öcalan, leader of the Kurdish Workers' Party, and she has especially championed the Kurdish women's movement. We live in a world where Rasmea Odeh, a Palestinian-American activist previously subject to horrendous forms of sexual violence by the Israeli military, was recently deported from the US to Jordan, where she continues to organize against the occupation.

Some of you may be aware that I was recently offered a human rights award by the Birmingham Civil Rights Institute in Birmingham, Alabama. And because I try to stand in solidarity with people all over the world, including the Palestinian people, the award was rescinded. I had been excited about this award because it was named after Fred Shuttlesworth, whom I had known as a child. I went to high school with his daughter, Patricia. Moreover, when my mother was alive, she was one of the institute's most passionate volunteers. Odessa Woolfolk, my Sunday School teacher, was the founder and the very heart of the Civil Rights Institute. While I am very sad that this controversy is affecting the reputation of the institute, I am excited that not only have on-the-ground organizers and activists in Birmingham stepped up to the plate (including the founder and my former Sunday School teacher!), but people all over the country and all over the world are speaking out. This response includes a significant number of Jewish people. For example, I just received a wonderful supportive letter from a large organization of Reconstructionist rabbis supporting me.

So what I'm saying is, I'm actually now glad that this happened—although I'm sorry that the reputation of the Civil Rights Institute has to suffer. I hope that they will be able to build that institution in ways that recognize what Dr. Martin Luther King called the *indivisibility of justice*.

But I don't think it is accidental that people are responding with support and solidarity at this time.

I want to close by pointing out that this is a very special historical conjuncture. And oftentimes we don't recognize these moments when we are directly experiencing them. We only recognize them later, once they have passed. But it is important to adopt a historical perspective when one is right in the middle of things. I think that this is a special time for challenges to misogyny, for challenges to racism—not only here, but throughout the world—challenges to anti-Semitism. And it is essential that we link struggles against anti-Semitism to struggles against racism. I would suggest that we combine our scholarship, our activism, with our collective passion and imagination. In this way we can hope to move forward in a confident way toward a far better future than the one that is currently imagined by those in the leadership of this country.

Thank you very much.

section 1

POSSIBILITIES

2

Conceptualizing Abolitionist Social Work

The Network to Advance Abolitionist Social Work

Introduction

The uprisings of the summer of 2020 became one of the largest protest movements in the history of the United States. The large-scale organizing and mass protests of that summer were made possible by many years of organizing work, done by the Movement for Black Lives and countless other groups across the country, and were propelled by centuries of struggle for Black liberation—from the resistance by enslaved people in the United States to the first abolitionist movement to end slavery to the Black Panthers and beyond. Conversation and action about mutual aid, resistance to state violence, and abolition surged broadly that summer, leading both to opportunities to build as well as unfortunate opportunities for the co-optation of abolitionist principles and strategies. Social work was held out by some as an alternative response to police and by others as an addition to policing models that could somehow "fix" the brokenness of the existing systems. These suggestions were often put forth with little to no recognition of the long history of policing by the social work profession itself.

The Network to Advance Abolitionist Social Work (NAASW) was one of many formations that took shape during the 2020 uprisings. It began as an effort to challenge the idea that social work and the police are ever compatible, and it seeks to explore the ways that social work both limits and advances the realization of a world where people have access to the things that are foundational to personal and community safety[1] and a world without police, prisons, and surveillance.

The roots of the NAASW date back to earlier anticriminalization organizing efforts and a long history of radical social work. In 2015, a group of social workers in New York City created a formation called Social Workers Against Criminalization (SWAC). Similar to NAASW, SWAC came together during a time of uprisings, following the police killings of Michael Brown and Eric Garner. SWAC was formed to challenge the social work profession's complicity in the criminalization of Black and Brown people. This was at a time when the social work profession was only beginning to use the term "mass incarceration" broadly and only starting to dig into the underlying realities of long-standing mass incarceration and mass criminalization. SWAC's vision was based on the shared analysis of its members at the time: that incarceration and criminalization were the problems and that social work continued to play a role in furthering both of those forces.[2] Although SWAC had ambition and useful analysis at the time, its ability to enact those ambitions fell short because of capacity. Fast-forward to 2020, and several of the founding members of SWAC came back together with other social workers across the United States to explore possible ways to intervene in conversations that proposed social work as the solution to policing.

Through much discussion, the NAASW was founded on the idea that not only should we challenge social work's carceral complicity, but we could also contribute to a different type of social work, one in which politics and practice align with the abolitionist horizon to which we were committed. The work of scholars like Beth E. Richie, Mimi E. Kim, and others offered us the concepts of *carceral social work* and *carceral services* as a way to understand not only the direct relationships between social work and carceral systems, but also the deeper carceral and punitive logics and relations that have been a part of social work practice broadly over time. So when the NAASW formed in 2020, not only did we have an understanding of carceral social work and experience attempting to dismantle it, but many of us had been a part of a growing abolitionist movement whose ideas and practices were more visible than ever before. The result of all of this was the push for a concept of abolitionist social work and an exploration of what that concept would mean in practice.

The term *abolitionist social work* has been recently introduced to discourse, is contested for a range of reasons, and is a term that many in the world of social work are grappling with for the first time. It is a term in early formation. Within the NAASW, there are differing ideas about the term's meaning and utility, as well as debate about whether we should be working to abolish social work altogether, rather than move forward a faction of social work practice rooted in abolition praxis. Despite this, there is a shared desire within our group to push ourselves and the social work profession toward anti-carceral and abolitionist politics and practice. What this means in the long term for social work is an unsettled question for us, but we believe that interjecting abolition into social work theory and practice will support more of us in working toward the world we dream of and aspire to.

In this chapter, we offer our contribution to the growing understanding of abolitionist social work gently, with acknowledgment of the term's contradictions and pitfalls and with acknowledgment of the possibilities offered by naming something and developing some shared understanding of it. We do not intend to draw sharp boundaries around what does and doesn't belong, but instead hope to share a porous scaffolding for bridging politics and practice for those in the social work field who seek to participate in freedom work that actualizes material change and structural transformation. We offer these ideas in the hope of growing abolitionist practice in our social work communities and creating more opportunities for rigorous and principled debate about whether and/or how social work and social workers can participate in the work of abolition.

Abolitionist Social Work Principles

At the most basic level, abolitionist social work is about bringing abolitionist principles and politics to social work theory and practice. As the title of this book suggests, this endeavor is full of contradictions and limitations, particularly in mainstream, majority-white social work institutions that are prone to a hyperfocus on the professionalization of organizing, advocacy, and care work. Still, we in the NAASW have been able to engage in abolitionist efforts in our own social work practices and have experienced the real changes that can come from doing this. At the time this chapter is being written, we can also still imagine a transformed social work, one that is rooted in solidarity over charity; one that is decolonized, deprofessionalized, anti-capitalist, and antiracist; and one that is committed to repair, accountability, and continual transformation.[3] As our colleagues wrote in 2020, at its best, "social work will be the chorus for abolition—partnering in the work of ending state violence, while supporting life-affirming relationships, practices and organizations."[4]

Toward the advancement of abolitionist social work, we offer the following principles, which bring together the ideas and practices of many scholars, activists, and organizers that have shaped our work and thinking and that we believe build a foundation for social work theory and practice that is truly aligned with justice, liberation, and freedom. We also recognize that achieving these principles in practice is often difficult, especially in professionalized social work. These principles act as both the horizon we seek to reach as well as a guide to support us in building the bridges from today to tomorrow, to the many years ahead.

Guiding Principles

Abolitionist social work is committed to being anti-carceral.
In their seminal piece *Defund the Police: Moving Towards an Anti-Carceral Social Work*, Leah Jacobs, Mimi E. Kim and their colleagues offered the concept and framework of anti-carceral social work. They understand carceral social work "as two interlocking components—the deployment of tactics, within social work, dependent on the same White supremacist and coercive foundations as policing, as well as direct partnership with law enforcement itself."[5] And thus, anti-carceral social work challenges both of these components.

Abolitionist social work is committed to anti-oppression.
Identity and power shape who has access to which resources, who is considered deserving, and whose humanity and dignity are acknowledged by social structures. Abolitionist social work fights for the dignity, freedom, and care for people of all intersecting identities—race, ethnicity, gender, class, sexuality, ability, nationality, immigration status, religion/spirituality—centering people and communities at the margins.

Abolitionist social work is committed to anti-capitalism.
Abolitionist scholar and activist Ruth Wilson Gilmore has taught many of us to understand capitalism, and more specifically racial capitalism, as a principal driver of violence and the core logic of carceral institutions.[6] Since its founding, much of professionalized social work has been subservient to the order of racial capitalism[7] and has attempted to mitigate its worst harms, rather than to transform the economic and social systems that create and sustain immense suffering. Therefore, an abolitionist social work toils against racial capitalism and struggles for economic and social systems rooted in mutuality, interdependence, and care rather than in domination and exploitation.

Abolitionist social work is committed to decolonization.
Many scholars and organizers, led by Indigenous people, including authors of a chapter in this book, have made clear that any just future must include Indigenous sovereignty and an end to settler colonialism and coloniality more broadly.[8] Craig Fortier and Edward Hon-Sing Wong offer practices for unsettling social work including disrupting historicization, working toward the repatriation of Indigenous lands, working toward deinstitutionalization, a return to mutual aid and treaty responsibilities, the ongoing reckoning of settler complicity, and promoting deprofessionalization as a way to return control to communities.[9]

Abolitionist social work is committed to deprofessionalization.
Social work's historical complicity in white supremacy, combined with its aspirations to be seen as a legitimate profession and the onslaught of neoliberalism over the last forty years, has led the field to become a gatekeeper of crumbs and a mediator of the worst consequences of systemic oppression, rather than a field committed to collective wellness and lasting liberation. The profession of social work has constructed professional boundaries built on hierarchies of worthiness and the primacy of legal liability. In addition, it has created a system of education, training, and licensure that has attempted to hold captive the means for wellness and care to the few who can access social work institutions. An abolitionist social work strives toward community self-determination and is committed to liberating the resources, tools, skills, and education that support all forms of healing, wellness, care, and transformation.

Abolitionist social work is committed to centering systems, structures, and ideologies as the problems, *not* people as the problem.
The profession of social work has adopted a practice of pathologizing individual behavior, rather than assessing and diagnosing the ideologies, structures, and systems that create and perpetuate human suffering, inequality, and violence. An abolitionist social work centers these forces, *not* people, as the problem and works with people to meet our individual and collective needs, to heal our individual and collective wounds, and to transform our social and economic conditions.

Abolitionist social work is committed to solidarity, not charity.
As Dean Spade and many others have taught us, solidarity is both the pathway to, and the result of, liberatory work,[10] and charity is rooted in maintaining inequality. Charity work is uninterested in facilitating access to what we need to get free: meaningful relationships, collective power, and changes to structural conditions. An abolitionist social work is committed to solidarity, which is rooted in interdependence and relationships and is centered around working together to meet our immediate needs while organizing collectively toward the world we deserve.

Abolitionist social work is committed to building life-affirming institutions and relationships.
Critical Resistance, Mariame Kaba, Ruth Wilson Gilmore, and many others have taught us that abolition is about building the institutions and relationships we need to be well and to thrive. Although social work has often been a partner to harmful systems and practices, we believe an abolitionist social work can play a role in building life-affirming organizations[11] and relationships that are rooted in care, mutuality, and interdependence.

Abolitionist social work is committed to self-determination and autonomy.
The Black Panthers and the American Indian Movement are just two of countless groups that have made self-determination and autonomy central tenets of liberation work. Carceral systems and ideologies of domination are sustained by control of, power over, and exploitation of people and communities. Abolitionist social work must be committed to realizing self-determination and autonomy in practice.

Abolitionist social work is committed to nonpunitive approaches to harm and abuse.
Responding to harm and abuse with more harm and abuse does not reduce it, nor does it create the pathways for meaningful healing, accountability, and transformation of individuals and communities. Punishment is a tool of domination, and carceral punishment is used to subjugate and control marginalized people. Restorative, transformative, and healing justice approaches have demonstrated that nonpunitive and noncarceral responses to harm and abuse are not only possible but necessary. An abolitionist social work struggles against punishment in all forms and works to bolster nonpunitive approaches to harm and abuse.

Practicing Abolitionist Social Work

Although the collection of principles offers an important grounding in the values, politics, and aspirations of an abolitionist social work, they mean very little if they are not applied in practice. And we know from our own experiences that bringing these principles into practice can be challenging for a whole host of reasons. From working directly for the state and working in organizations partnering with the state to working within the 501(c)3 structure and nonprofit industrial complex and its many limitations, pushing back against the status quo of carceral social work is not easy. Still, many are pushing back and practicing what could be considered abolitionist social work. Here we offer some frameworks, questions, and examples that we find helpful in bolstering our efforts to bring abolitionist principles to social work practice.

Against, Outside and Inside/Around the State

One framework we have found helpful in identifying where and how we can catalyze abolitionist social work uses our relationship to the state as a way to locate practices and strategies. Mi Gente, Interrupting Criminalization, and Cameron Rasmussen have written about this framework in some form that locates work against the state, outside the state, and in/around the state.[12] Here we use this framework primarily to think about how abolitionist social work practices work in relationship to the carceral state.

Against the state: This refers to work aimed at ending the harms and violence of the state and happens primarily through reducing the size, scope, and power of the carceral state. Examples of this include "closing jails, prisons, and detention centers; freeing people from these institutions (bail funds, sentencing reform, parole reform, clemency campaigns); reducing the harm of conditions inside these facilities (ending solitary confinement); organizing to get reparations for the harms of white supremacy and the carceral state; and organizing against family regulation policies and practices."[13] It is important to note that none of these strategies are social work specific, nor do they inevitably align with abolitionist aims.

Outside of the state: This refers to work that happens without engagement with the state. Many people are no longer able to rely on the state or have given up any hope that the state will adequately address their needs, whether that be the foundational necessities like food, shelter, and health care or the safety and justice needs that arise from violent and harmful acts (enacted on structural, community, and interpersonal levels). Many communities and groups have shown us how to create communities of care, safety, and interdependence outside of the state. These include but are by no means limited to Indigenous communities, Black liberation and Black feminist groups, antiviolence groups, and anarchist communities. Two of the most visible approaches outside of the state that are instructive for abolition and abolitionist social work are the practices of mutual aid and transformative justice, both of which understand the state as inherently violent and reject the notion that it is necessary for survival.[14]

Inside (and around) the state: This refers to working directly for, or in partnership with, state carceral institutions. Although the framework we are utilizing groups work inside of and work around the state together, we differentiate these into two distinct strategies. We believe that working directly for, by which we mean inside, state carceral institutions—police, jails, prisons, US Immigration and Customs Enforcement, law enforcement supervision (pretrial, probation, parole), district/prosecuting attorney offices, and child welfare agencies—is in conflict with the praxis of abolitionist social work. Although this work may at times provide meaningful support to individuals and may ameliorate real human suffering in the present, social workers in these positions are agents of the state and are responsible for policing, punishing, and surveilling people and communities. Many social workers working directly for the carceral state do not aspire to an abolitionist horizon; some are, to the contrary, staunch advocates for the carceral state, and still others choose this strategy based on the position that it mitigates harm of people in the present, including social workers who believe in abolition. We are not interested in gatekeeping who or who is not considered an abolitionist and find that questions about abolitionist identity can often distract from developing abolitionist practice. We are interested in concrete strategies and interventions that advance abolitionist social work praxis and believe that ending social work's direct partnership with the carceral state is one of these strategies.

We have witnessed ways of working around the state that we believe bring us closer to the abolitionist horizon. These include the long history of grassroots formations and nonprofits going into jails and prisons to offer needed support to the people incarcerated there. And some social workers have demonstrated tools for rejecting and/or reducing carceral practices in their practice by disengaging from harmful practices like mandated reporting and violating people back to incarceration while working in state-adjacent programs, organizations, or job functions. We have seen some diversion programs that have been able to wrestle some power away from the state to keep people from being incarcerated, while reducing the coercion inherently baked into alternative to incarceration programs. Still, we recognize that so much of the nonprofit work in and around the carceral state is controlled by mandates from the carceral state, is funded by the carceral state, and is limited in its ability to be in solidarity with, and build power with, the people and communities that are most impacted by the carceral state.

Although not as clearly in conflict with abolitionist social work praxis as work inside the state, work around the state is fraught and comes with many pitfalls and opportunities for co-optation. Still, we know that so many people and communities are under the thumb of the carceral state, and we are hesitant to suggest complete divestment from working *around* at least some of these institutions—court systems, jails, and prisons—in strategic capacities. Abolitionist social work around the state, if it can exist, must work to reduce social work's carceral complicity while building the power of communities and offering care and support that is as noncoercive as possible.

Discerning Abolitionist Social Work Praxis

Locating abolitionist social work strategies in relation to the state can be helpful in thinking through where and how individuals and groups can intervene. Still, it is not always easy to discern if and when, and to what degree, a particular strategy is working toward abolitionist aims. Fortunately, many abolitionist organizers and groups have sought to think through how we can analyze if and when something is aligned with abolition. In the fall of 2022, Interrupting Criminalization, Project Nia, and Critical Resistance published an extensive resource (*So Is This Actually an Abolitionist Proposal or Strategy?*) that compiled a range of assessments from a wide range of abolitionist organizers and grassroots groups.[15]

One assessment that has attempted to think through discerning abolitionist efforts for social work praxis is an adaptation of a series of questions developed by Dean Spade. Cameron Rasmussen and Kirk "Jae" James attempted to adapt Dean's questions to be applied to social work settings more specifically.[16] Although answering these questions will likely not produce an equation that gives you a clear yes-or-no answer to whether a particular strategy is abolitionist, it will help to analyze various ways in which the strategy is more or less abolition aligned. These questions include:

- Is the work accountable to the people it proposes to be working for and with? (I.e., does it include their leadership? Is it shifting power? Is it working to reduce and eliminate coercion?)

- Does it provide material relief? If yes, at what cost to one's agency and at what risk?

- Does it perpetuate dichotomies and ideologies of good versus bad, deserving versus undeserving, violent versus nonviolent, criminal versus innocent?

- Does it legitimate or expand carceral systems? (I.e., does it use, affirm or expand criminalization, incarceration, surveillance and/or punishment?)

- Does it center systems and structures as the cause of the problem (rather than individuals)?
- Does it mobilize those most affected for ongoing struggle? (I.e., is this building power?)

Instructive Organizations and Formations for Abolitionist Social Work

Finally, we'd like to highlight organizations and grassroots formations that have been instructive to our own abolitionist thinking and praxis. When we think about the questions above and consider organizations that have shown us how to apply theory to practice, we think of these organizations and of course many others that are not listed here.

Adalah Justice Project: This Palestinian-led advocacy organization is based in the United States and builds cross-movement coalitions to achieve collective liberation.

Center for NuLeadership on Human Justice and Healing: Founded by Eddie Ellis, NuLeadership has been a beacon for organizing with and building power for people directly impacted by incarceration.

Creative Interventions: This legendary organization in the transformative justice community, CI, founded by Mimi Kim, has helped many to build practical pathways to address harm and violence, bringing us closer to our noncarceral future.

Freedom Community Center: This Black-led organization in North St. Louis was founded to dismantle systems of oppression that inflict harm and trauma on Black communities in St. Louis City, particularly the police and the criminal punishment system.

Interrupting Criminalization: Founded by the abolitionists Mariame Kaba and Andrea Ritchie, IC has taught many of us about abolitionist praxis, about solidarity, and about experimentation and trying out many things.

Justice Committee: Founded in 1984 by former members of the Young Lords, the JC organizes against police violence while directly supporting people and families who have been harmed by the police.

JMACforFamilies: If you don't know Joyce McMillan, you do now. Joyce and JMACforFamilies are a powerhouse organizing against family policing and working to build the systems of support that keep families and communities together.

Movement for Family Power: This is one of several powerful organizations working to end the foster system's policing and punishment of families and to create a world where the dignity and integrity of all families is valued and supported.

upEND Movement: Along with JMACforFamilies and Movement for Family Power, the upEND Movement is working to abolish the family policing system and bring more social workers into this struggle.

S.O.U.L. Sisters Leadership Collective: Founded by Wakumi Douglas and sunsetting in 2023, SSLC has offered a powerful model of how to build a nonprofit that is committed to building power and dignity of young people with a strong focus on racial and gender justice.

The NAASW writing crew for this chapter included Michelle Grier, Vivanne Guevara, Sarah Knight, Nikita Rahman, Cameron W. Rasmussen, and Durrell M. Washington Sr.

3

Abolitionist Reform for Social Workers

Sam Harrell

Introduction

On January 3, 1901, Jane Addams, one of the most influential and well-respected women in the country, published an editorial in *The Independent* titled "Respect for the Law."[1] In an appeal to Northern white consciousness to stop defending Southern[2] lynching, Addams wrote:

> We would send this message to our fellow citizens of the South who are once more trying to suppress vice by violence: That the bestial in man, that which leads him to pillage and rape, can never be controlled by public cruelty and dramatic punishment, which too often cover fury and revenge. That violence is the most ineffectual method of dealing with crime, the most preposterous attempt to inculcate lessons of self control. A community has a right to protect itself from the criminal, to restrain him, to segregate him from the rest of society. But when it attempts revenge, when it persuades itself that exhibitions of cruelty result in reform, it shows itself ignorant of all the teachings of history; it allows itself to be thrown back into the savage state of dealing with criminality.

Five months later, Ida B. Wells-Barnett, the first person to use lynching statistics to show that violence against white women was "the excuse, not the cause" of lynching,[3] penned a reply to Addams titled "Lynching and the Excuse for It."[4] She wrote that Addams' argument relied on a dangerous presumption that white Southern mobs were lynching Black men in response to a "certain class of crimes" (i.e., sexual violence against white women). Wells-Barnett wrote:

> It is this assumption, this absolutely unwarrantable assumption, that vitiates every suggestion which it inspires Miss Addams to make. It is the same baseless assumption which influences ninety-nine out of every one hundred persons who discuss this question. Among many thousand editorial clippings I have received in the past five years, ninety-nine per cent. [sic] discuss the question upon the presumption that lynchings are the desperate effort of the Southern people to protect their women from black monsters, and while the large majority condemn lynching, the condemnation is tempered with a plea for the lyncher—that human nature gives way under such awful provocation and that the mob, insane for the moment, must be pitied as well as condemned. It is strange that an intelligent, law-abiding and fair minded people should so persistently shut their eyes to the facts in the discussion of what the civilized world now concedes to be America's national crime.

Contemporaries in Chicago, Addams and Wells-Barnett were two of the most important innovators in social welfare. By 1901, Addams was co-running Hull House in Chicago and working with other white social workers to develop specialized prisons and courts for children. Wells-Barnett was editing *The Chicago Conservator*, a Black newspaper she co-owned, and helping Chicago join the burgeoning Black Women's Club movement, extending organizing opportunities to women traditionally excluded from white social welfare organizations.

Their contentious exchange serves as an early lesson in the politics of reform. Although both Addams and Wells-Barnett wanted to see an end to lynching, they fundamentally disagreed on the underlying problem. Addams accepted the logic undergirding lynching—that Black men are predatory and a danger to white womanhood. Thus, she appealed to the concept of *alternatives*, suggesting that white Southerners capture and control Black men using more civilized, humane technologies.[5] Conversely, Wells-Barnett rejected the association between Blackness and violence, instead redefining the problem as the violence of state-sanctioned white supremacy.

Reform Is Not a Dirty Word

Like social workers today, Addams and Wells-Barnett wanted reform—changes that would improve the material conditions of people they lived with, worked with, and loved. But not all reforms look the same.[6] They exist on a spectrum.

On one end, social workers are advocating for and implementing changes meant to improve the prison industrial complex—or systems of overlapping interest that maintain surveillance, policing, and imprisonment.[7] They are mutating its outer appearance while extending its life, its ability to persevere under changing social and economic conditions. And they are uniquely positioned to do this work. The state relies on professionalized social workers to legitimize violence, collect and share information, and contract with systems of punishment (see Jacobs et al. on carceral social work).[8]

On the other end, social workers are advocating for and implementing changes to abolish the prison industrial complex. They are chipping away at the tools and logics that make imprisonment, policing, and surveillance possible and building new ones for a world we want to live in. The state has historically disincentivized and reprimanded this work (e.g., requiring licensure to access fields of work and opportunity; co-opting movement work through federal funding initiatives; and incentivizing specific areas of practice within professional education programs).

In reality, most social workers oscillate somewhere in between. Harsha Walia tells us that "every reform entrenches the power of the state because it gives the state the power to implement that reform."[9] And still, Walia continues, if we are ethically oriented toward emancipation, we can guide our reform work by asking, *does it increase the possibility of freedom?* With this question in mind, let's further explore different approaches to reform.

Carceral Reform

Many brilliant thinkers have offered frames through which to evaluate reform. The most reliable shorthand I have found involves the question of size–scope–power. Work that *sustains* or *grows* the life, scope, and/or power of the prison industrial complex threatens what Walia terms the *possibility of freedom*. Activist-scholars have given this work many different names (e.g., reformist reform, carceral reform, reformism). We can go as far back as the nineteenth century, when abolitionists working to abandon slavery and all the institutions and structures that relied on it fought against the popular idea of *gradualism*, which implored sympathetic white people to purchase and free enslaved Black people without targeting the foundations of slavery itself.[10] Those who advocated gradualism limited their goals and aspirations only to what was rational and practical within the institution of slavery, rejecting demands "incompatible with the preservation of the system."[11]

In their book, *Prison by Any Other Name*, Maya Schenwar and Victoria Law ask, "What does it mean to reform—to improve—a system that, at its core, relies on captivity and control?"[12] I want to extend this question beyond prisons. Some social workers find this question irrelevant because they cannot locate their own practice within a context of carcerality—of policing, surveillance, and imprisonment. In fact, the insidiousness of carcerality is that which Beth E. Richie calls a *prison nation*[13]—it reaches through the cracks of prison walls and toward nearly every aspect of our lives.[14] Take the following three examples from my own practice in a small, Midwestern city:

Increasing the power[15] of the prison industrial complex

I am codirecting the city's only low-barrier homeless shelter. The concept of offering a safe space to sleep without religious, sobriety, or warrant checks is controversial. Local leaders accuse the low-barrier approach of "enabling" a "homelessness crisis" and bringing people from nearby underresourced communities to "drain" county resources. In an effort to appease a growing moral panic, the interfaith council in charge of the shelter introduces the use of metal detectors. Small, personal weapons (e.g., pepper spray, pocket knives) were essential resources for many living without safe housing. Under the guise of protecting volunteers and shelter "guests" from an unsubstantiated risk of violence, guests (not volunteers) now undergo full-body screens from a metal detector wand operated by a paid security guard (at times, the only paid worker in the entire interfaith operation).

Although the metal detector often malfunctions and rarely detects weapons, its adoption significantly increases the *power* of both shelter workers and the state to police, surveil, and punish. Staff now have authority or permission to search bodies and belongings, creating new opportunities to identify criminalized or contraband possessions. Guests resisting body and property searches are frequently threatened with suspensions and bans, leading to an exponential increase in police calls and consequently arrests. Shelter workers, who are not subjected to body and property searches, adopt or further concretize the notion that by being housed, they are inherently safe and trustworthy. And vice versa—being houseless becomes an implicit threat.

Increasing the scope of the prison industrial complex
I am coordinating a department of a small domestic and sexual violence shelter and resource center. A resident of the shelter informed the director that she was physically attacked by a staff member known for hostile, intimidating, and punitive interactions with clients. The staff member denies the attack. Under the guise of "liability," the director quickly sides with the staff person, choosing not to believe or further investigate the questions of staff-on-client harm. Instead, agency leadership proposes the installation of new security cameras in the resident living quarters to prevent future "false accusations," to presumably exonerate future staff.

The proposal to add new security cameras threatened to increase the *scope* or reach of the prison industrial complex. Domestic violence shelters have long replicated tactics of abuse and control in interpersonal relationships.[16] In this shelter, there were few spaces where residents could be alone or not under the watch of shelter staff. Increasing the capacity of shelter staff to monitor residents, subjecting them to constant surveillance, would subsequently increase the capacity to identify contraband (e.g., drug use) and police behavior (e.g., children unattended). All of these enhancements would create new opportunities to subject residents to or compromise their ability to escape from formal systems of punishment (e.g., child protective services, police, probation).

Increasing the size of the prison industrial complex
I am directing a new reentry center for people leaving jail and prison. It is one of the few spaces left in town that provides daytime, low-barrier services without the surveillance of private security. One day, a woman walks into the center. I recognize her immediately by her uniform—she is unarmed, wearing a white polo shirt and black pants. Most people

called her a "white shirt" (cop) but the city preferred the title "downtown resource officer" (DRO). The introduction of DROs represented a revitalization of 1960s innovations in community policing intended to quell unrest from Black communities resisting systematic surveillance and detention.[17] Now, as Midwestern college towns invested in gentrification, the visibility of houselessness threatened capital investment (i.e., shopping). Reimagining the image of policing became a cost-effective way to remove people who are houseless from public spaces without investigating or disturbing the source of their economic insecurity.

I immediately escort the white shirt outside and tell her she is not welcome in this space. She explains that she is visiting local agencies to build connections with social workers. She and other police met regularly with a team of social workers to share information and coordinate their work. The expectation to collaborate with police threatened to increase the *size* of the prison industrial complex. As communities called to defund police in the wake of Michael Brown's murder, the DRO program created new positions to secure the place of policing in a potentially hostile future. A model relying on "collaborative problem-solving" and the investigation of "causational factors" of crime could not succeed without the buy-in of social workers. Social workers provided DROs with access to clients, coordinated information sharing, and a benevolent cover for violence.

It makes sense that social workers are drawn to carceral reforms. We are literally trained, in school and in the field, to defend and invest in the prison industrial complex. Our limited orientation to the history of social work in the United States usually centers on the improvement and expansion of systems of control (e.g., the juvenile justice system). We are trained as experts of care and therefore justified in the gatekeeping of life-sustaining resources. Neoliberalism demands an increase in contract-based work, and our access to those resources is reliant on our loyalty or "accountability" to our funders. And at the end of the day, nearly any work we do (no matter how carceral in nature) becomes rationalized under a malleable Code of Ethics and manipulated distortions of harm reduction.

With this in mind, I offer an incomplete list of signs that your social work practice, no matter how well intentioned, may be being used for carceral reform—to sustain or increase the life, scope, and/or power of the prison industrial complex:

(1) Your presence or involvement is being used to legitimize a system of surveillance, policing, or imprisonment (particularly when that system is facing a decline in public support).

(2) You are expected to collect new data for the state or expand its access to existing information.

(3) You are expected to expand the state's access to people (widening the net or helping the state locate and identify people they would otherwise not have access to).

(4) Your skills and tools are being shared with state agents (e.g., trainings, professional development) to make their surveillance, policing, and/or imprisonment work more effective.

(5) Your organizational budgets are being used to extend the life of or secure financial funding for surveillance, policing, and/or surveillance work (particularly when they are facing calls for defunding).

(6) You are expected to make the job of state agents easier or more efficient (e.g., policing client behavior).

See yourself in this list? You are not alone. Packed into your professional identity are an infinite number of outside agendas. In short, social workers are a hot commodity for the state—particularly in times of social unrest and rebellion. Although it might be easy to give in to the well-funded and well-argued traps of co-optation, there is a different way. In fact, for as long as the prison industrial complex has existed, people have designed, coordinated, and implemented systems of care not bound to the prison industrial complex's logics and limitations.

Abolitionist Reform

Abolitionist reform reduces the power of the prison industrial complex while exposing its inability or unwillingness to "solve the crises it creates."[18] These reforms strip "power and legitimacy away from the systems of policing, imprisonment, surveillance"[19] by decreasing their size–scope–power, changing current relationships and common sense, and building new systems and relations that actually support life. Abolitionist reform does not accept the state's definition of a problem and then simply find an alternative solution. Doing so has historically led well-intentioned people to simply transpose existing logics onto new tools,[20] changing the shape but not the function of the prison industrial complex. Abolitionist reform "does not base its validity and its right to exist on capitalist needs, criteria, and rationales," but instead on "what should be made possible in terms of human needs and demands."[21]

I find that many social workers struggle with the *idea* of abolitionist reform. Abolition requires relationality, experimentation, and divestment from success. All too often, social workers are taught to build walls between themselves and their communities, to ground their interventions in evidence-based models approved by academic experts, and to arrive at definite answers to questions/problems. Abolition asks us to use and adapt tools, approaches, and frameworks in ways that *increase the possibility of freedom* (e.g., de-escalation, policy evaluation, facilitation).

One practical model for using social work skills and practices to advance abolition is Critical Resistance's *dismantle–change–build* framework.[22] This framework illustrates three different, but equally important and concurrently exercised, strategies necessary for an abolitionist present and future. In short, *you do not have to do all the things*. Abolition as a long-term organizing strategy relies on relationality and cooperation. There is ample room to do the work that you are most passionate about in the communities you care most about, in tandem with others. Personally, I find myself most at home in Critical Resistance's "change" strategy, but like many readers of this book, I have practiced across the framework throughout my life. I pair a description of each strategy[23] with an example from my own practice:

Dismantle caging, policing, practices, and larger systems that harm, control, and impoverish communities
My friend, Matin Shahawar Siraj, is a Pakistani-American who was arrested on terrorism charges in 2004 following a now infamous post-9/11 entrapment scheme coordinated by the New York Police Department. Matin's case has been frequently cited as an example of the dangerous expansion of anti-Muslim surveillance and policing tolerated under appeals to patriotism and national security. Yet there has never been a

coordinated campaign for his release. Although Matin works with pro bono lawyers and legal clinics to secure his freedom through clemency or compassionate release, I am teaching myself website building and campaign skills to garner public support and awareness for his case. This is a small action toward *dismantling* the caging—an effort to have one less person in prison while we work to make prisons obsolete. You can learn more at freematinsiraj.com.

Change common sense, resource allocation, and practices toward empowerment and address harm and problems at their root causes
While coordinating a domestic and sexual violence prevention program, I became weary of youth-based interventions that centered on bystander intervention skills with strangers. Although strangers do commit harm and bystander intervention can mitigate that harm, the overwhelming majority of youth will experience domestic and sexual violence from people they know and oftentimes trust. With this in mind, I used a wealth of publicly available transformative justice resources[24] to reimagine a prevention curriculum based on accountability and youth autonomy. The new curriculum engaged high school students in tools and resources for navigating accountability with loved ones. It then asked students to imagine their best friend has caused harm. Recognizing that the majority of youth will not tell an adult or authority figure about interpersonal harm, they were asked to discuss how to hold someone accountable.[25] This new curriculum was significantly more challenging than its previous version—as it sought to *change* commonly accepted understandings of and responses to violence and empower youth to address harms that would otherwise go ignored.

Build practices, skills, relationships, and resources that address community needs, affirm life, and enable us to thrive
In 2015, I was following the work of what would eventually become Survived & Punished, a national prison abolition organization focusing on the criminalization of survivors and illuminating the relationship between state and interpersonal violence. I was working for a domestic and sexual violence shelter and resource center that did not serve survivors in the local jail and, at times, intentionally denied crisis calls from jails and prisons. I realized that if I were to meet criminalized survivors, there was

no existing infrastructure in my community to support them, nor to organize a campaign for their release (let alone, a larger mass campaign for decarceration). Hoping to *build* a network of organizations and individuals equipped to support criminalized survivors, I began contacting different organizations. I customized my messages to help organizations see criminalization and survival as *their issues*, appealing to the Black feminist organizing principle of multi-issue struggle.[26] These appeals were effective and unanimously accepted, bringing together staff and volunteers from LGBTQ+, prison entry, domestic violence, and reproductive justice organizations for monthly letter-writing nights, rotating organizational hosts. Initially, we focused on learning about the intersections of state and interpersonal violence and wrote survivors whose cases were highlighted by Survived & Punished. Over time, members built connections with local survivors and began imagining how to translate the campaign work of larger cities to our smaller Midwestern community.

The preceding examples illustrate small interventions intended to decrease the size, scope, and power of the prison industrial complex and increase the capacity of communities to take care of one another. They are not meant to be perfect or "pure" representations of abolitionist praxis (perfectionism has no place in an abolitionist present-future). I firmly believe that social workers—those trained by lived experience, familial and cultural tradition, iterative practice, and/or professional education to exercise intentional care and systems change work—have a critical role to play in an abolitionist future. I believe that many of the skills associated with professionalized social work are neutral. It's what we do with them that matters. I outline some of these skills and what I consider to be examples of their oppressive and liberatory potential:

Skills *can move us*	farther from *or*	closer to *the possibility of freedom*
active listening and empathetic communication	collect information for state authorities	listen for context and nuance, hold multiple truths, and help people move through conflict
crisis intervention	pacify resistance	de-escalate conflict, support people through trauma and healing
group work	implement court-mandated, deficit-oriented treatments that responsibilize and individualize structural harm	facilitate project-based work, form and coordinate coalition work, facilitate restorative and transformative processes

professional writing and communication	disclose criminalizing information in case notes	construct appeals for early release or to prevent detention or deportation
cross-system coordination	centralize control of service delivery and coordinate inclusion and exclusion of access	identify and dismantle cross-system barriers to safety and well-being
budgeting and organizational practice	define organizational priorities based on external funding opportunities and eligibility	identify and advocate for opportunities to divert money away from carceral systems and invest in life-sustaining resources
data collection and analysis	share data with carceral systems to maintain, secure, or access funding	understand, deconstruct, and make accessible the practices, policies, and impacts of carceral systems to inform effective dismantle work
policy design and analysis	write policy that increases the educational and/or licensure standards for social work to further restrict access to care work	understand the historical context of a policy, anticipate unintended outcomes, and ensure the most vulnerable are centered in its design
evaluation and needs assessment	evaluate an intervention based on indicators designed to produce data in service of state control (e.g., recidivism)	help a community assess and prioritize needs and implement a plan for meeting those needs

As we work to use our social work skills for more liberatory aims, we may find ourselves unable to materialize the changes we hope to see in our lifetime. This does not mean our work was not worth the struggle.

Records of Dissent

Abolition requires a divestment from success, from linear notions of progress. When social workers actively and intentionally engage in abolitionist praxis, they leave a *record of dissent*. Critical Resistance says that abolition is "both a practical organizing tool and a long-term goal." Our work is most sustainable when we situate it within a longer struggle, honoring both those who came before us and those who will come after. With this in mind, I want to leave you with one more historical anecdote, this time drawing from the archival work[27] of Natascha Toft Roelsgaard. Here is my best attempt at summarizing this anecdote from Roelsgaard:

Following the Civil War, slavery became legally permissible only as a punishment for crime. Chasing the economic advantage of a plantation economy and seeking to recuperate infrastructure losses from the war, the South turned to Jim Crow laws and convict leasing. This allowed southern counties to imprison masses of Black people without building or maintaining physical prisons; outsource violence work to leasees; recuperate plantation industries; and rebuild lost infrastructure at no cost. To rationalize this brutal system, Southern politicians continued to propagate stereotypes that made *Black* synonymous with *crime*.

In the early 1930s, the National Association of Colored Women (NACW), under the leadership of President Mary Church Terrell, organized to resist the convict leasing system. At a time when the mainstream white press openly supported the convict leasing system, the NACW used "the power of the press and counter narratives"[28] to shift the common sense and logic used to defend it. Terrell traveled the country to speak on the conditions of Black life in the South and found that white, educated social reformers (those often classified as social work "pioneers") had the privilege of being largely unaware of the horrors of convict leasing. Like her colleague Wells-Barnett, Terrell worked to systematically document and disseminate records of state-sanctioned violence. Doing so would ensure everyone, from social workers to governors, could not hide behind the illusion of ignorance.

Terrell led the NACW in three decades of written dissent of the convict leasing system in their monthly publication, *National Notes*. Their writings were republished in Black newspapers and, at times, white papers in the North. NACW members organized lecture circuits to educate the public on convict leasing and gave speeches at national conventions. Under Terrell's leadership, the NACW organized to repeal Jim Crow laws and convict leasing systems in several states.

No story is perfect. The NACW's anticonvict leasing campaign relied heavily on their larger strategy of respectability politics and "racial uplift" to secure social, political, and economic opportunities for Black women and families. Organizations, like people, are complex. And hidden in their histories are records of practices, tools, and innovations that moved us farther from or closer to the *possibility of freedom*. Let's commit to learning from those that came before us, fighting like hell while we're here, and leaving records of dissent and radical possibility for those that come after.

Notes

Mariame Kaba says that "everything worth doing is done with other people."[29] Thank you to my midwestern social work thought partners, in particular Donyel Byrd, Harsharn Kaur, Nordia McNish, Karlie Thomas, and Stephanie Waller.

4

Indigenist Abolition: A Talk Story on Ideas and Strategies for Social Work Practice

*Ramona Beltran, Danica Brown, Annie Zean Dunbar,
Katie Schultz, and Angela Fernandez*

Abolition is Indigenous. At its core, abolition is about imagination and creation beyond the colonial and carceral state. State structures create environments of oppression, violence, and disempowerment, which separate us from our humanity, ancestors, and Mother Earth. From an Indigenous perspective, it is important to dismantle that which no longer serves the community and to turn toward the development and creation of that which cultivates, nurtures, and sustains collective and planetary well-being. In this chapter, the authors use "talk story," an Indigenous method, to reflect on abolition as an Indigenous concept and offer strategies for practice. Talk story method is a circular, relational, and reciprocal process through which we identify and articulate practical and concrete strategies for Indigenist abolition praxis derived from our lived experiences as intersectional Indigenous, Black, queer, feminist, cis-gendered women. We define several terms to anchor the reader in our understanding of these concepts and how they are connected to abolition. We introduce ourselves to connect our ancestral lineages to the work we do in social work research and practice as scholars with various relationships to the ideology and practice of abolition. Finally, we introduce Indigenous story work methodology and how we use the talk story method as data for identifying and articulating Indigenist abolition strategies for social work practitioners, educators, and researchers.

Indigenous Abolition

Abolition is about addressing power; moving from authoritative power to shared or collective power. Morning Star Gali (of the Ajumawi Band of Pit River Tribe) says, "Abolition is more than an idea. Abolition is decolonization. Abolition on stolen land, as this is for Indigenous communities, is a radical dismantling of the carceral state."[1] Curley et al. use the term *settler-enslaver* to describe epistemologies and ontologies that "violently turn Black and Native life and land into objects of property and dispossession."[2] Settler-enslaver epistemologies view land and people as "potential property to further interests of capital, state-making, and whiteness."[3] Settler-enslaver epistemologies are the foundation for the colonial carceral state that continues to dispossess and criminalize Indigenous land, community, cultures and lifeways.[4] As such, the abolition of institutionalized systems of control is necessary for decolonization, defined by John and Brown as the "repatriation of Indigenous land and life."[5] Decolonization and abolition are inextricably linked. Therefore, we utilize the definition of abolition as a project of decarceration that replaces criminal law enforcement and related systems, including social work, with radically different institutional forms of governance and regulation.[6]

Power vs. Authority

Power is a personal trait resulting from knowledge, expertise, and lived experience, and authority is hierarchical and comes from outside sources or positions given by a doctrine (e.g. Doctrine of Discovery), organization (e.g. police, social workers), or another person (e.g. monarchy). Although a person with authority may have traits that give them power, their authority is derived from their institutionalized position.[7] Power is not inherently oppressive. In fact, many forms of power can be liberating when they are inclusive of the community and those affected by oppression. Authority, however, seizes individual and collective power and is used in damaging ways to perpetuate oppression.[8] In Western systems, authority is patriarchal and heteronormative and is derived from the idea that whiteness is paramount. Conversely, power is generated from trusting relationships, collective sharing, and nonhierarchical leadership.

Sovereignty and Self-Determination

Lumsden defines sovereignty as "a vehicle with which Native peoples stake a claim to a self-determined future."[9] Legal sovereignty for tribes includes the right to establish their own forms of government, determine citizenship, enact legislation, and establish law enforcement and court systems guided by their cultural worldviews and practices.[10] Cultural sovereignty considers the whole of tribal self-governance and self-determination outside of bounds and limits of recognition by the nation-state (but can also include rights guaranteed with legal sovereignty)[11]. Coffey and Tsosie state that tribes must consider their own internal definitions of "sovereignty" and "autonomy" and what rights, obligations, and responsibilities are included in relationships among tribal members, ancestors, future generations, and outside society as a whole.[12]

Self-determination is an important aspect of cultural sovereignty as it is the right of a group or political entity to determine what constitutes "traditional culture and how it will honor and practice that culture."[13] Despite tensions in definitions and processes associated with legal and cultural sovereignty, Indigenist abolition underscores that tribes and Indigenous groups must determine their future and how they will get there.

Relational Protocol: Introductions

Before we begin our talk story, we introduce ourselves. Introductions are an important protocol in many Indigenous communities. Introducing ourselves is a practice that acknowledges and honors our ancestors and is a demonstration of humility that recognizes wherever our location, we are sitting on the laps of those who have gone before us and claiming our place in contributing to the future of those who have yet to come.[14] It is a commitment to transparency of our origins and current positionalities.

Ramona: *Lios enchim aniavu.* May the Creator bless you all. My name is Ramona Beltrán. My family are descendants of Indigenous peoples of

Sonora, Mexico on my mother's side/Anglo European descent, originally from Northern Ireland on my biological father's side. I was raised by my mother so that is my cultural standpoint. I was taught to acknowledge all of my ancestors, even the painful and absent ones, as it locates me in the complicated history and current context of colonization. I identify as a mixed-race Indigenous Chicana, a dedicated mother of three, a dancer, activist, and scholar. I am newer in my relationship to abolition but I see it as a natural extension of Indigenous commitments to creation and innovation in community care.

Danica: My names are *Ahchishi Okshulba* "Honeysuckle Breeze," *Onnahinli Fichik* "Morning Star," and Aspen Leaves Turning Gold. I am Choctaw of the *Watonlak Oshi* "White Crane" clan and Scottish of Clan Ross, born and raised in Northern New Mexico. I come to this work as a multiracial woman, citizen of the Choctaw Nation of Oklahoma. I am an Indigenous autonomous anarchist whose worldview emerges from a deep love and respect for the People, our ancestors, and for *iholitopa pishki*, "our beloved Mother Earth."

Zean: My name is Annie Zean Rebecca Dunbar, and I was born in Monrovia, Liberia, and raised along the East Coast of the United States with my formative development in Lowell, Massachusetts. I come to this work through lineages of displacement, a deep love of my intergenerational and multiracial community, a commitment to Black queer feminist praxis, and a belief in the power of art and DIY practice. My experiences as a Black person, a parent to a precocious toddler, an artist, and emerging scholar shape my worldview, which centers the well-being of the whole community.

Katie: I am a citizen of the Choctaw Nation of Oklahoma with Irish and German ancestors. I write from Anishinaabeg lands where I am an assistant professor of social work. I engage with the idea of abolition as a Native woman, social worker, and academic researcher and as someone who was raised to believe in the promise of American democracy whose work also seeks to resist its deeply entrenched systems of violence and inequities.

Angela: *Pōsōh netāēhnawēmākanak*. Greetings relatives. I am Kenyukīw (Eagle Woman) and I am awāēhsāēh netōtāēm (bear clan). I am from the Menominee Nation of Wisconsin and am a multiracial woman with Menominee, Mexican, and European ancestors. I am a proud auntie of nine and relative to many. My love for all relatives of Mother Earth inspires my dancing, writing, teaching, research, and community work. I acknowledge all my ancestors' histories and their intersections, as well as the gifts, opportunities, and responsibilities they bring for my life journey and what I will leave behind for future generations.

Indigenous Story Work

Coined by Stó:lō First Nations scholar Joanne Archibald, *Indigenous story work* is centered on listening with your "ears and heart"[15] and is grounded by the notion that stories can uniquely educate the mind, body, heart, and spirit.[16] Story work is a form of Indigenous knowledge that is born of relationships with each other, the land, and our ancestors. Through the practice of Indigenous story work and oral traditions, Indigenous people learn to live in right relationship with ourselves, our families, our communities, our ancestors, and all of creation. It is also a way that power is shared and extended.[17]

Indigenous scholars[18] are increasingly calling for the inclusion of Indigenous story work into social work practice and research with Indigenous communities. It reflects Indigenous ways of knowing and is a sacred, indigenized research method with decolonial aims. Indigenous story work creates a body of knowledge that regenerates knowledge, while at the same time creating acts of resistance to colonization. It centers thrivance, which Blackfeet scholar Dianne Bauman describes as going beyond the "we are still here" survival narrative to "we are productive, vibrant, and contributors to today's world."[19] Plains Cree and Saulteaux First Nations scholar Margaret Kovach[20] emphasizes that Indigenous methodologies such as story work are reciprocal and relational to honor the interconnection between all creation as part of ecological and cosmological balance rather than extractive or exploitative. It is in this spirit that we utilize a "talk story" method to create a relational, circular, and reciprocal process to articulate concrete strategies for Indigenist abolition praxis.

Talk Story: Our Method

Based on the principles of Indigenous story work, talk story is an approach to research using dialogue and exchange of personal narratives based on mutuality. Exchanges often occur in a circle format and can be casual and conversational in process.[21] When we were envisioning what our contribution to this collection of works could be, we connected ideas of abolition to our own experiences through stories. With varying levels of expertise on abolition, from beginner, budding, aspiring, to lifelong autonomous Indigenous anarchist abolitionist, we found ourselves in a dynamic, circular process. The lead author took notes during conversations and documented clear motifs and corresponding strategies that emerged from the dialogues, despite varying degrees of abolitionist identity development. We realized we had been engaging in Indigenous story work and decided to formalize and document our talk story process to articulate the strategies that emerged from our conversations. We developed guiding questions: (1) What does abolition mean to you and how do you see social workers implicated in abolition movements?; (2) Tell us a story of when you felt dissonance between being an agent of the state and a social justice advocate or abolitionist; and (3) What are strategies for social workers rooted in land and place, restorative justice, and cultural innovations? We met via Zoom three times and recorded our conversations as our source of data. Along with detailed notes of our conversations, we downloaded auto-generated transcripts from the meetings and cleaned the data. We pulled out the most relevant talk story excerpts in relation to the questions and created a list of themes that corresponded to concrete strategies for social work practice. Here we share these strategies and the talk story exchanges that led to them.

Talk Story

What is abolition to you and how are social workers implicated?

Danica: I don't believe that these systems can be fixed; they are working exactly the way they were intended to. Abolition is the only way, and it has two parts: destroying or abolishing systems of oppression, including social work in its current formation, while building and/or replacing the institutionalized systems by utilizing mutual aid models. Without an imagination and vision of the future, we end up recreating those same oppressive systems. An important aspect of abolition is envisioning new and more empowered communities, systems, and institutions to support the health and well-being of the People, in a collective and healing way. I look to futurisms and speculative fiction, to inspire the collective envisioning process. Hope is a powerful medicine, and futurisms and speculative fiction give us hope, and they give us a road map for ways of being.

Katie: when Danica started talking, the first word I wrote was *imagination*. I consider myself a budding abolitionist, emerging or early stage. Two years ago, after the murder of George Floyd, I really started to think about what people had written about abolishing the police. Part of that involved imagining what that would look like. And that was hard. I understand we can't fix that (system), but what do I imagine replacing it with? It's about creation—creating a system that works equitably. But when you ask me what it should look like, it's hard to imagine those futures.

Ramona: I think we first start with learning and understanding. For example, I was recently contacted by an organization after the director had seen me give a presentation on historical trauma and healing, and he was moved particularly by the idea of intergenerational wisdom. He mentioned that he and his team were going to be in Denver and asked if I would teach them about these concepts. I suggested that we meet in downtown Denver so they could learn about "place" and the history of this land, specifically about the Sand Creek Massacre and the displacement of Cheyenne and Arapaho peoples. I took them to significant places that are part of the annual Sand Creek Massacre Healing Run and Walk. So when you [Katie] said that I just realized, it made me think of their responses to the walk. One person said, "You know it's devastating to be someone so educated and to not know this history." People always have big feelings about that. I said, "Well that's by design, right?" So maybe part of being an abolitionist is truth telling. We can't understand a world without the carceral or colonial state if we don't even know what got us here, right? If we start with learning or unlearning and relearning the truth, then we can create a foundation for imagining something else. But if we don't know what we don't know, then we are stuck to accept the systems put in place. And we can begin with learning "in place." I think it can be argued that every place, all land in this country (the United States), has history connected to genocide and displacement of original Peoples.

Danica: Yes, and for social workers in particular, we are often in roles of state authorities, with (state-sanctioned) power over the lives of those we serve. We are part of that genocide and displacement. Social workers have a responsibility to look at and understand how the field went from essentially serving the poor to serving the state. So, for me, I really want to unpack this shift of our field back to its origins to serve people in ways that are less reliant on the state, processes that are not punitive but unconditional. Move back to a more relational way of being and working. You have to be "clean and sober" to get access to substance abuse treatment. You have to be emotionally regulated to receive mental health services. You have to be in recovery to access housing. These are the conditions, and they are so counterintuitive. And they are in direct opposition to our Indigenous value systems, where we meet people where they are at and help lift them up.

Katie: I was thinking about the very important distinction between power and authority. It's an important piece of this discussion that we can't lose. In the context of the difference between power and authority, we must think about the language that forms the narrative of these systems, the language around "child welfare" or "criminal justice." In actuality, there is little "welfare," and "justice" certainly doesn't drive these systems. But in using these narratives, we're crafting a certain ideal of a settler colonial citizen when we serve these systems. A healthy person looks a certain way. A healthy family looks a certain way. Definitions of success in these systems serve settler colonialism and patriarchy. In this way, social workers are supposed to "help" or "fix" broken people and we are supposed to do it in line with these institutional narratives.

Strategies: Education/Conscientization, Truth Telling, Counternarrative

Education and Conscientization

Paolo Freire coined the term *conscientization*, which he defined as a "deepening attitude of awareness characteristic of all emergence."[22] Critical consciousness is key to articulating and understanding systemic social structures and is a crucial component in building a scaffolding toward action. Social workers must teach and practice with a clear understanding of the ways that power and authority function in society and encourage practices that disrupt systems of control and oppression in society.

Truth Telling

Truth telling is a process of developing critical consciousness and occurs through unlearning and relearning truths about history as documented by those who seek to maintain power. Many people are shocked to learn about the atrocities committed, and continuing, against Indigenous peoples at such late stages in education. Although difficult, it is important to know them as part of the fabric of Western society to develop new narratives and actions. Social workers need an understanding of the legacy of settler colonialism and its historical and current impact on Indigenous peoples to develop responses to remediate this legacy. Moving beyond the land acknowledgment, it is essential that social workers, especially those working in Indian country, understand and educate about tribal sovereignty and self-determination. Social workers must understand these concepts and the nation-to-nation relationship that tribal people have to the US government as well as tribal rights to culturally, politically, and spiritually create and produce themselves without outside interference.

Counternarratives

Counternarratives are narratives that emerge from the perspective of those who have been purposely marginalized.[23] For example, US federal policies stemming from manifest destiny defined Indigenous peoples as inhuman, savage, and expendable. These ideas negatively shape society-level and individual-level ideas about the potential of Indigenous peoples. Although historical truth telling is a first step, it is also essential to uplift the many ways that Indigenous and other minoritized communities not only survived these attempts at annihilation but continue to imagine, regenerate, create, and thrive. Social workers should center, support, and uplift stories of resistance, thrivance, and creativity from these communities.

Our Talk Story Continues

Angela: I never really had a lot of hope in these institutions growing up. But I also had an orientation toward healing. I was a person that people would share their stories with, so I was drawn to social work. I am thinking about the multiple intersectional identities within myself: my European, Mexican, and Indigenous ancestry. I'm thinking about the privileges and the traumas that I carry side by side within myself and my body. And in that complexity, I try to model transparency. I've seen it from all of us and in our interactions.

I have a friend who says, "I *am* my community." What he means is that being healthy and healing himself is healing our own communities. We have these intersections and conflicts inside, too, but part of managing those conflicts is to talk about them openly and with transparency. We talk about who we are and our positionality. As I tell my story, I model this practice for my students, and for my family—my nieces and nephews in particular.

Zean: As a person, one body can hold full histories of harm and violence and histories of being harmed, and so, how do we think about ourselves as these complex beings? What is the legacy that we are responsible for repairing? That relates to how I think about my relationship to abolition: I have a duty to whoever comes after me to repair the harm that my ancestors have perpetuated, and that involves daily practices of showing kindness to people, of being able to acknowledge my history and then also thinking about and listening to people who are being harmed the most.

Angela: We each have roles and responsibilities. Part of our work is understanding what those roles are, what gifts we bring to make change, and identifying the pathways we can use to make them. That involves ongoing healing and recognizing the dissonance or conflicts inside of ourselves. So when I talk to students, I talk about my privilege and how I use it, while I also talk about the traumas we have experienced. In doing so, I model for them what it looks like to be transparent.

Zean: How do we talk about our own personal histories? And then, what are the ways that we do acts of repair, as opposed to thinking about reparations as like one thing; one major act to right a tremendous wrong? I think reparations is a practice of daily working to undo these normative ways we perpetuate harm on each other.

Katie: This also makes me think of the protocols we have in community. We have times you're expected to show up in certain ways. In ceremony as children, it's your time to be adventurous and be cared for and that's how you learn. As adults you care for others, hold the work and structure of the ceremony. And then your role changes again as you become an elder. We show up in different ways over the life course. That resonates for me as an ideal—that healthy communities consider where you are in life and determine what role and responsibility you have related to those stages.

Danica: And this is related to community accountability and the importance of knowing your community. If you don't know your community, then you can't visualize yourself as part of something bigger than yourself, and then you have nobody to whom you are accountable. Quite frankly, I think that's where a lot of problems related to whiteness and white supremacy stem from—a lack of cultural knowing and belonging. How many times have you heard white folks say, "Oh, I'm just an American mutt"? Well, no, you're not a dog, you're a human being and that erasure is purposeful—that disconnection leaves you untethered and therefore without a role and responsibility to others. But, you know, you can also say, "I don't know my roots" and that's OK. The task, then, is to find out who you are, who your people are, where you came from, and where you belong.

Ramona: If I were to articulate a concrete strategy that is not just for Indigenous Peoples but for everybody, I would say, "Just *name* yourself!" Tell us who you are. Tell us what you know about your ancestors and your original land, even if you are just beginning to learn. I was conducting focus groups for another project outside of the university, and I noticed how all the people of color would describe their ancestors, land, or ethnic community. The white folks did not unless specifically prompted. Native peoples always introduce ourselves in that way. We say where we're from and we name our people or tribal nation. It's a sign of respect and relational accountability. I keep trying to model it for people, you know? But non-Native folks don't do it because they are not taught how to be in this kind of relationship to community. And that is also intentional. It becomes that whiteness is the center and the assumption is that it needs no introduction because it is the norm. But I really believe it is a simple strategy that immediately demonstrates knowledge, accountability, and a commitment to relational protocols. I think about your point, Katie, that we can be many things over the life course. I think this is actually an anti-capitalist practice because you don't have to be one thing for your life or develop this singular expertise. You can be many, many things. That is what nature does. That is how the seasons move, through change and cycles. In my naming ceremony, the elders had me kneel in front of this beautiful flowered altar. As I was kneeling, they had me taste traditional foods representing the different flavors—sweet, salty, sour, and bitter—with a specific teaching for each taste. They were telling me that this is how life is; it has all of these different experiences, and they were giving it to me in this sacred way with the message that as I took on my traditional name, I had a responsibility to myself and to my community through all of life's seasons. It was basically instructions for how to live my day-to-day life.

Katie: That reminds me of a paper where we talked about this within community connectedness. We described the purpose of naming ceremonies as protective because the ceremony and the name literally places you in relationship to the rest of your people. You're no longer this individual. You have been placed in relationship to community, and there are implications for your own health and well-being. Naming someone says you belong to this community in this capacity, in this relationship, and you have responsibilities to this community and, as a result, they also have responsibility to you. We *all* have naming ceremonies. When you graduate, you go from being a student to becoming a social worker. You go from being a PhD student to an assistant professor to an associate professor. These are naming ceremonies with associated roles and responsibilities. What we are often missing is community accountability and reciprocity. And in *those* naming ceremonies, we perpetuate hierarchy. Where are we serving a community and where are we serving a settler colonial system? We have an opportunity to reimagine this. We can reconsider our roles as we move through these positions in academia, and we can imagine how to better define and live our responsibilities to our communities. The same is true for social work practitioners.

Strategies: Naming and Claiming, Modeling, Transparency

Naming and Claiming

Naming and claiming is a way that we introduce our whole selves to a community. Like a positionality statement, when we name ourselves, our ancestors, our original lands, we are informing the individual or community with whom we are interacting of our legacies as well as our intentions. They may then decide how they will proceed in welcoming us, working with us, or not. Social workers should make this part of their daily practice. In doing so, we challenge whiteness as the center of normativity, and we make the first gesture toward building trust in relationships.

Modeling

When we name our identities and claim our communities and experiences with all of their complexities, we invite others to do the same. The more that we articulate how complex experiences exist within individual, community, and collective bodies, the more equipped we are to understand and identify alternative possibilities and practices. Social workers can do this work in clinical and nonclinical settings by showing others how to name their identities and claim their communities.

Transparency

Social workers are often discouraged from transparency and disclosure, but when practiced in a way that respects context and boundaries, it can be a powerful tool for building trust and shared understanding. It can be a form of representation where others might see themselves in an experience and consequently feel less isolated. Social workers should work to normalize the relational nature of giving and receiving help and social support. By destigmatizing that care within clinical settings or research spaces or in education as a common experience across and between people, we challenge settler logics of deservedness and dominion over other's lives and agency. This is a form of Indigenous story work, and it is sacred work.

Tell us a story of when you felt the dissonance between being a social justice advocate or abolitionist and an agent of the state.

Danica: When I was in clinical practice, I was working for the juvenile justice system. I worked as a mental health and chemical dependency counselor with juvenile probation for five years. When I started to work there, I went in with the attitude that I was going to be the "good" social worker. I was going to be the one person that they can trust and come to and put all their feelings in my counselor basket. I just had this very Pollyanna idea of what that work was going to look like. Part of the reason I became an anarchist and moved into a socialist perspective of working within and reforming systems and then to abolition was because of my time there. What became very clear was that I was not there to actually help them. I was there to punish them, to perpetuate this pipeline to the prison. Also at that point, I was working with the most criminalized youth that were looking at going to prison—whether it be juvenile prison or adult prison—so I had a lot of clients that were being direct filed as adults for homicide, drug dealing, or violent assault. I had very direct conversations with them about the nature of our relationship, and they appreciated the transparency and the realness of it. I told them that the best way to get off probation was just do what you need to do. Stop smoking weed for six months, for example. Consequently, I had a really high success rate, because my clients were like, "Oh, I can do that." So, at any rate, I think that's really when I started thinking about myself as a clinical social worker within a system intentionally designed to control the most marginalized, and that, I realized, is what needs to be abolished.

Katie: This makes me think about how we live multiple [professional] lives. You can do different things in different ways at different times in your life, based on the position, place, and power you have. I wonder if that's part of it too. We can contribute differently at different stages. Each stage you learn something that leads you to the next stage—just like you described, Danica. I am currently at a big public university. These systems are hierarchical and capitalist. But I chose to work here; how do I push back against that and how am I complicit in maintaining the current system? This makes me think of what it means to me to be an abolitionist. Maybe my role is staying in this academy. It's not the fire in the street, but there's some value to it. Sometimes it doesn't feel like enough and other times I think it's an important role to play. We can make an impact in different ways depending on where we are at a particular time and the roles that we play may change. I wonder if that's a helpful concept for people approaching the idea of abolition work, that our role in it can change over time.

Zean: Absolutely, I think that that speaks nicely to when I interned at a community-based organization during the summer between my first and second year of my master's program and we were protesting the university. I was getting paid, as a university student, to protest the inequitable treatments that the university was enacting on marginalized communities while I was also an employee of the university. And I think that was a really important political education moment for me as I considered that dissonance. It took me a long time to unpack and define my role of helping other people reach their own political education. That's kind of where I'm sitting with my role now. As an educator, I'm trying to get folks to move further left. In our political spectrum, I am trying to educate them toward a more progressive and critical way of thinking. So I think that's part of the tension of considering how we teach people and prepare people to engage in more radical or progressive movements from within these institutions whose very roots run deep as colonizing systems.

Angela: My mentor Ada Deer is a strong activist and a major leader in restoration of our tribal sovereignty after several decades of termination. Her slogan for her eighty-sixth birthday last year was, "I'm eighty-six and still in the mix and looking for some tricks." She was the first woman to head the US Bureau of Indian Affairs. While there, she said she tried to do as much as she could, as fast as she could, for as many as she could. She dealt with a lot of resistance and challenges as the first Native woman in this position. I remember as a practitioner when I was doing more crisis intervention, feeling the tension of using the Diagnostic Statistical Manual (DSM) to diagnose patients so that their treatment could be covered, yet also feeling the tension of how decontextualized and pathologizing these diagnoses could be. That tension made me feel frustrated and overwhelmed at times, and I wanted to work toward addressing structural root causes. Seeing how my dad and the other elders organized in the community with wisdom, knowledge, and advocacy to protect our land and sovereignty has really made me think about finding strategies. I remembered some of the wisdom of my elders, and when I felt that tension, I would ask myself, "Where are we right now? What can we do and how can we best focus our power at this moment?" I return to the present and consider what I can do in this moment—then in a clinical setting and now working in a research and educational setting with a focus on prevention at the structural level.

Danica: I would like to talk about disposability. The most recent political climate has created these reactionary processes, and social media exacerbates the mob mentality that comes for people who make mistakes and just throws them away—as if they are the whole of their one wrong action. That's exactly what the carceral state does. You commit a crime, you go to prison; you misuse substances, you lose your housing and your children. We have recreated these systemic values in our communities, too. That is how deep the colonization is. We don't talk about how to address and deal with conflict in any meaningful or healing way. How do we address and deal with harm in our communities? How do we create a space that's not just punitive, where you banish people from the community? Disposing of people is not our way. Banishment should not be the first option, but the last. When all else has failed. As Indigenous Peoples, we don't see people as disposable. We hold people accountable, yes, but we don't throw them away. Everyone has a role and responsibility, and something to teach and learn. We identify, as a community, what actions will restore learning to the perpetrator and peace to those impacted, and balance to the community as a whole. We do this by centering the needs and voices of those who are harmed in the process, to be survivor centered.

Strategies: Articulate Contributions, Act Accordingly, and Challenge Disposability

Identify and Articulate Strengths, Skills, and Contributions

Everyone has a role and associated responsibility and should act according to those responsibilities. When we identify and acknowledge the unique skills and talents of everyone, we transcend the hierarchical model of leadership and organization that often centers charismatic individuals and builds horizontal models of community contributions that honor individuals within the collective. Social workers should assist individuals and communities in identifying their unique strengths, talents, skills, and contributions and then should support and uplift those roles.

Challenge Disposability

Indigenous communities understand that people are in process and that we are surviving historical and intergenerational trauma and colonization. No person is the entirety of one singular action or characteristic. When people make mistakes, intentionally or unintentionally, we invite them into dialogue for repair or restitution. Sometimes this restitution requires banishment (for a time or permanently). But that is not the same as disposing of them entirely. We give them the opportunity to be supported in their learning and growing either within or apart from the community. Social workers must also challenge disposability and, in collaboration with communities, offer creative and collective approaches to repairing harm in a collective healing process.

What do you think are strategies for social workers that are specific to land and place, restorative justice, and cultural innovations?

Angela: What keeps resonating, again and again, is not only that focus on imagination and future but also on the present, by recognizing that we're already doing successful practices and interventions in our communities. We always consider how the past is informing the future. My first and only Indigenous Professor of social work in my undergraduate program, who's now retired, said, "You won't change anything but you'll have an influence over a number of people for a time, so do what you love." I think that spirit of acting in and through love is essential as we think about Indigenist abolition. Those Indigenist principles are based in love for community.

Katie: (laughs) Yes! Danica, I've come to realize that all your militant shit is so clearly rooted in love! That's what makes it powerful.

Ramona: Isn't that what abolition really is about? Imagining for our future generations is what our ancestors did. And I think it is what we are doing now and it is all out of love. When I think about it, I imagine my children and maybe my grandchildren and how much I love them and want them to live full beautiful lives. Ultimately, if I were to define abolition in a few words, it would be *creation, imagination,* and *innovation,* and I think those things are absolutely endemic to who we are as original peoples. We have always been innovators, always creators, always imagined something new and better in relation to our place and to the cosmos and we have always had these conversations.

Strategies: Imagining/Imagination
Imagining/Imagination
Eve Tuck describes mainstream approaches to research as "damage centered" as they uphold narratives of marginalized people as "depleted, ruined, and hopeless."[24] Tuck calls for "desire-based" research, which she describes as an antidote to the pain and suffering documented in damage-centered research in that it understands "complexity, contradiction, and self-determination of lived lives."[25] In this way, imagining is moving backward and forward in our thinking simultaneously to create new and more complex pathways, reflective of our past, present, and futures. Social workers should reject damage-centered research, education, and practice and should cocreate new methods for engaging with clients and communities that embrace complexity and imagine new possibilities.

Indigenous Futurism
Futurism is a practice of imagining and creating alternative practices and pathways toward a preferred future.[26] Anishinaabe scholar Grace Dillon first coined the term *Indigenous futurism,* which she describes as a renewal and regenerating process of envisioning the future using themes,

images, and technology of science fiction distinctly shaped by Indigenous Peoples' worldviews.[27] Through stories and story work, there is always guidance that helps us reimagine and envision a more just and distinctly Indigenous future as a living practice of abolition.

Discussion and Conclusion

In our current moment, it is difficult to imagine a world without authoritative power structures like law enforcement, child welfare, and prisons, which work in tandem with social work. However, there were systems of governance in place before the creation of what has become the current prison industrial complex. Ojibwe elder Art Solomon states, "We were not perfect, but we had no jails . . . no old peoples' homes, no children's aid societies, we had no crisis centers. We had a philosophy of life based on the Creator. And we had our humanity."[28] Social work as a professionalized discipline and area of study must grapple with our historical and ongoing relationship with enforcing institutionalized racism, dispossession, and criminalization of Indigenous land and life.

Social workers must develop new strategies that align our roles, responsibilities, and practices with our stated values. "At the level of direct services, an abolition praxis means that intervention programs and advocacy initiatives must avoid even the most subtle or indirect reliance on the punishment industry as a way to restore equilibrium to individuals or groups."[29] Abolition and decolonization provide a pathway for us to craft our aims toward liberation. Unifying the three principles of Indigenist research, resistance as the emancipatory imperative, political integrity, and privileging Indigenous voices together with abolition, we can begin to craft new practices that will build radically different forms of governance, community accountability, and collective care.

5

Abolition: The Missing Link in Historical Efforts to Address Racism and Colonialism within the Profession of Social Work

Justin S. Harty, Autumn Asher BlackDeer, María Gandarilla Ocampo, Claudette L. Grinnell-Davis

The profession of social work has historically struggled to address racism and colonialism. These efforts have failed, and will continue to fail, until social work critically examines the historical interrelatedness between racism and colonialism against people of color and attends to a missing link in the profession—abolitionism. In this chapter, we will analyze historical evidence of social work's struggles to address racism and colonialism as well as the profession's failure to link abolition to address both simultaneously. We will share a historical case example of a unified attempt by five Council on Social Work Education's Multicultural Task Forces (MCTFs) to address racism and colonialism within social work in the 1970s. Using content analysis of primary archival sources, we will discuss how the MCTF attempted to compel social work to address racism and colonialism through efforts that align with an abolitionist framework. Rooted in lessons from social work's past, we propose an integrated and historically sensitive antiracism, anticolonialism, and abolitionism framework we call the Critical Historical Antiracism, Anticolonialism, and Abolitionism Framework (CHAAAF). The CHAAAF leverages social work history to critically assess our profession's fragmentation and dehistoricization of racial disempowerment and colonial domination among people and communities of color. Our framework provides rationale as to why social work must concurrently address the unique needs of different populations of color, stemming from concurrent but divergent histories of racism, colonialism, and oppression. Last, our framework leverages a critical assessment of social work history and a unification of antiracism, anticolonialism, and abolitionism efforts.

Antiracism, Anticolonialism, and Abolition in Social Work History

In this section, we share social work efforts, or lack thereof, to address racism and colonialism within the profession. We also share social work efforts to leverage abolition to address racism and colonialism.

Historical Antiracism Efforts

Within the National Association of Social Work (NASW) Code of Ethics, an ethical responsibility of social workers to broader society is that "[s]ocial workers should act to prevent and eliminate domination of, exploitation of, and discrimination against any person, group, or class on the basis of race, ethnicity, national origin, color, sex, sexual orientation, gender identity or expression, age, marital status, political belief, religion, immigration status, or mental or physical ability."[1] Although not explicitly stated, this ethical standard can be unequivocally interpreted to mean that, among other things, social workers *should* be antiracists. Although racial justice can be considered at the epicenter of social work practice,[2] the profession has lacked sustained, concerted, and targeted antiracist efforts that reflect this prioritization. The profession in part has struggled with explicitly naming the many ways in which racism manifests in the profession, our practice, and in society more broadly. An NASW report notes that "the challenge for the profession is to have the courage to label racism as racism even though it is not comfortable."[3] This wanting courage has contributed to the lagging acknowledgment of the profession's responsibility to address racism.

For instance, despite the formalization of the profession in the late 1800s,[4] it was not until the 1980s that the NASW launched "Color in a White Society," an initiative to address racism across the system levels.[5] Although some system change resulted from this initiative, it was insufficient to effectively address racism in society. In 2005, the "need to address racism through social work education and social work practice" was formally identified at the 2005 Social Work Congress.[6] An NASW racism policy statement asking the entire profession to address institutional racism within the profession and society was published subsequently in 2006.[7] In this statement, NASW acknowledged the need for the organization and more broadly, the profession, to grapple with their complicity of maintaining white privilege and to commit to act against it.[8] In 2020, eliminating racism became one of the Grand Challenges for Social Work.[9]

Beyond these occasional calls for antiracism, which included recommended action steps, the profession has not taken innovative steps to meaningfully coalesce and organize social workers to collectively dismantle institutional racism, white supremacy, and other forms of oppression. This lack of mobilization on behalf of social work organizational bodies has resulted in stagnation, which "allows for the perpetuation of racist and oppressive policies and actions."[10] Unsurprisingly, racism persists, and the profession has much work to do to truly become antiracist. Ultimately, social work has historically struggled to take action against racial hatred, racial discrimination, and systemic racism within the profession.[11] Social work has, at various times, adopted antiracist approaches to address racism within the profession.[12] These efforts have centered on promoting awareness of prejudice, biases, and stereotypes held by white social workers initially toward Black populations, as well as awareness of the structures of power that produce and maintain racial oppression.[13] Antiracism has been expanded to include Black, Indigenous, and other people of color (BIPOC),[14] but anticolonialism has not been included in these efforts.[15]

Historical Anticolonialism Efforts

The history of social work education is deeply embedded within the dual powers of white supremacy and settler colonialism.[16] White social workers in the United States were integral to perpetuating settler colonialism and anti-Blackness.[17] This legacy persists today as social work continues its colonial and white supremacist legacies. Miller described social work ideology that characterizes its role in relationship to Black America as "philanthropic colonialism" by stating, "There may be an evil more terrible than racism, an enemy more powerful than ignorant prejudice, a doctrine more insidious than exploitation."[18] Coloniality is not to be confused with colonialism. Settler colonialism is an ongoing system of power that perpetuates the genocide of Indigenous peoples. While *settler colonialism* refers to the political and economic structures that perpetuate the eradication of Indigenous peoples and cultures to replace them with a settler society, *coloniality* is the long-standing patterns of power that result from this colonialism. Social work as a field operates from coloniality.[19]

It is critical to interrogate the origins of social work as a Western psychological project, an active extension of coloniality.[20] Manifestations of coloniality are namely systems of hierarchies (racial division), systems of knowledge (privileging Western knowledge as objective), and societal systems (state-regulated institutions that enforce hierarchies and knowledge segregation). Coloniality is also referred to as the colonial matrix of power, including the control of history, knowledge, health, and justice.[21] Social work perpetuates coloniality by whitewashing what counts as social work history, privileging Eurocentric forms of knowledge, ignoring health disparities of marginalized communities, and failing to live up to its purported mission of social justice. We cannot analyze oppression and subjugation without understanding coloniality and white supremacy. The field of social work bypasses both white supremacy and coloniality with shallow conversations about white privilege rather than directly addressing the structures that maintain these forces throughout the profession.[22] Social work education takes an approach of multiculturalism, namely through concepts of diversity and cultural competence, both of which enable the colonial construction of whiteness.[23]

Attempts to address colonialism within the profession of social work have centered around discussion—not action. For example, in 2002, the NASW published a policy statement entitled "Sovereignty and the Health of Indigenous Peoples."[24] Provided in brief bullet point format, a scurried presentation of settler colonialism is described in relation to various Indigenous communities; however, there is no mention of complicity or perpetuation of coloniality in social work. Two decades later, in the midst of cultural upheaval, the NASW[25] released an apology statement detailing how social workers have been complicit in colonial practices and furthering harm against Black and Indigenous communities. In 2021, the Council on Social Work Education (CSWE) published the "Statement of Accountability and Reconciliation for Harms Done to Indigenous and Tribal Peoples."[26] Authored by Indigenous social workers and advocated for by the Indigenous and Tribal Social Work Educators Association, this report is the first formal document published by a social work entity that addresses colonialism and complicity within social work in the United States. It remains to be seen what impact this report will have within the profession and what information, if any, will be taken up in social work education. Critiquing complicity without action will not lead to social change.[27] It is critical to grapple with coloniality and move toward embracing new and alternate histories and knowledge in social work.

Historical Abolition Efforts

Social work has not had coordinated efforts leveraging abolitionist goals or ideals. Most efforts aligning with abolitionism come from BIPOC communities and social workers resisting colonialism and racism within the profession of social work. Expanding beyond more contemporary expressions of abolitionism within social work, examples of abolition among BIPOC communities may be seen in historical efforts by Black communities in ensuring their social welfare needs when white dominant social work excluded Blacks from service delivery.[28] Additionally, Black political thought during the Civil Rights movement brought Afrocentrism into the domain of social work. "Although Afrocentric social work research is committed to abolishing all forms of oppression, it is primarily concerned with eliminating racial and cultural oppression because both pervasively affect the lives of persons of African descent."[29] Since the late 1960s, the National Association of Black Social Workers has centered Black liberation in their social work efforts. These contemporary social work efforts have focused on the profession's role in abolishing carceral systems,[30] child welfare systems,[31] and the general social work profession.[32]

A Case Example from Our Past: Council on Social Work Education's Multicultural Task Forces

In the early 1970s, the Council on Social Work Education (CSWE) recognized that social work needed to address the effects of racism and oppression on the profession. In an effort to address this issue, the CSWE established five Multicultural Task Forces (MCTF) tasked with creating a list of concerns and recommendations for social work to take up in an effort to address inequality within the profession, and social work education specifically. The MCTF was comprised of the American Indian, Asian American, Black, Chicano, and Puerto Rican Task Forces. In 1973, CSWE published all five of the MCTF reports that all contained lists of concerns and recommendations.[33] The CSWE MCTF reports serve as a historical snapshot into efforts by BIPOC social work students, researchers, and educators to compel the profession to address racism and colonialism on the heels of the Civil Rights movement.

A Historical Critical Content Analysis

We used the five MCTF reports as the texts for our historical critical content analysis. The five task force reports were scanned, digitized, and run through optical character recognition software to obtain textual data used for our analysis. We entered the textual data into qualitative data analysis software for analysis. We leveraged the MCTF reports as *explicit sources of evidence* representing direct concerns and recommendations for social work to address racism, colonialism, and abolition. We used first-cycle coding to analyze textual data using Boolean search terms for instances of racism (e.g., "racism," "racist," "racis*"), colonialism (e.g., "colonialism," "colonize," "coloni*"), abolition (e.g., "abolition," "abolish," "aboli*"), and liberation (e.g., "free," "liberation," "liberate," "liberat*"). The resulting occurrences were categorized based on the respective search term. For the purpose of our analysis, we nested occurrences of the term *liberation* within occurrences of the term *abolition*. Our rationale for the combined category stems from our operationalization of the term *abolition*. We operationalized *abolition* as efforts to liberate oppressed people. Therefore, we consider the two terms to be interdependent and of the same category. After creating categories (i.e., racism, colonialism, abolition) based on themes from the four search terms (i.e., racism, colonialism, abolition, and liberation), we used second-cycle coding to create three subcodes based on concerns or recommendations that were *general* to all BIPOC groups, *similar* to all BIPOC groups, or *different* among BIPOC groups. We share key findings of our historical critical content analysis next.

The Relatedness between Colonization and Racism

Results from our analysis demonstrate that, generally, the MCTF's reports reflect that social work's one-size-fits-all approach to addressing inequality was not sufficient to meet the needs of BIPOC groups leading up to the mid-1970s. This may be best understood from CSWE's Native American Task Force's description of the creation of the MCTFs:

> During its early planning stages, the [CSWE MCTF] Council recognized that certain problems were common to all the major ethnic minority groups under consideration: American Indians, Asian Americans, Blacks, Chicanos, and Puerto Ricans. It was also recognized that there were other problems and issues of special concern to individual minority groups and that these would most appropriately be dealt with by task forces from each of the minority groups.[34]

This quote demonstrates that although some issues and concerns around inequality were common among BIPOC groups, other issues and concerns were different among different BIPOC groups. But what leads to common and divergent issues among BIPOC groups that social work needs to understand? A passage from the Asian American Task Force provides an important explanation:

> Historically, America has tolerated and in some instances even welcomed minorities to the country during times of special need. Generally, this has consisted of a need for cheap labor. For example, the Blacks filled a need in the South to plant and harvest cotton; the Chinese filled a need to build the railways; and the Japanese, Filipinos, and Chicanos were needed for agricultural labors in the West. Yet, when these needs were met and the minorities began to compete for work with the whites, individual and institutional acts of racism came out in the open.[35]

This quote represents our fundamental argument. The differing forms of exploitation among BIPOC communities through varying forms of colonization leads to institutional racism.

Some MCTF concerns focused on the effects of colonialism and racism faced by all BIPOC groups. For example, the Black Task Force shared a concern that "neocolonialism and institutional racism have been built into all American institutions, structures, and systems. Social policies, as well as social work itself, have been both reflections of and instruments by which neocolonialism and institutional racism have been sustained and expanded."[36] This quote demonstrates that colonialism and racism are intertwined systemic structures embedded in social policy and social work affecting all BIPOC populations. Other concerns of the MCTFs regarding colonialism and racism reflected consequences that were unique among different BIPOC groups. For example, in sharing considerations that social workers should understand, the Puerto Rican Task Force discussed the resilience of Puerto Ricans during periods of colonization:

> Despite a heritage of years of Spanish colonial domination followed by seventy years of United States colonialist economic and cultural penetration, the Puerto Ricans brought with them a variety of strengths much needed for the trials ahead. They brought a fierce pride in their culture, language, and heritage. They brought a unity of family much needed to withstand the stress of transplantation to essentially inhospitable communities.[37]

This quote demonstrates how the effects of colonialism specifically affected Puerto Rican populations. The Black Task Force also shared the distinct effects that colonization and racism had on the Black community—"the growth and development of the Black community itself has been greatly deterred by institutional racism and colonialism."[38]

The Role of Abolition

Some recommendations made by the MCTF directly called for social work to adopt abolitionist ideals to address colonialism and racism. For example, the Asian American Task Force shared that:

[m]ovements for Black Power, Brown Power, Red Power, and now Yellow Power, guided by the colonial analogy, are proclaiming the objectives of "liberation." In practical terms this means the mobilization and application of political power to affect basic social changes that will benefit the masses of these peoples. Along with their Black, Chicano, and Native American brothers and sisters, Asian Americans are saying that their fundamental problems are systemic and structural, resulting from the oppressive nature of the nation's major political and economic institutions.[39]

The Asian American Task Force's statement embodies the essence of abolition through the idea that colonialism had created conditions in which BIPOC populations were oppressed. They ultimately argue that social work can create social change through the abolition of systemic and structural inequality within political and economic institutions. The Black Task Force made similar recommendations, albeit more focused on the role of the Black community: "[I]nstitutional racism has been conceptualized as a major handicapping force, and the Black community's thrust has shifted from civil rights to a goal of liberation. Liberation is seen here as 'self-determination, community control, and achievement of power.'"[40] Ultimately, the Black Task Force argued that social work should have, like the Black community during the 1970s, shifted focus toward abolishing institutional racism to ensure Black liberation.

Failing to Learn from Our Past

Results of our analysis demonstrate two key lessons from the MCTF as it relates to addressing colonialism and racism within the profession of social work. First, colonialism and racism are intricately connected. Racial and ethnic minority groups all have histories embedded in colonialism and racism. However, the form of colonialism that each group faces varies. Subsequently, each group experiences different variants of racism that are leveraged to justify associated forms of colonialism.

A dominant theme in our analysis was the need for social work to address colonialism and racism as part of the same enterprise, not separate aims. Second, key recommendations made by some of the MCTF groups included social work that leverage abolition and liberation to address the consequences of colonialism and the resulting systemic and structural racism oppressing historically marginalized racial and ethnic groups. As we demonstrate in the beginning of this chapter, social work historically struggled to address colonialism and racism. Perhaps social work would have had more success in addressing colonialism and racism if the profession simultaneously addressed both issues through a liberatory framework. We have developed a framework rooted in the MCTF's historical lessons to address our profession's inability to concurrently address colonialism and racism centered on abolitionist goals, which we will introduce next.

Critical Historical Anticolonialism, Antiracism, and Abolitionism Framework

We developed an integrated antiracism, anticolonialism, and abolitionism framework rooted in history that we call the Critical Historical Anticolonialism, Antiracism, and Abolitionism Framework. Our CHAAAF leverages colonialism typologies and their related forms of racism. The CHAAAF is grounded in the notion that racism legitimizes colonialism and antiracism struggles are essentially struggles against colonial domination, and vice versa. To address both colonialism and racism, the CHAAAF centers abolition to meet the liberatory and self-determinist goals of BIPOC populations.

Central to the CHAAAF is the understanding that colonialism and racism are both tools of white supremacy. Although most racial and ethnic groups experience colonialism and racism, the type of colonialism faced by each racial or ethnic group varies as does the kind of racism they experience. Nancy Shoemaker outlines different forms of colonization based upon the colonizers' motivations.[41] For example, Shoemaker's typologies of colonialism include settler colonialism, where settlers claim land and force original inhabitants out; planter colonialism, where colonizers exploit slave labor for the mass production of crops; and imperial power colonialism, where colonizers exploit foreign land and populations for expansion. Although the examples we supply are not exhaustive, it is clear how racial and ethnic groups have historically experienced variants of colonialism such as settler colonialism (e.g., Indigenous populations), planter colonialism (e.g., Black populations), and imperial colonialism (e.g., African, Mexican, Asian, and Indian populations). Accordingly, these racial and ethnic populations have experienced divergent forms of racism historically used to justify Indigenous land theft for settler colonialism, Black enslavement for planter colonialism, and political and economic dominance and exploitation of people with Native American, Alaskan, African, Mexican, Asian, and Indian ancestry for imperial colonialism.[42]

Implications of the Critical Historical Anticolonialism, Antiracism, and Abolitionism Framework for Social Work

The CHAAAF is informed by repeated attempts by BIPOC social workers to compel social work to engage in anticolonialism and antiracism efforts and our profession's inability to do either. The CHAAAF addresses ways that our profession has decoupled links between racism and colonialism, thereby ignoring connections between variants of colonialism and racism. We developed the CHAAAF in an effort to compel social work to simultaneously address colonialism and racism since separate, one-size-fits-all approaches are insufficient to address these issues as intended for different BIPOC groups. However, one essential question remains. How can social work meaningfully address colonialism and racism concurrently, given the fact that elements of both are either common to or unique among specific BIPOC groups based on the type of colonialism for which each group has been dominated and exploited? One approach would be for social work to work toward abolishing systems of colonization and racism.

To abolish forms of colonization unique to different populations of color, social work must make meaningful efforts to abolish variants of colonialism including settler colonialism, planter colonialism, and imperial colonialism affecting distinct BIPOC communities. Social work must also simultaneously target efforts in addressing racism and colonialism among populations of color consistent with universal abolition causes, including abolishing legal racism, systems of oppression, carceral systems, and family separation. Our profession must make efforts to achieve common abolition aspirations such as racial, social, economic, and historical justice. These efforts must also address divergent abolition goals including Indigenous land reclamation, Black liberation, and non-White immigrant citizenship. To abolish racialized systems of colonization affecting all populations of color, social work must abolish economic, political, and social structures oppressing BIPOC populations. This includes abolishing racialized carceral and policing systems that kill, repress, and suppress BIPOC communities. Furthermore, social work must make efforts to abolish racialized systems that enforce repressive social order among BIPOC populations through welfare programs and social services. Social work will continue to fail at addressing colonialism and racism among BIPOC populations if the profession does not work to abolish both concurrently. Furthermore, social work will continue to fail at anticolonialism and antiracism efforts if the profession is unable to meet common and divergent abolitionist goals of BIPOC populations.

section 2
PARADOXES

6
Is Social Work Obsolete?

Kassandra Frederique

I remember the crackling sound as the paper burned. I watched as he joyfully pushed the paper further and further into the fire. This group of friends laughed and cheered at their degree burning celebration. This person was burning their master of social work degree because of the belief that the degree was overpriced and worthless. I was surprised by how annoyed I was—it could be because the room was full of folks that were never denied an education, or it could be the part of me that still believed in the institution of higher education. But I couldn't ignore my resistance to his assertion that the social work degree was worthless. Anyone who knows me knows that I am a reluctant social worker in every sense. I went to social work school because there was no graduate exam for entry, I wasn't ready to work, and I thought it would give me two years before going to my real grad school goal of law school. Even when I was in social work school, I understood its temporal role in my life and identity. When I started my job in drug policy, I found it useful in some instances, and of course there was the benefit of being able to identify as a social worker on an issue that deals with the complexities of human behavior. But a feeling of ambivalence was never far behind. Social workers were always the people who put out the flames, but never the ones to prevent the fire or, more importantly to me, the ones to start one.

As an undergrad during my union summer internship, we knocked on doors looking for members and sometimes if we knew someone was home but not answering, we'd try, "We're from the union; we're not social workers." And sometimes it worked.

As I watched the letters crinkle in the fire, I realized that I was more attached to these institutions than I thought. Fire is a necessary element for light, for warmth, and in some traditions, for rebirth and transformation. In this chapter, I challenge abolitionist social workers to question whether or not we should hold on to the social work profession. Citing its history and pointing to its impact, I contend that professional social work as a discipline is misaligned with abolitionist practice and futures.

Is Social Work Obsolete?

In 1869, Helen Bonsanquet and Octavia Hill founded the Charity Organization Society in London.[1] This organization is often credited with professionalizing the social work discipline. Members of the organization believed they could help people do better for themselves and that, with limited government intervention, they could mitigate the effects of poverty. Although some would call them noble in their mission, their insistence on "self-help" and "limited government intervention" are a driving force in my assertion that social work as a profession and discipline should be abolished. Inherent in this vision of social work is the sole focus by professional social work on individuals and their actions as the reason for their poverty—when, in fact, it is government policies working to uphold a capitalist system rooted in exploitation and inequality that often create the conditions that limit the opportunities, and therefore the options, that some individuals have. The Great Depression in the United States offers a prime example in which social workers' prominence increased because of the eroding social conditions caused by the economic downturn.

In her book *Golden Gulag*,[2] Ruth Wilson Gilmore talks about land, labor, and the state in relation to the role the prison industrial complex plays in their protection. I argue that social work exists to protect capital, land, labor, and the state's capacity to ignore its citizenry. Since its inception, social work has focused heavily on casework and individual responsibility—which has played an outsized role in shaping how the general public thinks about those in need of support. The social work profession has focused so much on making individuals prove they are deserving of support, and in doing so, the profession has obfuscated and overlooked why the person is without. Social work's historic orientation has not and does not question the why. Its focus is on what to do now and, as a result, it serves as a benevolent distractor.

For example, in a place like New York City where we have over 100,000 New Yorkers who are homeless, mayors could use their power and resources to provide housing for everyone. Yet in 2023, Mayor Eric Adams pointed to shelters and private partnerships as the answer.[3] In one of the richest cities in the world, why would Adams and much of the public think that shelters—which by definition are temporary housing entities—could deal with a problem as massive as 100,000 unhoused individuals? This kind of approach is kicking the can down the road, and the profession of social work is aiding in pushing the can. Adams is outsourcing the responsibility of our citizenry to private and nonprofit institutions instead of looking at what the city can and should provide. Social workers in these institutions stand by Adams and assure the public that they can provide the resources instead of pointing to the role of developers who the city supports, or the rising rents that are pushing people out, or the lack of diverse housing options that need to be developed to support people with unmet needs. How is this the social work profession's fault? Well, social work is built on asking the wrong questions. Social work too often asks what the profession can provide instead of why this is happening. And when people don't go into the shelters, we ask what is wrong with the person, instead of what is wrong with the "help" that we are offering. The profession tries to nod to this responsibility in its code of ethics:

> Social workers should promote the general welfare of society, from local to global levels, and the development of people, their communities, and their environments. Social workers should advocate for living conditions conducive to the fulfillment of basic human needs and should promote social, economic, political, and cultural values and institutions that are compatible with the realization of social justice.[4]

Can we honestly say that this is what social workers are doing across the United States? Can we honestly say that the general public looks to social work as arbiters of social justice and a profession that sets and fights for the basic standard of human need? Or does society see our profession as the ambulance chasers after the harm or tragedy has occurred to keep society's train moving by getting the harmed individuals out of the way?

Some will read this and think, how does professional social work shape the thinking of the general public? Part of the answer is that people get to point to the social work profession as the entity in place to manage society's biggest challenges. Jane Addams, the person credited with founding social work in the United States, believed that settlement houses "laid the foundations for American civil society, a neutral space within which different communities and ideologies could learn from each other and seek common grounds for collective action."[5] Poverty isn't neutral—our failure to actively elevate, interrogate, and dismantle the roots of social work means that we are a generator of those same conditions.

When we think about the world we want to build in the twenty-first and twenty-second centuries, does it really make sense for us to have what should be public goods (mental health care, health care, housing, food, etc.) running through an under resourced and often privatized social service infrastructure? For example, there should never be a homelessness crisis in the United States; we have both the resources and the space to provide everyone a home, especially if we disincentivize the commodification of housing. There is a wide disparity between what is actually available versus what people are getting. To keep the obfuscation in place, a significant portion of resources is funneled through the infrastructure of social work—mental health, support for families, housing, food, and health care. My question is, why are nonprofits providing services and resources that the government should and can provide? There are basic human rights that the government can and should provide for but social work has taken the responsibility for instead. The privatization of resources that should be public goods makes it difficult for us to hold people and organizations accountable when needs are not met. At least with the government in charge of providing these resources, we can in theory vote out people who fail to meet our needs.

Deservedness, Inequality and the Failure of Social Work

Social work upholds the infrastructure of charity and philanthropy, both of which are based on economic inequality and hierarchies of deservedness. This premise is important because it reinforces the idea that our current society does not have the resources to support our communities, and there must be an entity that helps the have-nots. The history of social work has shown us that the degree to which we help those people is based on a scale of deservedness.

This notion of deservedness has been woven into the fabric of the United States and cemented the idea that not everyone deserves to have their basic needs met. US citizens don't live in a country that says, "Everyone should have the right to health care or have access to housing." The United States requires that we earn those basic rights, and our ability to earn them is deeply impacted by where we rank in our country's power hierarchy. Even then, unless you are in the upper echelon, you must perform actions to have rights. And to get help and to be deemed as deserving, you must acquiesce to rules that encourage achieving worthiness to get help. Examples include things like having a job, sobriety, attending parenting classes or other state-mandated programs. These rules are in place to maintain a prescribed social order, to surveil, and to ensure that the folks who don't need help never feel threatened by those who do. This has been true since the inception of social work. Even the founders of social work theory at the Charity Organization Society admitted that they use "scientific principles to root out scroungers and target relief where it was most needed."[6]

More disconcerting is this country's belief in the permanence of the subservience of certain groups of people. Those groups include but are not limited to people who use drugs or are sex workers, disabled, cis and trans women, cash poor, immigrants, Black, and other people of color. Social work is based on the idea that there will always be have-nots. This belief—that some people will always be without and therefore will always be in need of help—is what has made social work dangerous in the past, and what necessitates its obsolescence in the future. This belief is not just a consequence of social work: it is a central feature of it. I do not think there always has to be have-nots, nor do I want to work with an institution or people that do. This belief in the permanence of poverty must be part of what we're trying to dismantle as we create a new world. Our profession derives its pride in part from the belief that social workers are both the first and last lines of defense against harm. We're there when you first meet trouble and there when you are facing your most difficult and darkest time after a long history of trouble. And although there are times that at your first meeting with a social worker a problem can be solved, there are many more times where social workers give people the bare minimum to get someone through the day/week, but not enough that they no longer need social workers. This was one of the first lessons that I learned in social work school, when an administrator said, "If they are coming to you, you can't break them anymore than they've already been broken, so don't worry."

As Brooklyn-based abolitionist social worker Michelle Grier once told me:

> If I'm always in the power position, able to write a treatment plan for your life, then the power dynamic is always going to be there. There'll always be power dynamics in relationships. I think that's what you were naming with the harm component. I'm thinking a lot about the ways in which social workers have so much control over family, so much control over motherhood, parenthood as a part of our institutions that were created by social work. I think about this term that was often said in school, that *we should be social working ourselves out of a job*. I think that's a really interesting tag to have as you know that's something that's going to be said to you by your professors or folks, but really not having that conversation in the discipline (practice).

In building on what Michelle says, I contend that, although that might be a common social work tagline, nothing in our discipline demonstrates our desire to be nonexistent or to forcefully disrupt or dismantle the circumstances our "clients" face.[7]

In asking the question about whether or not social work should exist, there is another question—whether or not "need or gaps" should exist in our imagined new world. Are we dreaming expansively enough if there are still folks in need? Or is it naive to believe that we can aspire to a world without need? I also can hear the commentary that we need social work until we get to the place where there are people without need. When I strip this down, I wonder if it's the idea that both reform and abolition are needed at the same time. Can they coexist? I believe they can. But it ultimately depends on what kind of reform we are talking about. Abolitionists have done exceptional work on identifying whether a reform is harmful or if it works toward abolitionist aims. When it comes to social work, I believe the profession is inherently focused on quelling opposition by offering bare minimum supports as an excuse to not agitate against the ruling class. Social work is a harmful reform profession that must be abolished and should not exist in the world we are working to build, and in the interim we need to build different institutions and strategies to provide care.

I also contend that one of the theories that holds us back is the fantasy that social work was good before and that somehow it got captured. Some social workers who criticize co-optation of social work by the carceral state believe in social work's noncarceral origin. Social work as a profession has always been inadequate.

This reality is well illustrated in social work's relationship to the 2020 summer uprisings and how it offered itself as a solution to the violence of police. In a moment of massive social upheaval when people from all walks of life questioned the role of law enforcement and police in our daily lives, the National Association of Social Work released a statement that said:

> "Social workers already work alongside and in partnership with police departments across the nation. Strengthening social worker and police partnerships can be an effective strategy in addressing behavioral health, mental health, substance use, homelessness, family disputes and other similar calls to 911 emergency response lines.
>
> In fact, social workers are playing an increasingly integral role in police forces, helping officers do their jobs more effectively and humanely and become better attuned to cultural and racial biases. And studies show social workers help police excel in fulfilling their mission to protect and serve.
>
> Protests are happening across the nation and around the world. Protesters are demanding police treat people who are Black more fairly and end this pandemic of unarmed Black people dying while in police custody. We at NASW [National Association of Social Work] know social workers will play a vital role in helping law enforcement better serve their communities; the social work profession can help our nation achieve better public safety outcomes."[8]

Here social work tries to position itself as the great balm to society—"hey, everyone, trust us, we're neutral—we'll keep the cops in line but keep copping in place." For people who are OK with the status quo but are disturbed by the George Floyd killing, social work reinforces the idea that police killings are an aberration in need of modification but not proof that the institution of policing needs to be dismantled. The summer uprisings of 2020 broke open a conversation about the institution of policing: What was its purpose? Should it be invested in? Who is harmed? Is it just killings where we draw the line, or are we concerned by the harassment, surveillance, and the feeling of occupation that some communities experience? But instead of bearing witness to this, facilitating this conversation, the social work institution inserts itself to affirm the need for the institution of policing. The existence of police and policing is not immutable, nor is the existence of need. These are realities that could be changed with strategic pressure and revolution. I offer the summer of 2020 example to illustrate how the institution of social work works to quell disruption and offer its workforce as agents of complacency.

From Help to Support

There is a subtle, yet meaningful distinction between help and support. People use them interchangeably, yet social work is described as a "helping" profession. Merriam-Webster defines *help* as "to give assistance or support to (someone): to provide (someone) with something that is useful or necessary in achieving an end."[9] Although banal, I find the secondary definitions more astute: "to make more pleasant or bearable." Herein lies the main case for abolishing social work. Ours is a profession whose main purpose is to make the destructive realities of society more bearable. This is done in part by convincing the masses that through individual actions we can make our individual lives better, despite knowing that the odds are stacked against our clients. It would be irresponsible to ignore that social workers have helped people. That said, the social work profession assumes a neutral position even in the face of oppression and endless precarity. But the social work profession isn't neutral; it has positioned itself as a gatekeeping profession that makes sure that the social order can be maintained. And when individuals or communities interrupt that order, social workers intervene to either disappear or assimilate people into the status quo.

The profession is built on the idea that social workers understand the world better than their clients. As a result, one of the main tools of social work is psychological and structural gaslighting, making people believe they are the problem while doing little to nothing to address the structural causes of their circumstances. Oftentimes what people need as help is for the state to provide them with the resources without hoops. Not only is the profession complicit in watching people drown, social workers are positioned to be lifeguards in the face of oppression and of assimilation, pulling people out just before they die but leaving them in the same place while doing little to tell folks that the tide is too high for swimmers.

In Angela Davis's book *Are Prisons Obsolete*,[10] she talks about John Bender and his study on penitentiaries during the English Enlightenment. Bender describes how the purpose of prison is to impose order, classification, cleanliness, good work habits, and self-consciousness. Prisons were seen as necessary to ensure order by removing unsightly people from society with the hope of rehabilitating them to be reintegrated into society, ready to be a part of the social order, rarely questioning whether or not what was deemed unsightly was a function of the individual or the rules. This is the starting point of the social work profession. This rationale for prisons is the same rationale for the establishment of settlement houses—to "civilize" immigrants and kidnap Indigenous children to teach them Christianity. It is the same rationale we now use against parents in family courts to dictate what is considered good parenting and when one can regain custody of their child. What's more, it is the field of social work that formed the institution of child welfare. Social work used the English Enlightenment's metrics as a way to decide if people are worthy to be in society, to be disciplined and corrected, or to be cast aside and alienated. Dr. Davis was talking about prisons, but we also must consider the role social workers play in maintaining a violent social order veiled in ideas of individualism and help.

In a world so intrinsically violent, we need coconspirators. This requires a reckoning for those that want to use their life to "help" others. The people you want to help should be people that you see yourself in, and as Desmond Tutu says, "my humanity is caught up and is inextricably bound up in yours."[11] Merriam-Webster defines *support* as a verb—uphold, advocate, back, champion. But the secondary definitions further solidify this distinction: "to promote the interests or cause of"; "to uphold or defend as valid or right"; "to argue or vote for"; "to provide with substantiation"; "to pay the costs of"; "to provide a basis for the existence or subsistence"; "to hold up or serve as a foundation or prop for."[12] Some may call the distinction between *help* and *support* semantics, but if we do not develop and nurture an analysis and practice around rigorous support, we will not have the practice and power necessary to build the new world that will buttress an abolitionist future.

The human experience is complex and layered. Even if we achieve everything we want as abolitionists, people will need support. For that support to exist, there is a need for us to invest our time in building bonds between each other. Those bonds aren't possible within the current infrastructure of professional social work. Between the nonprofit industrial complex, whose business model is dependent on people in distress, and the norms of professional boundaries, social workers are not positioned to have their freedoms tied to that of the client. In the world I am fighting for, we are facilitators, guides, conspirators. We organize with people because we share similar experiences. We do not have a profession that is instructed to stand on the sidelines claiming neutrality while community members get pummeled by the state, often the same pummeling that a segment of the social work workforce goes through in their own lives but cannot divulge because of professional boundaries.

In this new world, I am dreaming of communities of support for people. These communities are working together to identify their needs and organizing to transform their realities. I am imagining a state that has more responsibility and is unable to pass its responsibility off to nonstate actors that lack the resources to transform the situations. But even in this dream, I struggle to picture what we would need in the world after punishment. What would we actually be advocating for? What is the space in the middle as we move closer to utopia? Is it a bigger state infrastructure? I'm not always sure that works best for people who are historically marginalized—a bigger state feels scary. The other option is a world with less state involvement wherein we let people fend for themselves, which I believe would not work for people who are purposefully under resourced. Is there a middle ground where the state has an infrastructure that fulfills the universal needs of our communities: food, shelter, housing, accessibility, education, health care, transportation, utilities, and basic income? How does the existence of our current nonprofit and social work infrastructure dilute our power to demand these basic needs?

As an abolitionist policymaker with a master of social work degree arguing for the obsolescence of social work, I'm reminded that our most successful campaigns have been when we actually change the material conditions for people without passing a bill—when we can show that policymaking isn't the end goal. When deliverables and outcomes demand that success is measured by the passing of bills, we prove to ourselves and our community that what we need to do is change the contours of the conversation. We actually need to make policy less powerful, not more, and build our success based on a metric that's actually generative for and by our community. This is my metric for social work.

Building Communities of Care and Support

So what do we do? How do we provide care? How do we build communities of support?

One concept that's interested me during my own journey toward abolition is the idea that abolition doesn't mean harm won't happen. It was pretty disorientating for me and I was confronted with a ton of questions. Abolition doesn't mean utopia? Abolition isn't a destination? Abolition is a practice? I am organizing toward a new way of engaging harm? I can reduce harm by engaging in addressing structural inequities? Even if we can bring down incidences of certain kinds of harm, harm happens because people are people? As I have learned in my lifetime, people are complex, imperfect, and self-interested. People can commit harm for all types of reasons, including when they feel challenged, unsafe, threatened, angry, shameful, and so on. Understanding this and still organizing through an abolitionist lens demonstrates a commitment to humanity, believing we can move through difficult situations through collective actions in lieu of individualism and alienation.

If we abolish social work, how do we provide support in a world that will continue to include harm but not include as many (if any) structural inequities?

I want us to have a conversation about what we are striving for. Social workers consistently say, "I want to work myself out of the job," but how exactly do we measure that? Is our job complete when a child is snatched from their home and placed in a stranger's house? Or when we find housing for a mother and child in a dilapidated, under resourced shelter? Or is it when we help someone get a low-wage job that is known for terrible work conditions, limited opportunities for growth, and no health insurance? Yes, I purposely picked the underbelly examples of our profession because I want to ask the question: What is the point of social work? What is the job or profession that so many find "selfless and honorable"?

The purpose of this chapter is to provoke the conversation about if social work should exist when we achieve the world of abolition. I believe the answer is no. Social work as a profession should not exist in the world after the dismantling of cages both literal and felt. Why? Because social work itself is a cage masked by presumed benevolence. It is important to imagine a world where people have what they need, and we no longer need to teach people how to survive the world. I imagine a world where folks are thriving, have what they need, and have the space to embrace and explore the fullness of themselves. Some might describe this as utopia, but I know this world is real because I have seen it in places where people's basic needs are met, and they can experience the fullness of life. This human condition should not only be limited to the people that have the resources and space from the state to experience it. This chapter aims to provoke a conversation to color in what is needed for a world where we are all free—physically, materially, emotionally, and spiritually. We cannot have a free and just society if the profession of social work exists. If it does, it means that our imagination was stunted and that we conceded to what we could achieve in the existing order of things. Some people may find this exercise upsetting and disturbing. Why lob a grenade without a plan for escape? To those looking for a how-to, my response is that my ancestors didn't have to know freedom to know they wanted freedom. Sometimes realism is the enemy of liberation.

I am arguing for radical imagination that cannot hold both the social work profession and abolition.

Abolishing the field of social work does not mean we do not do care work. In fact, many people point to the fact that many nonwhite communities have always had institutions of care work that weren't explicitly named social work. Through the professionalization of social work, we took on the role of gatekeepers and perverted traditions of care work and care workers in our communities. Uplifting these traditions reminds us that abolition is about the reclamation of our humanity and our ability to see our worth tied to one another. How do we democratize the knowledge that we have? What are the ways that we can disrupt the systems and processes that we have to go through to get the things we need? How do we reduce their power?

Haven't we as social workers grown tired of having to do everything with nothing? I have, and for me the only thing left to do is light the match.

7

Abolition and the Welfare State[*]

Mimi E. Kim and Cameron W. Rasmussen

The Welfare State: Definitions and Discernments

As Ruth Wilson Gilmore has offered, "[A]bolition is not absence, it is presence."[1] That is, the work of abolition is about building and making present the relations, practices, and structures we need, rather than just abolishing the harmful systems and forces that exist. Our work is not just toward the absence of oppression, but realizing the presence of well-being. The last two decades of abolitionist organizing have surfaced significant discourses and strategizing about what that "presence" is or could be. Since the global protests of the summer of 2020, sharpened analysis, bolder demands, and new opportunities urging real-time negotiations with elected officials and state agents have shaped emergent on-the-ground examples of abolitionist-inspired policies and programs. From defund to refund, to divest/invest campaigns, to treatment not trauma, and to counselors not cops, there are numerous efforts struggling both *against* the carceral state and *for* transformative shifts in the presencing of abolition.

Protest against the *carceral* state has been front and center, and, indeed, forms the prominent backdrop for abolitionist values, frameworks, and actions. Antipolicing politics—informed by radical street protests of the 1960s, the platforms and actions of the Black Panthers and the Young

---

[*] This chapter is adapted from "Abolition and the Welfare State: Implications for Social Welfare," published in *Affilia: Feminist Inquiry in Social Work* 39, no. 1 in February 2024.

Lords, and the writings of Angela Y. Davis, Ruth Wilson Gilmore, Beth E. Richie, Michelle Alexander, Andrea Ritchie, Naomi Murakawa, and a host of critical activists/scholars—have produced a rich conceptual and empirical knowledge base on the carceral state. In the past two decades, initial convenings and ongoing organizing by abolitionist organizations such as Critical Resistance, established in 1998, and Incite!, founded in 2000, have further contributed to the popularization of abolitionist discourse on the prison industrial complex, the prison nation, mass and hyper incarceration, and other phenomena falling within the now common parlance of the carceral state.

In this present political moment, those advocating for the abolition of the carceral state have come to recognize the centrality of the punitive state to the reproduction of the capitalist state—leading to important writing and debates on the relationship between abolition and the state, more generally.[2] As activists continue struggles against and, in some cases, at the edges of or even within the state, contemporary reflections on the work of André Gorz[3] about the possibility or impossibility of abolition through reform** are fueling productive discernments guiding on-the-ground struggle.

What then can we say about abolition and the *welfare* state? Although the welfare state has already been deeply implicated as a disciplining arm of the capitalist state,[4] it does provide functions—albeit in ways that stigmatize the poor; provide more salutary benefits to the middle class; and ultimately benefit capitalism—that abolitionists also demand. As Mariame Kaba argues:

> We should redirect the billions that now go to police departments toward providing health care, housing, education and good jobs. If we did this, there would be less need for the police in the first place.[5]

Indeed, what Kaba's words point to is that the guarantee of "health care, housing, education and good jobs" would make policing as it exists today obsolete. What is further implied is that the provision of these basic needs is foundational not only to abolition, but to an abolitionist future. Just as calls to dismantle the carceral state have elicited reimaginings of "community safety" and abolitionist means toward those ends, like

---

** See discussion of reformist reforms vs. nonreformist reforms in chapters 2 and 3.

transformative justice and community accountability, a wholesale demand for the abolition of the state altogether raises questions about the means toward provision of health and mental health care, housing, education, childcare, elder care, and so on—the very things that our current welfare state has cobbled together in some form since the advent of modern industrialization and through these postindustrial times. Such a broad range of social provisions does not require a uniform answer or form of governance. However, an unpacking of our notion of the welfare state and a better understanding of welfare state components and functions can better inform both contemporary abolitionist demands and future-facing strategies. In furthering our understanding of the welfare state, this chapter begins with a brief reintroduction to the welfare state and its history in the United States, offers an introductory analysis on the relationship between abolition and the welfare state, and sets forth a series of questions that is intended to catalyze further inquiry, study, and action.

A Brief History of the Welfare State

The term *welfare state* first appeared in Britain in 1945, as World War II came to an end and a landslide election ushered the Labour Party into power. During these heady times, the promise of the "abolition of poverty" and the "conquest of unemployment" was palpable, although the mechanisms through which they might be achieved were more platitude than concrete policy.[6] In fact, the progenitors of the British welfare state as well as those formations emerging through Europe preceded the United States in the forms of poor relief, secularizing social provision away from the church in the UK, and social insurance programs first established in Germany in the nineteenth century to counter the advance of socialism. Building upon nascent frameworks and institutions guiding the UK's establishment of its welfare state, the United States created initial, pre–New Deal social provisions for those (white, emancipated) individuals seen to be both "deserving" and in most dire need, for example, widows left with no source of income and the poorest class of women with children.

In the United States, the term *welfare state* has not been embraced beyond academic social work, sociology, and political science. However, the notion of *welfare*, of course, is one that has taken a winding and ignoble path. Emblazoned in the first line of the US Constitution, the promotion of the nation's "general Welfare" was foundational to those establishing the nation-state. However, interpretations of the role of the state vis-à-vis the nation's general welfare has been the subject of ongoing and unrelenting debate. The protection of private property was and continues to be seen as a central role of the US state *and* as a guarantee of the greatest general welfare for the majority of (white, property-owning) citizens. The realities of profound poverty, unemployment, and lack of basic needs, often a result of capitalist development, prompted a need beyond that managed by family, church, and, eventually, local governmental jurisdictions. The history of the development of the US welfare state is one of the contradictory impulses to sustain market capitalism and manage its deleterious consequences—all while maintaining the tenets and the ongoing sustainability of the former.

Grounded in the principle vigorously expressed in the early foundations of the welfare state in the UK—that material provisions to those most in need never exceed the wages of the poorest laborer—the United States followed with an even more constricted version of its welfare state, characterized as the extreme remedial end of the continuum of modern industrial welfare states. In his classic treatise, *The Three Worlds of Welfare Capitalism*,[7] Esping-Andersen emphasized the means-tested and stigmatizing nature of the US welfare system as representing an ideal type that Esping-Andersen identified as *liberal*, not in the sense of a progressive politic but rather in the free market–based sense of the word. Juxtaposing it to the generous, universal *social democratic* system of Sweden and other Nordic nations and the *conservative*, traditional social insurance models of such countries as Germany, the United States represents the welfare state regime that is characterized by the highest levels of poverty, the greatest economic inequality, and the lowest percentage of governmental material support.

The construction of what we now know as the welfare state in the United States followed in response to the financial crisis of 1929 and the Great Depression. Though relatively egalitarian in its purported goals, the actual implementation of the series of reforms embodied in the New Deal—legislated in enduring if embattled programs such as social security, agricultural assistance, aid to families with children, and public works—were bound not only by ideals of free market individualism but by the profound anti-Black sentiment that continues to imperil even the most modest welfare gains in the United States.[8] Postwar prosperity in the United States and throughout the industrialized world fueled a period of relative balance between the drive for profits and a limited belief in the common good. In the 1960s, Johnson's War on Poverty and Great Society programs expanded Medicare, Medicaid, housing supports, job training, and food stamps—enduring conservative attacks and leading to documented reductions in poverty.

The 1970s marked a new period of US economic decline and the rising rhetoric and political prominence of conservative (often bipartisan) forces, pushing back against prior Civil Rights movement and welfare gains with a highly racialized agenda that has successfully mobilized the rapid growth of the carceral state, on the one hand, and the retrenchment of the welfare state, on the other. Indeed, just as 1973 marks the *punitive turn*, marking the beginning of an over fivefold increase in rates of incarceration in the United States, the period of the early 1970s is also characterized by the decline and increasingly punitive nature of an already disciplining system of social welfare provision. These conservative forces, already on the rise, ushered in the US election of Reagan in 1980 (along with Prime Minister Thatcher in Britain in 1979) and the advent of a neoliberal era that vilified poor, Black beneficiaries of public assistance, broke labor union power, dismantled public housing supports, slashed taxes, and set the stage for what would become a hegemonic veneration of private market forces and the demonization of welfare and the "undeserving" racialized poor. By the time Clinton reached the US presidency in 1993, the tenacious hold of neoliberalism led this Democratic leader to pass the draconian Violent Crime Control and Law Enforcement Act, or crime bill, of 1994 *and* the Personal Responsibility and Work Opportunity Reconciliation Act that dramatically reversed welfare gains only two years later.

Functions and Components of the US Welfare State

Public discourse around the term *welfare* and policies established to promote what the Constitution states as central to the nation have suffered a level of confusion and rhetorical embattlement that continues to obscure the scope, benefits, limitations, and even—for the greater portion of the US population—the very existence of the welfare state. In fact, the welfare state in the United States persists as a variegated conglomeration of a patchwork of policies, procedures, programs, agents, and institutions constructed, in large part, to both solve immediate social problems as they arise and to mitigate against the ever-present excesses of US capitalism. Despite the unique US failure to grasp the rudiments of what the welfare state is or does, it remains an institutionalized feature, if precariously so, within the contemporary US state.

Garland's breakdown of what he refers to as "five institutional sectors"[9] delineates distinct categories of the welfare state, which helps to clarify its beneficiaries and its scope. According to his categorization, the first sector of the welfare state is the *provision of social insurance*. That is, all citizens of modern states face certain risks—those associated with uncertainty inherent to the variable market forces of capitalism, such as unemployment, and those universal risks that are a part of the human life cycle but that can impede one's capacity to participate in the labor market. These latter risks include illness, accidents, disability, pregnancy, early child rearing, and old age. Under some interpretations of social insurance, participation in the military and identification as a veteran needing or entitled to certain services can be classified under this category. One function, therefore, of the welfare state is to provide government provision of resources to assist in these situations.

The second sector is *social assistance* or what is commonly known as *public assistance* or, more simply, *welfare*. Though this is not by any means the largest sector of the welfare state, it is that which occupies the largest portion of the public imagination. This politically volatile category of welfare activities includes general assistance, Temporary Assistance for Needy Families (TANF), food stamps, Medicaid, Earned Income Tax Credits, Child Tax Credits, and Supplementary Security Income (SSI). These also include guaranteed income programs that have been the subject of recent political debate and experimental localized pilot programs.

The third sector is made up of *publicly funded social services* that constitute age-old public goods proffered by city-, county-, state-, and federal-level government in the form of free or subsidized education, libraries, parks, museums, transportation, childcare, health care, legal aid, and other universal goods that are often subject to budget priorities and restrictions but that have also become a normal expectation, at least to some extent, of modern governments.

The fourth sector is what Garland refers to as *social work and personal social services*. Similar to the category of social assistance, this sector is often subject to means testing and often performs a particularly disciplining function. Individuals and families that may fall out of what is considered "normal" functioning or that cannot have such needs taken care of within the private domain of one's personal or family care may seek or, alternatively, be identified for welfare support. These forms may be variably subject to stigmatization or pathologizing and range from such services as free or subsidized child care or care for the elderly to mental health interventions, interventions addressing child abuse or other forms of family violence, or postincarceration services. Balanced precariously between notions of care and discipline, choice and mandate, family support and family regulation—this sector is also politically volatile and subject to polarizing discourse.

The final sector is *government of the economy* or "the operation of large-scale government controls on economic life."[10] Although this aspect of governance is rarely considered part of welfare state functions, particularly because of its economic focus, Garland argues that the regulation of fiscal and monetary policies, wage and income management, the organization and working conditions of labor, and so on are central to mitigating the adverse effects and crises inherent to capitalism and, hence, subject to the necessary management of the welfare state.

Although the sectors of the welfare state most associated with poor racialized classes in the United States prompt the most public and polarizing attention, a review of these various sectors also demonstrates the diverse class interests engaged across sectors. In the United States as in all welfare state regimes, middle classes also gain from certain activities of the welfare state and specific benefits offered. Some of these welfare benefits may be particularly appealing to middle classes and may be the basis for ongoing middle-class support. For example, such programs as mortgage tax credits and social security benefits pegged to income level provide significant material advantages to those in higher income brackets. The wealthy are also recipients not only of universal welfare benefits but of *corporate welfare*—that is, specific and, in many cases, significant tax benefits, the result of tax policies increasingly weighing in favor of corporations and their highest salaried employees and investors. Though public discourse is continuously drawn to welfare benefits for the noncontributing and what are considered the "undeserving" poor, these forms of advantage to the middle class and wealthy are often hidden in the minutiae of tax codes or are considered outside the scope of what is commonly considered to be welfare.

Finally, the source of welfare state benefits is not only through direct provision via governmental service delivery but has been largely shifted from the scope of state activity through contracts to nonprofit, faith-based, and increasingly private agents. US preference for private enterprise and decades of neoliberal policy have devolved and diminished essential welfare functions of the state to activities driven by profit and distributed and rewarded through quantitative outcome measures.

The Disciplining Welfare State

Although critiques of the disciplining functions of the welfare state are not new, close examination of the relationship between the carceral state and the welfare state has been surprisingly rare. In 1971, Piven and Cloward argued in *Regulating the Poor*[11] that the central purpose of welfare had little to do with alleviating poverty and was instead offered to mitigate the danger that poor people posed to economic, social, and political stability. Although these earlier theories of the welfare state were tied to the mitigating effect on the cycles and excesses of capitalism, they were siloed from discussions of what is now known as the carceral state.

Garland, known more for his scholarship on the carceral state, drew early attention to the punitive functions of the welfare state, noting that modern phases of capitalism necessitated variable forms of punishment—in softened forms of amelioration of the carceral state's harshest interventions or in regulating forms of care. In 1981, Garland wrote that the policing of individuals, families, and communities was more so governed by agencies of social welfare—social work, education, insurance, and child care—than traditional systems of crime and punishment.[12] Although critiques of the disciplining nature of welfare was central to the work of those in the radical social work tradition, direct ties to the punishment of policing and incarceration were largely left out of these conceptions of the welfare state.

Fifty years of neoliberalism along with the rise of the carceral state brought further and more explicit enmeshment between the carceral and welfare states and increased the policing functions of welfare institutions. Inquiry and scholarship from Garland,[13] Wacquant,[14] and Abramovitz,[15] among others, have illuminated the relationship between state punishment and the welfare state, analyzing the growing interconnectedness between these forces. Garland's theory of penal welfarism suggested that prior to the 1970s, penal institutions in the west were largely organized around the ideal of rehabilitation and presumptions that the criminal legal system should play a welfare-like role in the lives of those under their supervision. The punitive turn, starting in the early 1970s, brought a departure from the rehabilitative ideal, and began the marked growth of mass punishment and what would later become known as mass incarceration. Wacquant examines these early years of neoliberalism as the United States adopted new forms of governing the poor, moving away from Keynesian economics and redistributive social policies and toward workfare (tying welfare benefits to work) and prisonfare (punishing those who did not abide by the workfare policies). Together, workfare and prisonfare led to what Wacquant called *double regulation*, integrating social and penal regulations toward a cumulative punishment of individuals who are poor and disproportionately Black.

Within the field of social work, Abramovitz, using the lens of social reproduction, aptly captures how the impacts of this period and neoliberalism "supplemented the diminished welfare state with punitive programs that favored economic production over social reproduction, accumulation over legitimization, and regulation over liberation."[16] That is, the era of neoliberalism privileged the free market above all else, diminishing the limited but somewhat equalizing power of the welfare state, and as economic insecurity grew, so did the carceral and punitive systems and responses.

Other critical feminist critiques of aspects of the caring professions and the carceral state emerged in critiques of the antiviolence field addressing domestic and sexual violence.[17] Building upon the anti-carceral and abolitionist social movement formations of Critical Resistance and Incite! and informed by political struggles as practitioners within what has been named as a *carceral feminist* antiviolence sector, these activist-scholars point out the close relationship between the carceral state and the caring state—or what Garland referred to as the fourth sector of the welfare state, that is, the disciplining social work and personal social services sector.[18] These conceptual and empirical studies demonstrated how even emancipatory social service sectors can succumb to the logic and institutions of the carceral state through the conflation of perceived social goods such as safety or protection with the monopolizing violence of the state. They also revealed how nonstate, nonprofit actors have expanded the carceral web through collaboration with law enforcement. Examination of the antiviolence sector yielded an important case study showing how welfare functions inside and outside the state directly tie to increasing criminalization and the growth of the carceral state. Related work on transformative justice and community accountability as abolitionist praxis addressing the harms of domestic and sexual violence have moved beyond critiques of carceral feminism and the state to reimagine and build abolitionist praxis divested of ties to the state in its welfare or carceral forms.

Despite the persistence of a small strand of social workers and social work scholars in the continued analysis of the punitive functions of social work, neoliberalism's hold across the field and the elevation of individualized, clinical forms of social work hide its disciplining functions under the platitudes of social work's commitment to professionalism and a nebulous notion of *social justice*. More recent attention to the disciplining nature of social work as an arm of the system of social/public assistance, child welfare, and other regulating systems of care have unearthed radical traditions in social work and built upon more recent praxis and scholarship that both critiques social work and points to abolitionist possibilities.

The US welfare state has always been rooted in racial capitalism and the punitive impulse (and structures) that have provided both the justification and means by which racial hierarchies and capitalism have been maintained. The carceral and neoliberal boom of the last 50 years brought the disciplining functions of the welfare state into full view as the double regulation and punitive policies of both the welfare state and the carceral state increased dramatically. And yet, the welfare state, both historically and today, has provided meaningful and necessary relief to tens of millions of people during any given period. We can legitimately critique the welfare state, its history, and the punishing force it has played, while at the same time acknowledging the critical role it has played and continues to play in meeting (some) people's needs. In this way, the welfare state is paradoxical, representing what Bourdieu referred to as both the left (caring) and right (punitive) hands of the state but increasingly held within a grasp that is decidedly punishing.[19] Nonetheless, this persisting paradox leads us to abolitionist questions about whether a noncarceral state is possible, and more specifically, about the role of the welfare state in the abolitionist horizon.

Abolition and the State

Abolitionists are fighting for an end to the carceral state and the prison industrial complex. This is an unequivocal abolitionist position. Still, as this chapter reveals, other aspects and functions of the "caring" state—such as public education, health and mental health care, and housing—are not immune to the forces that produced the carceral state. Any brief course of critical study illustrates how welfare state institutions have been constituted by white heteropatriarchal supremacy and punishment since their inception and have become more punitive throughout the era of neoliberalism. However, a closer examination of the welfare state's myriad functions and expansive scope is imperative.

Among abolitionist scholars and organizers, questions about the possibilities of a noncarceral state or alternative systems of governance are growing. In *No More Police: The Case for Abolition*, Mariame Kaba and Andrea Ritchie ask, "[I]s there an abolitionist form of stateness? What might a state look like if it's unyoked from racial capitalism and explicitly organized around abolitionist priorities?"[20] Although no singular answer is offered, they review differing ideas about the abolitionist possibilities and limitations of the state. Some, like Ruth Wilson Gilmore and Craig Gilmore, believe the state can be changed and remade to meet material needs at scale, respond to large-scale crises, and leveraged toward participatory governance and liberatory education.[21] Others, like Dean Spade[22] and William Anderson,[23] argue that the state will always be a "technology of extraction" and that the violence of the state is not an unfortunate by-product of the state, but an essential element to ensuring its continued existence. Kaba and Ritchie map a set of possibilities regarding abolitionist state formations or systems of governance but do not resolve what, if any, the role of state will be in the abolitionist future. They do, however, offer some foundational principles that can help in shaping further inquiry into questions about abolition and the state, including the welfare state. They write, "For us, two things are clear 1) The carceral, racial capitalist state cannot be reformed, or captured and repurposed, and 2) abolition and racial capitalism cannot co-exist."[24]

In confronting the possibilities and limitations of the welfare state's abolitionist ends, there are substantial structural questions about whether the state, in general, and the welfare state, in particular, can exist beyond racial capitalism and without the carcerality that has been so central to the existence and governance of the state. Notions of an *abolition democracy* have been offered by W. E. B. Du Bois in 1935[25] and, later, by Angela Y. Davis in 2005,[26] informing aspirations for a state no longer captured by racial capitalism and carceral dominance. Although we, like Kaba and Ritchie, do not offer an answer, we see the clear articulation of these larger questions as critical as we consider how relationships to the welfare state today further or hinder the abolitionist horizon.

Current and Future Considerations

History has demonstrated that the welfare state in and of itself is not emancipatory. More than anything else, the welfare state has existed to "save capitalism from capitalism"[27] rather than to ensure the welfare of all peoples, and in various ways has played a disciplining role in the social regulation of people at the margins. At the same time, in societies with capitalist economies like the United States, provisions from the welfare state like social insurance have played a significant, though uneven, role in keeping many people out of poverty and providing some level of economic, social, and political security. Given this, it makes sense that many in the work of abolition are ambivalent about the role of the welfare functions of the state but are reluctant to dismiss engagement with the welfare state. In the present, this may translate into demands for the continued or increased social provisions that welfare states have offered and should offer—social/public assistance, health and mental health care, housing, childcare, elder care, education, disability access and supports, living wage jobs, and guaranteed basic incomes. Given the critique of the welfare state under capitalism, do these demands further translate into struggles for a stronger and larger welfare state, with greater universal programs, like health and mental health care? Or do demands for a stronger welfare state in the contemporary context distract us from the work of abolition?

Welfare Functions in an Abolitionist State

As we imagine our abolitionist future, how is it that we imagine our future state or form of governance? It is here that Garland's articulation of the sectors of the welfare state may assist in prefiguring and building what might be necessary under any form of governance—and that which may no longer be needed or warranted under a noncapitalist system.[28] For example, human risks as articulated under the welfare state notion of social insurance may still be necessary—serious illness and debilitating accidents will still occur regardless of state formation. What form would social insurance take in an abolitionist future? How would we effectively care for those facing these conditions of financial instability that accompany common risks? What role would the state or other form of governance play in such situations?

The provision of at least basic minimum needs such as adequate housing, food, clothing, health and mental health care, education, transportation, recreation, and so on may be central to an abolitionist future—but how would these actually be determined, produced, and distributed? Likewise, what Garland refers to as *publicly funded social services* or the infrastructure of parks, libraries, and so on as aspects of the welfare state would certainly constitute an abolitionist future. What role, if any, would we expect the state or another form of governance to play in providing for basic individual and community-based needs?

Will there still be interpersonal violence, conflict, and abuse? Although we could anticipate that these forms of harm would be significantly reduced in an abolitionist future—and that nonviolence and mutual respect would be central at all levels of social relations—we can also imagine that violence and abuse would not disappear. How would these forms of violence prevention, intervention, accountability, and care be handled in an abolitionist future? Would these be considered functions of an abolitionist state? If so, what would be its role?

And if we expand to Garland's conceptualization of a more overarching management of a well-functioning economy as an essential part of the welfare state, then how do we see this unfolding in an abolitionist future? Of course, this points to grander questions of our future mode or modes of production—and the best form of governance to maintain and sustain the health and well-being of all humans and other beings. Although these are questions that require a collective vision of what we together can dream, we argue that this must also be grounded in an understanding of the historical trajectory leading us to today.

Although we no doubt agree that everyone should have access to the goods that allow for well-being, we also want to clear space for discussion and questions about the role of the welfare state in the abolitionist future. When we prefigure the world we want, how do we envision the role of what we now experience as the welfare state? And how, if at all, does that change how we relate to the welfare state today? How can the demands we make of the welfare state today help us to chip away at racial capitalism and ideologies of supremacy and punishment? And relatedly, how can our approaches to the welfare state today support us in transforming social relations and the building of community power and care for tomorrow?

Abolition and a Future State: Further Questions

The work of abolition is, in part, the work and politics of prefiguration. When it comes to the future of the state, in general, and the welfare state, in particular, we are engaged in ongoing debates about whether their existence is possible outside of racial capitalism. There is much to learn from the study, politics, and organizing of anarchism and socialism, as two seemingly opposing orientations to the state. In oversimplified terms, anarchism argues for the abolition of the state, and socialism views the state as a possible and necessary institution to regulate social, economic, and political systems. Today, some of us may find ourselves in the ambivalent middle, suspicious about the likelihood of a state that is truly in service of well-being, while at the same time cynical about the ability of more decentralized and localized forms of governance alone to meet large-scale needs. If we can not definitively prefigure the role of the welfare state at this moment, what other questions can be engaged toward the work of prefiguration?

If, as Gilmore and Gilmore[29] have argued, the state can be remade in service of the people's welfare, what will it take to realize this transformation? The welfare state, which developed in response to the failures of the free market economy, has been constituted such that its own survival is dependent on the success of the free market. As abolitionist efforts work to diminish racial capitalism and shift away from a free market economy, we must ask, can universal social programs be remade such that their success is not dependent on endless capitalism? How does a welfare state change when its purposes grow beyond mitigating the failures of capitalism? And, if fortifying the best of the welfare state is our goal, how if at all does that change our approach to and goals of organizing?

If, as Spade[30] and Anderson[31] have argued, the state will never exist to support self-determination, collective care, and widespread well-being, what can come in its place? How can the practices of mutual aid and collective care meet the scale of needs that exist in modern society? What is needed to remake our social relations such that this shift away from the state becomes more possible? And how then should abolitionists approach what the state is already offering vis-à-vis social insurance and the rudiments of basic needs?

As we negotiate and analyze these possibilities and the ambivalent in-between, we also wonder if there is a realm in which both a robust welfare state and widespread practices of mutual aid and collective care can coexist? By default, this is the vision that many of us are already struggling for without, we argue, a clear understanding of the components that constitute well-being nor a clear analysis about the future state we are or are not building toward. If this is the default position of many, how can this framework be made clearer in the intersecting goals and strategies of building collective care inside and outside of state?

Conclusion

In this chapter, we seek less to provide answers or remedies and more to shape and sharpen questions for continued inquiry, study, and action. Although contemporary social and political conditions have reinvigorated radical social work traditions and coupled them with abolitionist critiques of the carceral state, we have been troubled by the lack of attention to the welfare state in our considerations of an abolitionist future. The welfare state, we find, has played a necessary and contradictory role in the maintenance of racial capitalism. It has mitigated the excesses of capitalism, thereby offering course corrections to capitalism while assuaging critical forces that might have otherwise disrupted or even usurped capitalism and its capitalist ruling classes. It has blunted analysis of the structural causes of social problems—poverty, homelessness, mental illness, chronic health disorders, and so on—in favor of a focus on individual misfortune or, more likely, individual failures. It has championed charity and supremacist delusions of rescue over mutual aid, self-determination, and public goods. It has colluded with forces of discipline, exclusion, capture, and death in the name of care and social justice. And yet, the welfare state and the institutions and agents of social work have offered acts of care and compassion that have, despite the welfare state's oppressive function, offered sustenance, and saved lives. On the other side of the welfare state's contradictory role and carceral collusions are the lessons it lends to our understanding of social provisions and supports for well-being in the future.

Although this chapter is far from offering robust recommendations, it makes small steps in examining a sector of the racial capitalist state that has remained too long in the shadows. As Garland claims,[32] the welfare state is short on charismatic champions—rather, it remains in the mundane world of administrators and civil servants. Despite the quotidian, bureaucratic, and denigrated world of the welfare state, it has served an important role not only in the maintenance of capitalism but in addressing, even if poorly, social needs—a function that will continue to be necessary and important no matter what our future holds.

8

Ending Carceral Social Work*

Alan Dettlaff

As a profession, social workers are called to challenge injustice and oppression. This critical aspect of social work has been enshrined in the National Association of Social Worker's (NASW's) Code of Ethics since its earliest origins and fundamentally distinguishes social work from other helping professions. This commitment was strengthened in 2021, when revisions to the Code of Ethics added new language stating, "Social workers must take action against oppression, racism, discrimination, and inequities"—becoming the only phrase in the Code's Ethical Standards using the word *must* and affirming social work's responsibility to take direct action against injustice.[1] Yet throughout its history, the profession of social work has been deeply embedded in the systems that are directly responsible for perpetuating oppression, racism, discrimination, and inequities—particularly prisons, policing, immigration detention, and child welfare. Although our collaborations with these systems have been called into question in recent years, social work has remained steadfast in its commitment to them.

This is most explicit in the profession's commitment to the child welfare system. Although the child welfare system is viewed by many as a benevolent system that protects vulnerable children from harm, this perception is far from the reality of the outcomes this system produces. In reality, the child welfare system is a vast system of social control with

---

*   This article is an edited, reprinted version of an article published in *Inquest* on June 15, 2022.

significant power to surveil and punish families. Every year, the child welfare system forcibly separates hundreds of thousands of children from their families for reasons largely related to poverty.[2] Rather than protecting children from harm, nearly 70% of children in foster care are seized from their parents due to a vague and expansive category referred to as "neglect," defined as a failure to provide for basic needs including food, clothing, education, and shelter.[3] Yet rather than being provided with aid, families who are unable to meet these needs are charged with "neglect" and their children are taken from them.

The harm that results from these separations is immense. An abundance of research shows that forcibly separating children from their parents results in significant and lifelong trauma, regardless of how long the separation lasts.[4] This is true when parents are incarcerated, when children are separated by immigration authorities, and when children are forcibly taken by state child welfare systems.[5] Beyond the trauma of family separation, the harm associated with placement in foster care continues as children are sent to live with strangers and receive little to no information on when or if they will be returned home. As a result, children who spend time in foster care experience severe hardships as adults including poverty, houselessness, joblessness, substance use, mental health concerns, and involvement in the criminal punishment system.[6] The state is well aware of these outcomes. And the state is aware these outcomes occur disproportionately for Black children.

For more than 60 years, since the earliest origins of the modern child welfare system, the surveillance and separation of families by the state as a means of social control has been used disproportionately against Black families. Due to intentionally vague mandatory reporting laws, the child welfare system surveils Black families to the point where more than half of all Black children in the United States are the subject of an investigation by their eighteenth birthday.[7] Once investigated, Black children are forcibly separated from their families at a rate nearly double that of white children.[8] In some states, Black children are represented in foster care at a rate more than three times their proportion in the general population.[9] This destruction of Black families acts as a cycle. Poverty, houselessness, joblessness, substance use, incarceration—each are the outcomes of child welfare intervention. These outcomes then drive families' continued involvement in the system through the surveillance and policing that occurs in Black communities. Although the system purports these separations and surveillances are based on the need for "protection," the outcome is the same—the subjugation of Black families at the hands of the state.

Although these harms have been known to Black families for decades, for some, the harms of this system only recently came to light following Texas governor Greg Abbott's directive in 2022 to investigate and potentially separate families for providing gender-affirming care to their children.[10] The national outrage over this directive and the stories of families who were impacted brought new awareness to the harms of this system and also brought new awareness to the power of the state to weaponize mandatory reporting laws against certain families or communities based on the whim of those in power.

Mandatory reporting laws derive from the 1974 Child Abuse Prevention and Treatment Act (CAPTA) in response to national alarm over the physical abuse of children, driven by media attention to a phenomenon described by researchers as "battered-child syndrome."[11] Although CAPTA established mandatory reporting laws for all states, it also established minimum federal definitions of maltreatment. However, CAPTA allowed states broad discretion to expand on those definitions, resulting in laws that vary widely by state and often reflect current social issues within those states. The result is an immensely vague set of laws that can be used at any time by those in power as a means of targeting a marginalized group for political gain. This is happening now to families in Texas with transgender youth, but this has been happening to Black families for decades, such as when "crack babies" were removed en masse from Black parents upon birth despite the lack of any evidence those babies were at risk of harm. The ability to weaponize mandatory reporting laws by the state is the reason these laws were written so vaguely. At any moment, the state can decide a particular behavior or way of existing is undesirable, and at any moment, that behavior or way of existing can be defined as maltreatment and subject to coercive state intervention.

Although some social workers have stood against the directive in Texas and pledged to not report families for providing gender-affirming care as this is against their social work values, the reality is that reporting any family to a system known to result in harm and oppression is against our values. The harm that will result from reporting parents of a transgender child is no different than the harm that will result from reporting a poor Black family whose child comes to school slightly dirty and in need of food. Yet this is the result of mandatory reporting laws, and this is the result of a profession of social work that has collectively failed to see its complicity in the harm produced by this and other carceral systems.

In the summer of 2020, following the murder of George Floyd and others at the hands of the police, many conversations occurred about the role of social work in policing and the potential for social work to reduce the racist outcomes of policing through increased collaborations. This presented an opportunity for a significant turning point for social work. Decades of racist violence against Black families and the collective national outrage we experienced in summer 2020 presented a moment for social work, and the profession's leaders, to stand against this violence and to stand against our historic complicity in this violence. It presented a moment for social work to disavow itself from the police and to clearly and unapologetically state that social work would no longer be complicit in the harmful and racist outcomes this system produces. Yet this did not occur. In response to these conversations, Angelo McClain, then CEO of the National Association of Social Workers, affirmed the importance of social work collaborations with police, writing in an op-ed titled "Social Workers Cooperate with Police Forces":

> Social workers already work alongside and in partnership with police departments across the nation. Strengthening social worker and police partnerships can be an effective strategy in addressing behavioral health, mental health, substance use, homelessness, family disputes and other similar calls to 911 emergency response lines. In fact, social workers are playing an increasingly integral role in police forces, helping officers do their jobs more effectively and humanely and become better attuned to cultural and racial biases. And studies show social workers help police excel in fulfilling their mission to protect and serve.[12]

If the events of summer 2020 could not serve as a catalyst for the social work profession to reevaluate its role in supporting the police, despite all the violence and evidence of harm, clearly social work lacks any awareness to recognize the glaring inconsistency between its professed values and the reality of social work practice. Today, social workers continue to debate whether we should collaborate with police, whether we should work in jails and prisons, and whether we should be part of crisis response teams where social workers walk hand in hand into communities with the police, the very people responsible for murdering and terrorizing them. As a profession, social work continues to support and cooperate with a system of policing that is responsible for the murders of countless Black Americans, yet despite this blatant inconsistency with our professed values, social work continues to be complicit in this harm.

Similarly, social work has yet to meaningfully consider its complicity in the harms that result from the child welfare system. NASW recently acknowledged and apologized for the bias among social workers that contributes to "the disproportionate impact of the child welfare system on families of color."[13] Yet the organization made no commitment to stop engaging in the practices that result in this disproportionate impact. In fact, NASW recommends that an undergraduate degree in social work be a minimum requirement for all child welfare workers.[14] Thus, the position of the largest membership organization of social workers in the world is that the child welfare workforce be entirely comprised of social workers.

These professional stances suggest that social workers who recognize the harm and oppression carceral systems produce must act outside of our professional organizations to bring about change. Further, social workers need to stand together and not only disavow the carceral systems we've historically supported, but also completely remove ourselves from these systems and work from the outside toward their abolition. For decades, social workers have been fooled by the idea that we can create change from the inside. We have tried to collaborate, we have tried to reform, but this has not led to meaningful change. At this point we are complicit. The idea that we can create change from the inside is simply a lie that we can no longer accept.

Change can begin in schools of social work in both our curricula and our practicum experiences. Within our curricula, schools of social work must include content on the racist origins of carceral systems, the harms these systems produce, and the ethical conflicts that result from our participation within these systems. For decades, schools of social work have presented content on carceral systems as if they are essential systems within society that contribute a needed, benevolent function and our work within these systems is simply one of many career choices. This practice cannot continue. We cannot continue to turn a blind eye to the harm and oppression these systems produce and our decades-long complicity in producing this harm and oppression. Within this conversation, we can recognize that many social workers have dedicated themselves and their careers to working within these systems in efforts to bring about change from the inside. We can also recognize that these efforts have likely led to small changes and even helped many people along the way. Yet within this recognition, we can also acknowledge that these efforts have not brought about the changes needed to significantly alter the harms that continue to result from these systems. Within this recognition, we can acknowledge that despite decades of valiant attempts, our efforts to create change from the inside have failed, and it is now time to look for alternative strategies.

Similarly, within practicum education, we must begin to model our commitment to our professional values by disallowing student placements within carceral systems. This should begin with police, prisons, district attorneys' offices, and other aspects of the criminal punishment system, but this must also extend to placements within child protective services. For too long, schools of social work have been guilty of accepting hundreds of thousands of dollars from the federal government to lure students into working within this system under the guise of Title IV-E "training" programs that provide a tuition benefit for students who commit to full-time employment upon graduation. We have justified our complicity in these programs by focusing on the needed financial benefit this provides to many students. Yet we must recognize Title IV-E programs for what they really are—a system of forced labor that preys upon vulnerable students who might otherwise not be able to afford an education and then forces them to work in a system that forcibly separates over 200,000 children from their parents every year. Despite our decades-long complicity in the harm this system produces, we must begin to take a stand against this system, and this stand needs to begin in our educational spaces.

The profession of social work is at a crossroads, where its professional credibility is at stake. Our continued support of and collaboration with racist systems that produce harm is not a position social work can continue to uphold while espousing a commitment to justice and a mandate to act against injustice and oppression. As it stands today, our Code of Ethics is merely a performative statement of aspirational thinking that sorely differs from the reality of social work practice.

Yet there is a resistance forming. Social workers across the country are adopting anti-carceral and abolitionist stances, and social workers are leading movements calling for abolition of carceral systems. Those of us who are true to our values know that taking action against injustice and oppression means taking action against the *systems* that are responsible for injustice and oppression. As social workers, we must be clear in our goal, and that goal is liberation. This begins by liberating ourselves from the NASW, which continues to be complicit in its collaborations with harmful, oppressive systems. This is followed by social workers wholly disavowing and removing ourselves from systems of harm. It is only when we are no longer complicit in these systems that we can begin to work with communities toward their abolition. And abolition is the only solution. For social work to remain viable as a profession—a profession whose practice aligns with its values—the abolition of systems of oppression is the means to liberation and our only professional path forward.

9

Social Work and Family Policing: A Conversation between Joyce McMillan and Dorothy Roberts

Joyce McMillan and Dorothy Roberts

Caitlin Becker from the Network to Advance Abolitionist Social Work: What brings you to this conversation about social work, abolition, and family policing?

Joyce McMillan: What brings me to this work is my lived experience knowing that social workers didn't help, my understanding that reform hasn't changed anything, and my admiration for Professor Roberts, who wrote books regarding this very topic before I was ever impacted or understood the harms this system brings to families and communities. It is your turn, Ms. Roberts. You can start talking about why you wrote that book in 1997.

Dorothy Roberts: It's interesting that you went back to 1997 because that is kind of the beginning of how I got here. I published a book called *Killing the Black Body* in 1997. I was doing research for it about the punishment and regulation and disparagement of Black mothers. I was focusing on the regulation of Black women's childbearing in the United States from the slavery era until the 20th century, and although I was focusing on the criminalization of Black mothers who were being prosecuted for being pregnant and using drugs, I discovered there were many more Black mothers, thousands and thousands, having their newborn babies taken from them based on a positive drug test. I had not encountered the

SOCIAL WORK AND FAMILY POLICING   117

so-called child welfare system before. I was living in Chicago and was shocked by the level of intense state involvement in Black neighborhoods and that the public was not up in arms about it. It was so obviously a racist system. That's what led me to write my next book, *Shattered Bonds*. After that, I worked on a lot of reform efforts, including spending nine whole years on an expert panel that was supposed to implement a class action settlement in Washington State where a judge declared the child welfare department was violating the constitutional rights of children in foster care. And I learned from that experience that the department was not interested in hearing what parents and families had to say. I tried while on that panel to get parents involved in the changes, and nobody wanted to hear from them. That was an indication right there that something was wrong with this reform process. Over the years I have come to realize that the system cannot be fixed, and I have been inspired by people like Joyce and other impacted parents who were at the forefront of a new movement. Families have resisted for a long time but they are now coming together as a recognizable movement to abolish this system and that's what brings me here today.

Joyce McMillan: How does it feel to know that the books you have written have been so affirming to parents like myself? Prior to knowing you and your writings, I had never felt affirmed in what I experienced, and knowing that the system didn't help, knowing that the system created barriers to pipeline me from one system to the other, and knowing that it created barriers to prevent my family from reunifying and to create a track record that would always make me subject to further investigations.

Dorothy Roberts: I feel that I could not have written any of my books, especially *Killing the Black Body*, *Shattered Bonds*, and *Torn Apart*, without engaging with the people who have been harmed by these systems. How dare I write about it without engaging with them? The reason I could write *Shattered Bonds* is because I got to know Black mothers in Chicago who were fighting to get their children back, and it was their stories that gave me the knowledge of how the system operates and what it is designed to do. Back then, and this would have been around 2000, I met with a group of Black mothers in a church basement in Englewood, a Black neighborhood in Chicago. They were just trying to support each other and survive this system and get their children back. They described their experience as a form of slavery and kidnapping of their children. Those are the kinds of ideas that helped me understand what this system was really about, and so I cannot pretend to write completely on my own.

I am inspired by people who have been fighting to abolish these systems even before they or I had the language of abolition.

I just gave a talk a couple nights ago, and someone in the audience said, "America is never going to have radical change so we have to have this system to keep children safe." I know that's not true. And how do I know? It is not from the studies, even though there are lots of studies that support the need to abolish this system. It is from people like you who have experienced it and know that it has to be abolished. I refuse to ignore that. I think it's essential we work with each other. There are certain skills that I have and also luxuries that I have as a university professor, including the ability to take the time to do this analysis and to write books. But I don't have the same skills that you have, Queen Joyce, and so, we have to work together. We mutually support each other. We can't do it on our own but collectively we are so much more powerful.

Joyce McMillan: The strangest thing to me is how this system has flown under the radar for decades and how people continue to say they are protecting children as if they are blind to the outcomes and blind to the data. They are blind to children aging out homeless. Those who have failed out of school because of all the transfers from schools and homes and the mental stress on them that has caused them to develop mental health issues, the substances they pick up to try to mitigate what they are feeling from the mistreatment that often happens in the stranger's homes where they place children to live on a contract. What is the difference between contracting a child into a home and straight selling them as they do at the OCFS [Office of Children and Family Services] website here in New York, which is another story. They sell children under the cover of "Heart Gallery." They sell kids on the heartshare website and rent to foster people. Kids for Cash! Some of the children on the website wear hearts in the picture that say "on hold." Why would you not want to abolish a system that does this? OCFS runs around touting protecting children and what are they being protected from? They are being protected from success because pimping poverty is the way that America survives. Pimping poverty is the equivalent to slavery. And this is forcing more people into poverty, and in poverty people are surveilled more by all of the systems, and each of the systems leads to the child welfare system as they chose to call it because it is the family regulation system, it is policing of Black bodies.

Dorothy Roberts: You were talking about the harms to children and how ridiculous it is that people support this system despite knowing the harms it inflicts under the guise of protection. The harms are well documented. First of all, anybody working in the system knows about them. Those people working in the system are lying if they pretend that they have not seen data on the outcomes, as well as with their own eyes. Just like when I started going to family court, when I first became aware of the family policing system in Chicago, and I could see that the only people brought before the judge were Black mothers and their children. How can you sit there, day after day as a judge, as a caseworker, as a prosecutor, as a public defender, and not be aware that this must be a racist system?

Joyce McMillan: Destabilizing children, changing their living quarters, schools, doctors, and so on regularly and placing them in congregate facilities that mimic prison environments.

Dorothy Roberts: So-called residential therapeutic centers are like prisons. They are violent places where no child should be. I got an email from an angry person because I wrote a piece in the *Washington Post* called "Five Myths About the Child Welfare System." She accused me of ignoring all the good that it does. But she was ignoring all the bad that it does. She criticized me for writing that a third of teenagers in foster care spend time in an institutional setting because that means two-thirds don't—why didn't I mention the two-thirds? I thought, isn't it bad enough that a third do? I think it is sickening.

Joyce McMillan: The family policing system is one of the only systems where we train—and I will utilize *train* because there is a difference; you train dogs and teach people—but the systems readily use the word *train* in their world of child welfare, they *train* parents to work with them. There is no other sector where we encourage people to work with the same people who have caused them such harm and damaged children so deeply. And I just think it is really a very sick thing to come up with the idea that it is good to have people work under the umbrella, encourage it, and finance it. Here in New York, Administration for Children's Services (ACS) right now has an RFP [request for proposal] I believe they just completed around this whole parent advocacy thing. The ACS is looking to gather people who have been harmed and give them a little hush money, because otherwise these people are not employable because employees of the ACS, who caused them harm, put them on a registry that prevents them from being employed, so now working with the system that caused them harm is their only option of employment, and those employees of the ACS bring them in to further abuse them. That is real sick, careful, deliberate, malicious, hateful thinking.

Dorothy Roberts: Yes, I agree. That is despicable when you take the people you have made to suffer and force them back in under the guise that you are helping them. One of the most pathological things about this system is that it has this veneer of helping people when in fact it is harming them. At least the prison system admits it is punishing people. It is a pathological place too, but at least it admits its purpose is to punish people. As long as family policing officials pretend to be helping people with their services, they can do anything to them.

There's another really important point, which is to blame the people who are harmed the most by structural inequalities—structural racism, poverty, sexism, discrimination against people with disabilities, people who use drugs, all of these hierarchies that actually cause the most harm to children—and then blame their parents and family caregivers for that harm as a way of continuing these exploitive, unjust systems. And then pretend that the state is really solving the problem by taking children away from their families—creating and ignoring the trauma being caused by these invasive and predatory investigations and separations. It is so infuriating to read these backlash studies and commentaries that are coming out against abolition that ignore the harm. Ms. Joyce, you asked how can people continue to support this system? The propaganda around it is so strong, but also a lot of people want the status quo. They are invested in it.

Joyce McMillan: When you say invested, I look at Casey Foundation and all the rest of the Casey's. Full of shit, right? Basically because the foundation has the most money of any foundation that I know, but most of its money goes to supporting these systems. If you were smart enough to make the type of money you made to have a foundation the size of the Casey Foundation, then you have to know you don't invest in failing things.

You know why the Casey Foundation has all that money? That money comes from a long history. It goes back generations, and when we go back generations we look at free labor and a lot of that money was made by free labor, and the foundation wants to keep the status quo. Casey, I am calling you out and calling out the rest of the foundations because you guys need to start supporting the community. If you got money to give away, give it to the people who need the money and not those who are taking the money to create more harm and using it to make it more difficult for people who look like me to live.

Dorothy Roberts: That's such an important point, Ms. Joyce, that we cannot keep supporting a system that is, like you said, failing based on the outcomes but clearly doing what it's designed to do, causing devastating harm. There is a deep pathology in the way people approach this. All the harm that's caused by family policing gets hardly any attention. But when a child known to the system is killed at home or in foster care, the response in either case is that we need to give more money to caseworkers so they can investigate more homes. It is nonsensical. These are cases where the system has failed to protect children. How many times do we have to see that it has failed to protect children and in fact affirmatively harms children and their families before we decide we have to dismantle it? It can't be fixed. Instead of providing the resources that would actually meet families' needs, including cash payments and community-based resources, the government spends billions and billions of dollars investigating families, taking children away, and maintaining them with other people—it is willing to pay other people to take care of children instead of their own families.

Joyce McMillan: Here is the thing that gets me. Of course, I have a conversation with ACS. I haven't called out the prince of child welfare, Jess Dannhouser. I know that he has a clear understanding of the harms of the system. I don't want to put it all on him. Maybe he has a good heart and wants to make change, but once you enter that machine, it is not up to you alone, and the vast majority of people are not going along with you to create change because they believe that creating change means they won't have a job. When they should be saying, we can keep our job and change what we do so that we actually supporting and helping families, right? Maybe we become resource workers, getting resources to the family and getting paid; maybe we become the person who picks up the child from school—there are things you can do for the community versus causing the community harm.

In addition, ACS is not supporting families in knowing their rights, which is really problematic to me because if you are looking to keep me from knowing my rights, that means you are seeking to violate my rights. ACS wants to cover it up by using the word *safety*. That's the magic word. Children are not going to be safe but I need to say for everyone to understand, parents knowing their rights cannot be conflated with an agency doing its due diligence to ensure that a child is well. We should be concerned with a child's well-being, but ACS is never concerned with a child's well-being. ACS never did anything that supported me or my children. It snatched my children out of the home even though my children were well taken care of and there was no evidence I utilized anything in front of my children. It caused me to spiral my life in a downward way. ACS doesn't want families to know their rights. Had I known my rights, I would have never taken that test and my children would have never been unnecessarily removed, but more importantly it is our Fourth Amendment and constitutional right. ACS in New York City wants to come into peoples homes, and *after* entering their homes, ACS want to tell them their rights.

ACS is saying it needs to come in first because there is a child that may be in danger but here is the thing: when a person calls the state central registry to report a concern about a child and/or a family, the first thing they get is a recording that says if this is an emergency, please hang up now and dial 911. That same person we are trusting to report a concern does not hang up and call 911. The caller does not hang up and dial 911, they stay on the line and they get an operator from the New York state OCFS, the state agency that oversees the child protection offices throughout the state of New York. The caller speaks to the live operator from OCFS, and the operator takes their complaint, their concern, whatever you want to call it. At no point does the caller or the OCFS operator deem the call to be an emergency, but suddenly when it gets to the "field" office every case is an emergency, and the OCFS weaponizes the armed police against families who are simply exercising their Fourth Amendment right to refuse entry without a court order, making reports to the police that there may be a child in danger. You know that it is not an emergency because it just went through two test runs where it was verified not to be an emergency. Take your ass down to the court and get a court order. The reason OCFS wants to enter people's homes without the court order is because it gets to operate in the shadows of the judicial system. You want to go to court because then you have somebody who is supposed to hold the OCFS accountable to what the letter of the law is, especially if you have a good organization working with you like Brooklyn defenders, Bronx defenders, neighborhood services of Harlem, right?

Dorothy Roberts: Community Legal Services in Philadelphia. Shout-out to my local family defenders.

Joyce McMillan: Absolutely. In my opinion, you want to be in court. The ACS creates all these backdoor mechanisms without judicial oversight, such as coming to a child safety conference, so what ACS workers didn't extract from you in your home they can extract and twist in their office during "friendly" conversation. They make you come to their office so they can interrogate you more under the guise of creating a safety plan. Don't go. You already have an attorney and more than likely are already in court. Stay away from them. You would never sit down with a prosecutor in a criminal case and convince them you didn't do what they are accusing you of. Keep your mouth shut when ACS investigates you. If you keep your mouth shut, they will have nothing to say about you. Stay quiet and know your rights. You don't have to let them in. This is a Fourth Amendment right and they will threaten to call the police and when the police come, you ask them, "Where is the warrant?" There is no safety issue and no indicators that says there is an emergency happening in my home, so you, Mr. Officer, need to go get a court order too.

Dorothy Roberts: A really important point you are making, Ms. Joyce, is how the family policing system can have greater powers than criminal law enforcement. The police know they are supposed to get a warrant, and the public knows they are supposed to get a warrant. That doesn't mean the police always respect constitutional rights, right? But at least they don't have this blanket exemption to the constitution that caseworkers are allowed. The false idea that a child is always in imminent harm in the home has allowed them to run roughshod over our rights. I think a lot of people might be surprised when you say the Fourth Amendment applies. The Fourth Amendment applies to any government official who wants to enter your home. You do not have to let them in without a warrant based on probable cause.

Joyce McMillan: Say it again, law professor.

Dorothy Roberts: There is a reason we have constitutional rights. Most people wouldn't say we should abolish the Fourth Amendment to allow the police to come into everybody's home whenever they want to. You know that would not get support from most people and yet, effectively the Fourth Amendment protection against unwarranted government searches has been abolished in the realm of child protection. I want to emphasize that caseworkers not only work hand and hand with the police, but they also bring police officers to the home. In my book, *Torn Apart*, I describe violent—even lethal—cases that have happened when police showed up on routine child welfare investigations. Officers can ride the caseworker's coat tails to enter the house because the caseworker has not only this effective constitutional exemption, but also the threat of taking your children away.

The Supreme Court of Pennsylvania recently issued a decision holding that the Fourth Amendment warrant requirement applies to caseworkers! Caseworkers have to go to court and show probable cause to search a home, especially when the search is based on an anonymous tip. The case was brought by a wonderful housing rights activist in Philadelphia named Jennifer Bennetch, who advocated against homelessness and for secure housing. She was instrumental in the encampment in Philadelphia that won the right to housing in a certain part of Philadelphia, and she recognized the connection between the lack of housing and state separation of families. During one of her protests in front of the Philadelphia Housing Authority, somebody anonymously reported her to CPS [Child Protective Services] on the suspicion that she may not have fed her child for the eight hours she was protesting. It was a totally baseless accusation likely made by somebody retaliating against her for her protest. CPS sent a caseworker to her house, and she refused to let them in.

She knew her rights. Then they came back with a police officer trying to terrorize her into letting them in. When she still wouldn't let them in, they went to court and got a judge to issue an order to allow the caseworker into her house. Ms. Bennetch took her case all of the way up to the Supreme Court of Pennsylvania, which ruled that the court order violated her constitutional rights, and the Supreme Court made it clear that the Fourth Amendment applies to family policing just as much as it applies to law enforcement. Caseworkers have to obtain a warrant based on a showing of probable cause and a nexus between the accusation and the need to search the home. They can't invade somebody's home based on an anonymous tip with no support to back it up. This ruling should be applied everywhere, and people should be informed of their rights. Ms. Bennetch tragically passed away in February of COVID-19 complications and I want to lift up her name. I promised some of her comrades that every time I talk about this case I will mention her activism. I want to stay true to that.

Joyce McMillan: They (ACS workers) have a union. They should be going to their union. Their union leader Anthony Wells's job is to protect its employees, not to ensure they get into homes. That's not the union's job. Protect the employees' safety. Anthony Wells, you are a union leader and I know what union leaders do. You protect the safety of the employee on the job. You don't stand against a family knowing their rights because your worker needs to get into their home.

Dorothy Roberts: You are pointing out that there has to be collective action among social workers to disrupt family policing.

Joyce McMillan: ACS employees want to mistreat communities, mistreat children, mistreat parents, treat us like we are stupid by violating our rights and acting like the fourth amendment never existed for our communities. Whoever is causing that type of harm under the guise of doing a job, something is wrong. I don't want a job that does that.

Dorothy Roberts: I absolutely agree. You have to decide: Where am I going to work? How am I going to act? Who am I going to stand with? Those are questions of integrity. Are you just going to bow down and do what you know is wrong under the excuse that your supervisor told you to do it?

Caitlin Becker: I appreciate this. It is certainly caseworkers new to the field and following instruction, but it is also social workers who are causing great and particular harm in this system, therapists and the managers at ACS and the child protective agencies, the ones making the decisions, and they have social work degrees. They are causing great harm. We are causing great harm. This is a social work audience so I want to offer that to both of you, what are the particular harms that social workers are causing at each point in this system?

Joyce McMillan: We all know what we are doing wrong. It is called gut instinct. Don't ask these rhetorical questions where you want me to alleviate the pain you are feeling from within because you know what you are doing that's wrong. I am not going to answer that. You know if you are not giving a person any autonomy, if you are judging a person, if you are not believing and not trusting of a person, if you are thinking the worst of them. That's what you are doing as social worker that's wrong and that's helping to create and strengthen this system.

Dorothy Roberts: I could add to that the social work scholars who now are trying to defend the family policing system against abolitionist movements and principles and visions. They have been saying that abolition is going to harm children and we have to rely on this system to protect them. As I said before, they ignore all the harms the system inflicts on children and they pretend it is actually helping them. What is really important is the possibility that we can build something better.

Joyce McMillan: We don't even need to be building anything better. Just have the money infused into our community where we can care for ourselves. If I have the money to pay for a babysitter, if I have the money to order out because I am a single parent and not feeling well and can't cook, if I have the money to get a babysitter and can get a break, if I have the money to send my clothes to be laundered after working two jobs all week . . .

Dorothy Roberts: I agree. When I say build something better, I don't mean build another system. I just mean build a different approach, which includes what you are saying, Joyce.

Caitlin Becker: Are there policy efforts that we should be endeavoring to push forward?

Joyce McMillan: In New York, we are pushing for families to know their rights. Miranda Know Your Rights for Families and the bill number is NY State Bill 2021-5484B. That ensures that whenever CPS or any officer knocks on the door, they would have to advise people of their right to have an attorney, right to remain silent. We are not asking for new rights. We are just asking that the rights the families have be told to them.

Second is confidential reporting, which is the antiharassment bill that is to prevent people from reporting anonymously. We know that most calls to the state registry that are made anonymously are malicious calls, and although the number of cases that are founded are very low, and they are going to be lower now because new data came out that show it is minuscule. If you are calling, you are calling because you are being malicious, and I want it to align for the community the same way it does for a mandated reporter. If a mandated reporter calls, they have to give their name and their name does not trickle down to the family they called on. If a person calls confidentially, they will not trickle down, but it will prevent a repeated calling without the person who mans the registry hotline from knowing. They will know you have called five times on the same person before. That bill number is NY State Bill 2021-S7326A.

The last one is informed consent bill number S4821A, and informed consent is Miranda rights in the hospital setting where they cannot just strip-search your bodily fluids for the sole purpose of reporting you to an agency that can't help you even if you do have a substance abuse problem. Even if you are overusing, CPS cannot help you with that. The hospital setting is the right place to administer some support for that. That's where it should be handled. The CPS should not be farming you out to this third party. It makes no sense to me. And this is what we have been going along with for a long time, but we going to work together, and take this shit and not allow the CPS to keep disrupting our community and we are going to disrupt the CPS simply by telling the truth.

Dorothy Roberts: If I can add a few things; one is abolishing mandated reporting altogether. It doesn't do any good. Some people think if we abolish it, who will report their suspicions of child maltreatment? But the people who are mandated reporters are supposed to be supporting families; so all mandated reporting does is have them move toward this punitive system instead of exercising their professional skills to support families. Ending mandated reporting doesn't limit its support; it allows the reporters to do what they were trained to do. Social workers are supposed to be helping. Doctors are supposed to be helping. Teachers are supposed to be helping. They are not supposed to be turning people over to a punitive system. We should get rid of it all together. Another important support for families is high-quality legal defense for parents and other family caregivers from the very beginning, just like wealthy families have. If a caseworker comes to a wealthy family's door, which is extremely rare, the parents call their lawyer and they won't usually get to the point of taking children from the home or maybe even searching the home. All families should have high-quality legal defense like multi-disciplinary family defense units in Brooklyn, the Bronx, Harlem, and Philadelphia. Here is a place where social workers should be working.

Caitlin Becker: How do you recommend starting an abolition movement around the family police system in an area or jurisdiction in an area where it hasn't been started?

Joyce McMillan: I did a fellowship with Law for Black Lives and what I learned was to divest in systems and invest in communities and that everything that I think about should encompass shrinking the system. If you want to start a movement, I think you should start thinking about what you could do, what you can contribute, to begin to shrink this system, and ask others to join you.

Dorothy Roberts: I want to highlight the work that Joyce has done founding JMACforFamilies and then bringing together scholars, family defenders, legislators, and system-impacted parents and youth to build a collective network of people to strategize. Go to JMACforFamilies' website and look at all it has been doing. I hope to work with Ms. Joyce to build a network of organizations like hers around the nation where people who have questions like this—What do I do? How do I start? How do I build an organization—can turn to for advice and support. We can be stronger by sharing our strategies and putting them in place all over the country, both locally and nationally.

We could form more of a collective effort, I think, that would be super powerful, where it would be helpful to have a national campaign, like repealing the Adoption and Safe Families Act. I am not saying these efforts are not already going on, but I think working together we could make them even stronger.

10
Reaching for an Abolitionist Horizon within Professionalized Social-Change Work

Sophia Sarantakos

Part I: Edges as Interfaces
Edge One: The Limitations of Paid Work

In the introduction to *Golden Gulag: Prisons, Surplus, Crisis, and Opposition in Globalizing California*, the abolitionist scholar Ruth Wilson Gilmore writes, "Every geographer knows, edges are also interfaces. For example, even while borders highlight the distinction between places, they also connect places into relationships with each other and with non-contiguous places."[1] This understanding of edges as interfaces is a crucial starting point for professionalized social-change workers[2] laboring toward prison industrial complex (PIC) abolition. Before we can reach within ourselves and our professional contexts for an abolitionist horizon, we all need a firm grasp of the structural arrangement that creates the contours of our paid labor. Knowing the shape and imposed boundaries of the spaces we're laboring in provides us with the vision we need to move transformatively within and beyond the borders, and ultimately eliminate them.

As the organizer, educator, and curator Mariame Kaba says, we all live under the weather of settler colonialism, racial capitalism, and white supremacy. These technologies of domination shape our shared world and impact the ways we navigate it. Most people need paid work to survive under racial capitalism and, in some cases, have the resources to self-select into types of labor that is connected to something that they value and want to contribute to. For instance, many people who come to professionalized social-change work see it as an avenue to "do good"[3] *and* get paid. What I'd like to offer here, with Gilmore's quote in mind, is that the *getting paid* part shouldn't be viewed as merely compensation for our labor, but rather a key boundary, or edge, of our work. The truth that too few professionalized social-change workers, and no schools of social work, recognize or act with in mind is this: *paid work will never be freedom work*.[4] In other words, labor that is paid for, regardless of where it is done, is not work that threatens the status quo in a meaningful way, because people with wealth and power will not pay workers to do things that challenge their wealth and power. This is an important truth for professionalized social-change workers to grasp, because if they don't understand the contours and intentional limitations of their paid work, an abolitionist praxis within that realm is not possible. This doesn't mean that paid work can't contribute to liberatory movements and practices, but this work, on its own, will not bring about the economic, political, and social shifts PIC abolitionists are committed to.

As human beings in the world, we're all enmeshed, to different extents, in the oppressive systems that shape that world. Workers in the profession—particularly white workers—can take this entanglement to mean that everything they do will always be tainted and not enough and that liberatory work is futile. I hear my predominantly white students ask all the time, "How can I ever do good work in such a problematic field, under such oppressive systems?" The first part of my response to this question is, "You can't control the profession and world at large, but you *can* control how you function within them." Every day that we're alive, we can choose to "do what we can, with the resources at our disposal, within our capacity, to lessen suffering where we are, for as many people as we can."[5]

The second part of my response to this question is, "If we collectively decided to function differently, and chose to be in solidarity with people over systems of power, the possibilities would be endless." Thinking critically about our individual actions, and the political commitments we uphold through those actions, is only the first step. To advance structural change, our personal behavior needs to be in alignment with the world we're reaching for and be combined with the clear-eyed actions of others. Individual activism will never bring about the world we all need and deserve; only collective movements can do that. This brings about the second edge I see as an interface within the sphere of professionalized social-change work: understanding to whom the master's tools belong and how they can collectively be used differently.

Edge Two: To Whom Do the Master's Tools Belong?

The act of "professionalizing" social-change work immediately compromises and complicates it because the desire of people in power to keep the profession toothless, to maintain its legitimacy and survival, will always be in direct contest with some workers' desire to truly transform the landscape. But just because it's complicated and we're all painfully entangled doesn't mean that we can't and shouldn't shift the way we function within the profession to a more solidarity- and liberation-focused way of doing things and caring for one another. Laboring in the field of professionalized social-change work means functioning at the boundary of survival and harm: Our own survival and the survival of those around us and who will come after us is at stake, and we're working under the weather and with the tools—as they're currently wielded—of structural harm. But what if the roughly 700,000 professionalized social-change workers in the United States decided to take ownership of the field and do things differently? The key questions to help us think through this edge are: Who controls professionalized social-change work, and to whom does it belong? These two questions don't yield the same answers.

In her essay "Public Enemies and Private Intellectuals: Apartheid USA," Gilmore wrestles with the main message of Audre Lorde's famous speech "The Master's Tools Will Never Dismantle the Master's House." Gilmore says, "The issue is not whether the master uses, or endorses the use of, some tool or another. Rather, who controls the conditions and the ends to which any tools are wielded?"[6] Throughout this essay, I've been using the phrase *professionalized social-change work*, and in this section I'll get even more specific. There are many lineages of social-change work, both inside and outside of the profession (e.g., Black radical/Indigenous/queer social-change work). The genealogy of professionalized social-change work that's been legitimized by people in power, taught and practiced most widely, and caused the most immense harm is *white* social-change work. In her book *The Black Power Movement and American Social Work*, Joyce Bell recalls a conversation with Jay Chunn—the first official president of the National Association of Black Social Workers—where he urged Bell to refrain from using the term *mainstream social work* and instead call it what it explicitly was: "white social work."[7]

Since professionalized social-change work's inception, white people who are committed to upholding the white supremacist status quo have controlled the field, but here's the edge: the work of building a better world, even within the confines of paid labor, doesn't belong to the oppressive few. The work of building a better world belongs to the workers, who can change the "conditions and the ends to which any tools are wielded."[8] In a discussion on the podcast *Millennials Are Killing Capitalism*, Gilmore further clarifies the point she made in her 1993 essay: "What belongs to whom is what matters, and the apostrophe in *master's tools* is what matters more than anything. Does that mean that anything that oppressive forces and forces of organized violence do would change magically if we could seize those means? Of course not ... But thinking about the possibility of how things can be used differently is, to me, the heart of everything we're trying to do now in the 21st century."[9] It's Gilmore's last sentence here that I think needs more attention as we work toward changing the core practices of our field and incorporating a radical intention into our approach.

Mariame Kaba reminds us that "the most important thing you can do is to improve your questions and stop trying to find the answer ... the questions that you ask are very, very important because they'll lead you to some response that will be better than a response that a bad question might enable."[10] Here are some of the questions I'm urging professionalized social-change workers to wrestle with:

- How might clearly seeing our field's edges illuminate avenues for subversion, disobedience, and disruption?
- What are the many ways we can seize white professionalized social-change work and use the infrastructure and workers to achieve the economic, political, and social aims of PIC abolition?

Working collectively to build responses to these questions can move us toward dismantling the master's house "so that we can recycle the materials to institutions of our own design, usable by all to produce new and liberating work."[11] It's long past time to seize the field from the clutches of the powerful few in support of a fascist order, strip it for parts, and use those parts to reach for an abolitionist horizon. As a white worker in this field, I see this capturing and retooling of professionalized social-change work for abolitionist means as an ethical obligation. I'm not certain that it will work—there is no certainty in organizing and experimentation— but I'm committed to trying, because the alternative is a harmful arrangement that I refuse to live with and function within.

Part II
Reaching for the Abolitionist Horizon within Professionalized Social-Change Work

The language and imagery in the title "Reaching for an Abolitionist Horizon" are important. The convergence of the COVID-19 pandemic with the enduring issue of racist state violence has thrust the word *abolition* into the area of professionalized US social-change work more so in the past two years than at any other time. Some schools of social work have been organizing panels to discuss PIC abolition's connection to social work and incorporating the framework into their curricula. These discussions and actions have the potential to yield powerful shifts within the field. However, the profession's and the academy's fast-paced uplifting of abolitionism and focused attention on the *label* instead of the *labor* of it present complications and limitations as well. What this rapid uptake often seems to be missing is the fact that abolition is "not a trademark, it's not an identity, it's also not an outcome. It's an ongoing commitment to praxis and to collective creativity.... It's about being, the liberation of being against the oppressive imposition ... that this civilization has forced on people."[12] As the field of professionalized social-change work engages in the collective project of radicalizing our practices (meaning, addressing root causes and opposing power instead of appealing to it), workers who are new to PIC abolition must concern themselves less with the task of self-identifying as an abolitionist and more with studying, questioning, and practicing the ideas and work that PIC abolition calls people to commit to. And those of us within professionalized social-change work who are, and have been, deeply committed to an abolitionist praxis should be inviting others in, with care, to learn, unlearn, and build with us. Just as people held the door open for us to explore, question, and practice a radical politic, we must pass on this invitation and openness. The only way forward is together.

I appreciate the phrase *abolitionist horizon* because it implies a continued journey for all of us, a constant reach for something better, more beautiful, more righteous—not a destination. We can gain great clarity when we put aside the idea of becoming a "PIC abolitionist," and/or building an "abolitionist social work," and think mainly about the work that needs to be done to move professionalized social-change work from being "proximate to power" to "antagonistic to oppression."[13] At the end of the day, the goal isn't (or shouldn't be) increasing the number of professionalized social-change workers who identify as PIC abolitionists, but rather building a workforce unwaveringly dedicated to our collective liberation. What the workers call themselves is no matter—what matters is the work that's being done and the commitments shown through that work.

In the following two subsections, I'll offer some of the ways that I believe professionalized social-change workers can act—internally and externally—to shift our commitment from the survival of the profession to radical social change.

Reaching within Ourselves for the Abolitionist Horizon

"What are you pretending not to know today?"[14]

This question, from Toni Cade Bambara's essay, "The Education of a Storyteller," takes us from looking internally to interrogating the stories we tell ourselves about our external world. Bambara writes about an elder, whom she called "grandmother," asking her this question, which she often did in moments when Bambara was "[playing] like [she] wasn't intelligent."[15] I think this question is simply phrased and unsettling in the best way. I've been turning it over in my mind quite a bit, especially over the last few years.

It's a question that white people in particular need to be asking themselves, but it's one we all could benefit from ruminating on. Many people likely don't ask themselves this question because the answers frighten and overwhelm them, and they see no way to make meaningful change. We've never had time for this head burying though, and we certainly don't now. I think about how many of us are pretending not to know, for example, that the United States is a fascist nation-state committed to death and destruction, particularly the death and destruction of marginalized people and communities.[16] We are three years into a pandemic, and we've seen no concerted and sustained federal effort from people in power to minimize infection and save lives—the response of racial capitalism is always profits before people, death before life. After one of the most violent, deadly years of police killings on record in 2022,[17] President Joe Biden's response was to increase the overall budget for policing[18]—again, death before life. We've had decades of data showing that we're heading toward climate collapse, and what we've been witnessing isn't inaction but a forging ahead toward ecological destruction[19]—people in power have acted, and they've chosen death before life, time and time again. And within our own profession, we have endless historical and present-day data proving how the field has largely been used as an arm of the white supremacist, carceral state.[20] The first step toward a radical politic, whether we identify it as abolitionist or not, is transforming ourselves, as the organizer and scholar Grace Lee Boggs said.[21] We all must face the truths we've been pretending not to know and act from this new understanding.

Reaching within Our Contexts for the Abolitionist Horizon

The second realm of action looks outward, to our different paid-labor contexts, with a particular focus on social-change workers in direct practice and academic settings (conducting research and/or teaching).

Political Commitment #1: Refuse norms and metrics that problematize people and cause harm, and work to change them.

A key norm in this category would be mandatory reporting. How can we say that we value people's inherent dignity and worth, recognize the central importance of human relationships, help people in need, and challenge social injustice (our purported values) while pulling a lever that we know causes irreparable harm, particularly to poor/Black/Brown/Indigenous/queer families? Not only do practitioners within professionalized social-change work largely abide by this violent mandate, but educators in higher education continue to teach social-change work students that being a mandatory reporter is essential to their "professional identity" and "responsibility." Mandatory reporting is a mechanism of the carceral state that relies on social-change workers to be loyal foot soldiers and respond to harm and need with further *harm*, not *care*. By following this mandate, we become cogs in the machine that helps perpetuate violence.

An example particular to academia is how social-change workers often cosign the harmful processes of university disability services that put the onus on students to achieve certain "official" statuses for their learning needs to be acknowledged and met. As the abolitionist writer and organizer Kelly Hayes has said, "If you ask someone to prove they need accommodations, that's not accessibility."[22] We need to think critically about the norms in our contexts and ask ourselves, is this centering care? Am I doing the dirty, violent work of the state/people in power by upholding this norm? Practices that do not center care, that maintain inequities, and that perpetuate violence must be broken.

Another example in the research area of the legal punishment system, on which I focus, is scholars choosing to uphold metrics such as "recidivism" and "criminogenic risk." These metrics problematize people and are completely void of a structural analysis. We should refuse measures and language that intentionally disregard this country's foundational practice of hypercriminalization: "The expansion of the carceral state is targeted, not random. It affects different groups in the population differently, with a clear disposition to aggressively target socially vulnerable groups and those that politically threaten the system controlled by power elites."[23] Researchers within professionalized social-change work should be talking about structurally focused concepts like *recriminalization*, not recidivism and criminogenic risk, which rates people across several static and dynamic categories to decide a person's "level of criminal risk." We have to reject these metrics wholesale and engage in work that humanizes and cares for people and punches up at the structures that are abandoning, harming, and branding particular people and communities (Black, Brown, Indigenous, queer, transgender, undocumented, disabled, poor) as "criminal" and "risky."

Political Commitment #2: Leverage our personal, institutional, and organizational resources to support directly-impacted people, organizers, and existing movements.

We need to stop thinking in hierarchical ways and ask ourselves, what can I offer my community to help us get closer to a world where we all thrive? Part of how I think we get to this mindset is understanding that those of us within professionalized social-change work are not exceptional. I may have a PhD in social work, but at the end of the day, I'm a worker, community member, and fellow human. The aim should always be to offer ourselves, our knowledge, and openness to others to help move the collective to something greater, healthier, and more beautiful. This is the mentality I try my best to share and pass on to my students.

Once we have this mindset, the question then becomes, what do I have access to that others need? Organizers on the ground need space, computers, printers, money, volunteers, and so much more. Agencies and schools of social work could open their doors and share their resources in important ways. Clinicians can provide free or extremely low-cost mental health care to organizers; they can run groups for organizers experiencing burnout. This type of thinking and redistribution of capital centers care, collaboration, and collectivity and directly opposes individualism, competition, and recognition. The state wants us to stay siloed and fight with each other over scraps, whether that be funding or some other resource we're told is scarce. In all contexts that we're in, we need to find ways to deepen our connection and commitment to one another. How can we come together, build together, organize together, amplify each other's work?

Political Commitment #3: Expand what we think of as the sites of struggle.

As I mentioned earlier, *paid work is not freedom work*. People in power will never pay us to do truly transformative work, work that aims to upend the status quo and threaten their existence. Because of this truth, we need to not only think of ways to be subversive and disruptive in our paid work environments, but also find different, less limiting sites where we can strategically fight, build, and apply outside pressure to the agencies and institutions that hope to confine us.

Part of this important work is teaching students the truth about the nonprofit industrial complex and the academy and how work in these sectors has severe, intentional limitations. We need to be challenging the idea that we can completely change systems solely from the inside. Mariame Kaba's response to that notion, lifted up from the organizer and scholar Ella Baker, is, "Who are your people?"[24] Meaning, "[W]ho are you accountable to in this world?"[25] Are you connected to people in the community who experience the harm of the system you work in? Are you listening to their experiences and supporting their larger organizing efforts that may be in direct contradiction to the paid work you do? The revolution won't be started or won within the agencies and institutions that are all interested in maintaining their survival.[26] The bigger, more impactful work happens outside of these spaces.

Political Commitment #4: Refuse the commodification of radicalism and commit to "slow work in always urgent times."[27]
Part of what I've witnessed over the last several years, as social work has quickly taken up its language, is the commodification of abolition. It's gaining in popularity in some ways, students are interested in learning more, and the natural impulse of the academy is to ask, how can I package this and sell it to students? Some of the ways that this commodification happens are through the development of certificates, pathways, or focused learning opportunities. Those of us who are studied and practiced in and committed to a radical politic need to help others understand that this is not the way forward. We must hold the line and help people understand that PIC abolition, transformative justice, decolonization, and so on are not career tracks. They are ways of being in the world and unwavering political commitments. They're a constant practice of learning, unlearning, being in better relationship with one another and the land, and working to shift the world in material ways. A certificate in PIC abolition does not make you an abolitionist and is antithetical to an abolitionist praxis. We need to be focused on the slow, steady, behind-the-scenes work of approaching everything we do from

these radical lenses—all interactions, all teaching practices, all policies, all curricula, everything.

Part III: Onward with Love and Rage

I want to end this essay by saying how deeply hopeful I am. I first started moving in abolitionist ways at fifteen, after my first painful experience with the PIC, and my learning, hope, and praxis has only blossomed since then. The challenges before us—within the profession, in the United States, and globally—are great, but there are more people who want a livable, better world than those who are gripping and defending the ruins of the old one. As Bobby Seale, the cofounder of the Black Panther Party for Self-Defense, said, "We're not outnumbered—we're out-organized."[28]

The entire premise of professionalized social-change work is distorted, as is every other system and institution under the weather of settler colonialism, racial capitalism, and white supremacy. We can spend our time debating whether social work is obsolete and should end, or we can come together in this distortion; try our damnedest to take control of it with a shared, relentless commitment to liberation; and twist the field into something new.

section 3

PRAXIS

11

Staying in Love with Each Other's Survival: Practicing at the Intersection of Liberatory Harm Reduction and Transformative Justice

Shira Hassan

How do we end social work's addiction to the state? How do we end prisons and police? How do we find sustainable community-based solutions to interpersonal and systemic violence? As an antiviolence activist with a history of drug use, life experience in the sex trade and street economy, complex PTSD, and both learning and physical disabilities and as a devoted self-injurer, I forced myself to make it through a master's program because I believed that there were solutions to end suffering to be found within mainstream social work. Radical activists like me (and you) often make the decision to become social workers in an attempt to divert resources to our people and fight the system from inside.

This strategy of reducing harm from the state and increasing access to critical help is a kind of harm reduction applied at the system level. Harm reduction teaches us how to practice the politic—No One Is Disposable—demanded by transformative justice, a blueprint developed by Black, Indigenous, and people of color activists searching for solutions to end violence without using state systems. Liberatory Harm Reduction is a love letter from our ancestors. It teaches us that we are not the problem; we are the solution.[1] Social workers must *understand and believe* that harm reduction is the street-based revolutionary's gift back to our larger community and that the intersection of harm reduction and transformative justice can hold possibilities for personal and political transmutation.

What Is Harm Reduction?

Harm reduction, like many radical philosophies, was co-opted by institutions of public health, social work, and the medical industrial complex. Activists fighting for the rights and safety of people who use drugs, people in the sex trade and street economy, people involved in sex work, and people with chronic illness and disabilities sought to make the philosophy of harm reduction a part of the United State's public health strategy to stem the spread of HIV/AIDS in the late 1980s. As a result of the successful work of these revolutionary organizers, some of you may have heard about syringe exchange, the most popularized example of harm reduction.

What you may not know is that although the risk reduction strategies embedded in harm reduction (condom use, syringe exchange, etc.) did eventually become part of public health's standardized approach to HIV prevention in most states, much of what actually makes up the daily practice of saving our own lives—the core values of the philosophy of harm reduction—was stripped away inside these institutional settings. Harm reduction is not a public health strategy (and yes, I know this statement pisses off many people). Although it improves public health dramatically when used in its whole and un-co-opted form, it is a multifaceted, trauma-centered approach to mutual aid.

Harm reduction was designed and created by drugs users, sex workers, feminists, trans activists, people with chronic illness and disabilities, those of us working to end violence without the police, and those of us working to end prisons and the violent state. It is a practice steeped in joy, in living into the beauty of our lives no matter how messy they may (appear to) be.

This article and all of my practice is grounded in Liberatory Harm Reduction[2] (LHR) as an abolitionist and transformative justice praxis, meaning we understand that the prison industrial complex directly threatens the health and well-being of entire peoples. This belief is foundational to harm reduction in communities most affected by the War on

Drugs. This chapter will not be discussing "public health harm reduction." Instead we will be talking about its origins as a liberation practice—LHR—and how it intersects and pushes social workers to find a place for all of us in the work.

Redefining "Risky" and Reclaiming Trauma-Centered Practice

To understand the philosophy of harm reduction, we have to interrogate our understanding of the idea of "risky behaviors" and reimagine our trauma-centered practice. The strategies survivors use to fight back, heal, cope, and yes, seek pleasure are highly stigmatized and criminalized. Drug use, involvement in the street economy or the sex trade and sex work, self-injury, or not using prescribed (psychiatric or other) medication are often criminalized.

Those of us whose survival strategies have been deemed morally wrong or criminal are made even more vulnerable by social workers who lack a complex trauma analysis. We have become targets of a system that cannot make sense of us and seeks only to control us. Sometimes I think these systems have little help to offer, and other times I think these systems hoard resources from our communities intentionally and force us to fight each other for what little access we have. Depending on a person's age, race, and/or gender presentation, the judgments of institutional representatives, including social workers, can and often do have carceral implications.

To counter stigma and criminalization, we are forced to lie to social workers about our drug use, sex work, housing, medication adherence, and more to cover our tracks as much as we can. Even if we want to stop using drugs and seek out rehab or other forms of assistance, we are subject to humiliation and monitoring of our bodies that is designed to reduce caseloads and keep costs down.

When seeking medical assistance therapy like methadone or suboxone, the average person can wait months or even years to get into a medical assistance therapy program and then must be free of other drugs to stay in the program. I have had several friends who intentionally became pregnant for the sole purpose of getting into rehab or onto methadone because pregnant people have access to priority placement. If you felt shock or judgment come up when you read that statement, I invite you to answer it with curiosity and compassion. What is life like when becoming pregnant is the best option for someone who wants to get off drugs? What does it mean when the system is so violent that extremes become logical options?

When I was finally able to find a doctor who prescribed me suboxone, which is how I effectively stopped using heroin (but not all opioids) in my thirties, I was able to get into a program at my local syringe exchange. The program required few hoops because it was in a harm reduction setting. This is far from a common experience, and I know that my community relationships are what kept me alive.

What Is Liberatory Harm Reduction?

The definition was collectively created in the book *Saving Our Own Lives: A Liberatory Practice of Harm Reduction*:

> Liberatory Harm Reduction (LHR) is a philosophy and set of empowerment-based practices that teach us how to accompany each other as we transform the root causes of harm in our lives.
>
> We put our values into action using real-life strategies to reduce the negative health, legal, and social consequences that result from criminalized and stigmatized life experiences such as drug use, sex, the sex trade/sex work, surviving intimate partner violence, self-injury, eating disorders, and any other survival strategies deemed morally or socially unacceptable.
>
> Liberatory Harm Reductionists support each other and our communities without judgment, stigma, or coercion, and we do not force others to change. We envision a world without racism, capitalism, patriarchy, misogyny, ableism, transphobia, policing, surveillance, and other systems of violence.[3]

Liberatory harm reduction is true self-determination and total body autonomy.

LHR disconnects the ideas of sobriety and healing. We center all of our lived experience and don't create false hierarchies with sobriety at the top. We honor decisions to use herbs as medicines, engage in the street economy though the sex trade or selling drugs. We hold each other close and fall in love with each other's survival and survival strategies.

The idea of keeping our community safe from harm through the practices of abundance, love, joy, and welcoming each other as whole people is deeply rooted in the cultural practices of many Black, Indigenous, Latinx, and other people of color who find ways to survive in the United States. LHR emerged as a daily practice to address the long-term impact of white supremacy, cisheteropatriarchy, ableism, and structural violence.

Where Does Liberatory Harm Reduction Come From?
Liberatory Harm Reduction Focuses on Transforming the Root Causes of Oppression That Cause the Actual Risk for Illness, Death, and Incarceration

In the United States, the story of the evolution of harm reduction predates the AIDS crisis. Parts of LHR came through Marsha P. Johnson and Sylvia Rivera and through activists like Miss Major Griffin Macy, trans women of color, people who were sex workers and street based, and people who created shared housing, syringe exchanges, and sex work safety information. Parts of LHR came through the Black Panthers creating free breakfast programs to feed and nourish a revolution and the Young Lords taking over Lincoln Park Hospital in the Bronx to demand—and ultimately create—community-accessible drug treatment programs. It comes from drug users, underground abortion providers, Indigenous resistance fighters, and AIDS activists.

LHR came to be because people in the sex trade, people of color, queer people, transgender people, gender non-conforming and two spirit people, people with disabilities, people who were houseless, and fat people and drug users saved our own lives. It is a collective story of "Bad Date" sheets passed between sex workers to warn each other of dangerous customers. It is the story of clean syringes, "liberated" from empathetic doctors' offices and then passed between punks in squats in the East Village by women like Isabel Dawson and Kelly McGowan—early AIDS activists—who made sure that everyone had syringes and knew how to use them in 1983.

Although it is difficult to say who started the first ever harm reduction projects for certain because of the underground nature of syringe exchanges, Catlin Fullwood in Seattle and Women with a Vision both began Black and queer/lesbian harm reduction projects led by people with life experience using drugs and in the sex trades in 1986.[4]

Much of the mainstream harm reduction movement that operates alongside public health has historically treated people in the sex trade as an afterthought, as though the most important intervention ever contributed to the field of harm reduction is syringe exchange and as though sex workers, even those of us like me who also shot drugs, are not a central part of the creation of this life-affirming philosophy. The few books that are written about harm reduction barely touch on sex work and focus entirely on drug use. *People in the sex trade, sex work, and survivors of all kinds are the breath of LHR* because, as uncomfortable as this sounds to many, as people with life experience in the sex trade and sex work, we place the importance of relationships and care work as a core practice in everything that we do.

Liberatory Harm Reduction Hinges on the Depth of Relationships We Have with Each Other
What Is Transformative Justice?

There are any number of books, articles, and zines that should be read about transformative justice and prison abolition before you begin your work to end violence without police, prisons, and the state. From *Beyond Survival: Stories and Strategies from the Transformative Justice Movement* by Ejeris Dixon and Leah Lakshmi Piepzna-Samarasinha to *We Do This 'til We Free Us* by Mariame Kaba to the books that started it all—Angela Davis's *Are Prisons Obsolete?* and *The Color of Violence* and *The Revolution Will Not Be Funded* by INCITE! Women of Color and Trans People of Color Against Violence[5] and the Creative Interventions Toolkit stewarded by Mimi Kim and an entire collective of people practicing community accountability. Each of these books gives us a foundational framework and real-life examples of how we can respond to violence without relying on the state.

As defined by Young Women's Empowerment Project in 2009, transformative justice means:

> acknowledging that the state can and will cause harm in our lives, so we work to solve problems together that don't rely on police or social services. We believe that we will reduce violence in our lives and community the more we build together. We believe that we have to confront systems when they stop us from getting the help we need—this is called attacking the "root cause" of violence. We believe that state systems are the ones most responsible for what causes violence in our lives. We believe that survivors use harm reduction every day to survive violence.[6]

Just as harm reduction was created by the people, so was transformative justice and community accountability created by women of color and trans people of color who were antiviolence activists working in domestic violence shelters, rape crisis hotlines, and peer-based counseling projects for survivors. In recent years, we have begun to think of transformative justice as a broad philosophy that can encompass everything from having our own safety teams at conferences and marches to safer workplace culture to safety planning for sex workers. Put simply, transformative justice names the role of state harm in the lives of Black, Indigenous, and other people of color and requires us to find solutions outside of state systems to solve problems. Miss Major Griffin-Gracy, an early harm reductionist, prison abolitionist, transgender activist, and sex worker organizer, said:

> The interesting thing is, by the time I got to prison, and I was talking to Frank Smith [the leader of the Attica prison uprising], I realized the stuff we were doing to try to keep the girls safe was good, but it wasn't enough. We didn't have enough information about what harm was being done to us, and until you understand how oppression works, where it's coming from, and what it means, it's really hard to fight it because you didn't understand what the fight is all about.[7]

It is this naming of structural violence that is essential to our liberatory practice of harm reduction, and it is the everyday, sometimes small things that we do to keep ourselves and our communities safe that makes harm reduction inextricable and necessary to our understanding of transformative justice.

If LHR is what we do on an individual level to increase our daily safety and personal accountability and to build deep relationships, transformative justice is what we do on a community level to address the root causes of violence and create alternative solutions to calling the police and depending on social services. What many people who are newly attracted to the work to end prisons and policing do not realize is that most activists who have been working on transformative justice and community accountability for the last two decade have also been grounded in harm reduction philosophy, and they use it to weave their politics and practice together into tangible action. This is in part because LHR is nonbinary and helps guide us in the release of things like "innocence" versus "guilt" and "good people" versus "bad people," "clean" versus "sober," and so on. Releasing these concepts and the trappings of the success-or-failure dichotomy is essential to our work in transformative justice.

In my community of drug users, people in the sex trade, trans and queer people, young people, and people who are Black, Indigenous, or People of Color, harm reduction is how we make daily life. Sexual violence and harassment from law enforcement are common experiences, and calling the police for help is almost impossible without risking rape, arrest, or death. As a survivor of multiple forms of violence that started when I was very young and spanning to the last time I experienced sexual violence, a few years ago during a date with someone I was attempting to partner with, I am writing from a perspective of complexity. A phenomenon I have noticed recently among people newer to transformative justice and prison abolition work is blaming survivors for calling the police, blaming survivors for responding violently, or just blaming survivors, period.

I believe that survivors of sexual violence have a secret stash of power; we grow our insight out of a need for protection, out of a need to anticipate a violent swipe or someone grabbing us off the street. Some people also form this sixth sense out of generational understanding and awareness of how to escape white racist predators, and they hone psychic practices that allow us to apprehend danger. The survivors I met doing antiviolence work were building underground networks of safe houses that ignored traditional social service models, including domestic violence shelters, because so few people got help from those places. Drug users, people in the sex trade, transgender people, and LGBTI people were thrown out or refused help by shelters, hospitals, police stations, and even soup kitchens every single day—all the places we were socialized to believe would help and protect us only criminalized us further and trained us to lie to get our needs met.

I began to see that all the shelters where I worked or stayed were not reducing problems but making them worse. I saw the shelters fight to expand carceral strategies, from mandated reporting laws to sentencing for people who purchase sex to the expansion of domestic violence courts. It was the mid-1990s, mass incarceration and drug arrests were rampant, and I could not wrap my head around how to be a feminist who did not believe in the state or institutions supported by the state. I was experiencing what Emi Koyama describes in her essay, "Disloyal to Feminism: Abuse of Survivors Within the Domestic Violence System." Emi writes:

> Feminist movements have struggled to confront abuse of power and control within our very movements, even as we critique and resist the abuse within this sexist society. On a theoretical level, at least, we now know that not all of our experiences are the same nor necessarily similar, that claiming universality of experiences inherently functions to privilege white, middle-class, and otherwise already privileged [people] by making their participation in these systems of oppression invisible. We now know, for example, that fighting racism requires not only the obliteration of personal prejudices against people of different races, but also the active disloyalty to white supremacy and all of the structures that perpetuate systems of oppression and privilege.[8]

Koyama's foundational essay shows the deep flaws in the ways that the state and the nonprofit-industrial complex address sexual violence and purport to support survivors. It is clear that a person's identities are surveilled, policed, and punished in the person's attempts, simply, to live. Emi's own thoughts helped me to understand my struggles reconciling my feminist ideas and the stated feminist goals of the shelter. My feminism is rooted in transformative justice, LHR, and abolition; it is clearly anti-carceral and anticolonialist/prorematriation and pro-Black, Indigenous, and other people of color; pro-trans; pro-queer; pro-sex work/pro-ho. The shelter's ideas of feminism were based on perfect, passive, submissive victims needing help from the state; they subscribed to carceral feminism. In my own practice, and in key collaborations, I've attempted to take to heart many of the lessons and methods Koyama lays out.

Emi Koyama's zines were some of the first writings I found that linked the antiviolence work and violent world I was living in with harm reduction. The National Harm Reduction Coalition gave us the principles for US harm reduction practice, which are still radical and rarely fully practiced in public health settings.

Emi took the principles from the National Harm Reduction Coalition and updated them to reflect the trauma-based work done by those of us who identified as survivors. Focused on intimate partner violence, domestic violence, and violence in the sex trade, in sex work, and in the street economy, the following chart is taken word for word from her zine written in the late 1990s. When I reread what she wrote, I am painfully aware of how relevant it is, how little has changed, and how necessary it is for us to have a clear understanding of the role of violence, trauma, and survivorship in our harm reduction practice. See image on page 153.

Tensions for Abolitionist Social Workers Practicing Liberatory Harm Reduction

The practices of LHR and transformative justice are guided by several frameworks, including those that are anti-capitalist, anti-carceral, anti-racist/colonialist, pro-Indigenous/no borders, healing justice (no medical industrial complex); they respect and support total body autonomy, self-determination, the values of disability justice, and empowerment theory; they are trauma centered and prioritize reproductive justice and trans justice; and they are sex work positive and drug use neutral.

There are tensions in the abolitionist praxis of social work that cannot and should not be resolved. The tensions must inform our practice, keep the work sharp, and keep us uncomfortable with the application of our values inside of state and nonprofit institutions. Moreover, abolitionist social workers must also walk the tightrope of applying the values of transformative justice and LHR without allowing the philosophies and practices to be further co-opted by the state and nonprofit systems in which many of us work.

SURVIVOR-CENTERED HARM REDUCTION VALUES

ACCEPTS THAT SURVIVORS LEARN TO COPE IN WHATEVER WAYS THAT REDUCE THEIR PAIN & INCREASE THEIR SENSE OF CONTROL, INCLUDING THOSE TRADITIONALLY VIEWED AS "UNHEALTHY"

MINIMIZES HARMFUL EFFECTS RATHER THAN CONDEMNS OR IGNORES

 ALCOHOL & DRUG USE
 STAYING OR MAINTAINING CONTACT W/ ABUSER
 IRREGULAR EATING & SLEEPING PATTERNS
WRIST-CUTTING & OTHER SELF-HARM
SURVIVAL SEX & SEX WORK

ESTABLISHES QUALITY OF INDIVIDUAL & COMMUNITY LIFE & WELL-BEING - NOT NECESSARILY CESSATION OF ALL ACTIVITIES DEEMED "UNHEALTHY" OR "UNSAFE" — AS THE CRITERIA FOR SUCCESSFUL INTERVENTIONS & POLICIES

UNDERSTANDS EACH METHOD OF COPING AS A COMPLEX, MULTI-FACETED PHENOMENON

SOME WAYS OF DOING IT ARE SAFER THAN OTHERS

A CONTINUUM OF BEHAVIORS

CALLS FOR NON-JUDGMENTAL, NON-COERCIVE SERVICES & RESOURCES TO PEOPLE WHO ARE COPING WITH THE EFFECTS & AFTERMATH OF ABUSE & THEIR COMMUNITIES

NO ACTION — RECKLESSLY EXTREME

 END CRIMINALIZATION OF SURVIVORS!

ENSURES THAT SURVIVORS ROUTINELY HAVE A REAL VOICE IN THE CREATION OF PROGRAMS & POLICIES DESIGNED TO SERVE THEM

AFFIRMS SURVIVORS AS THE PRIMARY AGENTS OF REDUCING THE HARMS OF VARIOUS COPING METHODS AS WELL AS THE AUTHORITIES ON THEIR OWN EXPERIENCES & SEEKS TO EMPOWER THEM TO SHARE INFORMATION & SUPPORT EACH OTHER IN STRATEGIES THAT MEET ACTUAL CONDITIONS OF SURVIVAL & COPING

RECOGNIZES THAT THE REALITIES OF POVERTY, CLASS, RACISM, SOCIAL ISOLATION, TRAUMA, SEX-BASED DISCRIMINATION, & OTHER SOCIAL INEQUALITIES AFFECT SURVIVORS' VULNERABILITY TO & CAPACITY FOR DEALING WITH THE EFFECTS & AFTERMATH OF ABUSE

WE ARE EXPERTS IN OUR OWN LIVES

DOES NOT ATTEMPT TO MINIMIZE OR IGNORE THE REAL & TRAGIC HARM & DANGER THAT CAN BE ASSOCIATED WITH CERTAIN COPING METHODS SURVIVORS MAY EMPLOY

— **EMI KOYAMA** —

Illustration by Lizartistry

At the end of the day, public health, social work, and medicine are not concerned with putting themselves out of business, and they are not concerned with building our collective power.[9] Keeping the lights on and thousands of people employed, keeping the institutions lawsuit free and the system intact, is the primary purpose of hospital administrators and the vast majority of mainstream nonprofits. And although I do, in fact, want both systems of health care and social services to center harm reduction, we need to acknowledge that liability laws make the application of LHR almost impossible. In the words of Sarah Daoud, an anti-carceral queer and trans Arab social worker who works with LGBT houseless young people in Chicago:

> So often, we can't use liberatory harm reduction. Liability laws and other bureaucracy make the practice of honoring what people want to do with their bodies nearly impossible. We'd get fired, licenses revoked, maybe even arrested. So, we're given public health harm reduction, and told that it's the same thing. That it's good enough. It's like what they say in cooking shows—if you can't make your own, store bought is fine. But most of the time, state-sanctioned harm reduction isn't fine. It's the site of harm.[10]

Common Praxis Contradictions

(1) Self-determination: How do abolitionist social workers respect our choices to go off prescribed medication? Our self-injury practice? Our suicidal ideation?

(2) Behavior change: LHR requires no change in "risky behaviors." This means we do not have to be "sober" to get housing or a bus card.

(3) Peer led: LHR programs should be led by and for those whose survival is criminalized and stigmatized.

(4) Reformist reform: Many social workers who are focused on policy propose ideas that grow the carceral state.

(5) Cooptation: Public health has already co-opted harm reduction. To not further this co-optation, abolitionist social workers need to acknowledge they cannot use a liberatory practice of harm

reduction or transformative justice within most nonprofits unless they are small, community-controlled grassroots organizations.

(6) Boundaries: We must honor the complexity of relationships by honoring survivor boundaries and our own boundaries as people who intend to be fighting alongside our community for the long term.

(7) Nonprofit policy and liability: Liability laws undermine relationships. How can abolitionist social workers reduce this harm and prioritize our people with daily practices?

(8) Collaboration with state: When, how often, and at what personal cost will your resistance come? Abolitionist social workers need a personal and professional plan to help them map the impact of their decisions to resist forced hospitalizations, mandated reporting, and cutting people off from services for noncompliance.

Practice Recommendations

LHR helps abolitionist social workers to be directed by individuals and survivors who are criminalized/stigmatized and who directly experience the impacts of structural violence and oppression. Furthermore, LHR demands that abolitionist social workers:

(1) Center the impact of trauma in all work and always give people an opportunity to be their best self and show up a new way. To do this well, we must acknowledge that change and healing isn't linear and we cannot fit people's lives into grant cycles.

(2) Negotiate by/with community to develop and manage programs and create interventions that are led by and for people with lived experience at every level of the organization—not only front-line workers.

(3) Value an investment in long-term relationships over the rules of the agency/organization.

LHR helps abolitionist social workers to makes clear boundaries and relationships through the belief that people can be accountable, grow, heal, and change:

(1) We believe in the whole person—not just the "worst" part or mistakes.

(2) We learn practices and strategies from people in the sex trade and street economy.

(3) We are all teachers and learners. We are creative, imaginative, and focused on both the long-term transformation of our lives and the world and short-term crisis resolution.

(4) We focus on what people actually want and not what the grant requires.

Conclusion: Liberatory Harm Reduction Is a Resilience Strategy

Abolitionist social workers are tasked with maintaining the contradiction of working both inside the system to protect our people and outside of it to dismantle the state. We need to reduce the harms of institutional violence and neglect while simultaneously working inside and outside of the system to end prisons and police and to move us toward a world without violence. Those of us who have been working in social services and also are (or were) stigmatized/criminalized survivors deserve the space to focus on our own resilience methods—how do you fight back and heal on a daily basis, both inside and outside the system you are working in? How do you honor at once the impact of intergenerational trauma and the impact of intergenerational resilience in your own life and in your community?

We must continue to diverge from public health's focus on our bodies as sites of disease by releasing our shame and embracing each other as we are. This means our organizing and praxis strategies must include people who are high in meetings, who are high in therapy, who are in the sex trade and sex work, who are making decisions about their mental health and wellness that may not fit into mainstream social work model of "success." We must continue to demand a trauma-centered practice that is more than "trauma-informed care," one that does not profit from our pain or use liability as an excuse for institutional violence.

While we are working toward our collective freedom, we need to remember that LHR is a love letter from our ancestors who gifted us these hard-won, critical strategies so we can stay alive. These teachings reinforce the idea that every coping tool we use to resist state and interpersonal violence is a miracle. LHR is the daily practice of transformative justice, of abolition, because it helps us place the power back into the hands of people who have systematically been silenced by public health, the medical industrial complex, and carceral social work. By allowing us to be in control of our choices, LHR reminds us that we are not required to do anything but take our next breath and remain in love with each other's survival.

12

A Conversation with Charlene A. Carruthers about Social Work and Abolition

Charlene A. Caruthers and Mimi E. Kim

Charlene A. Caruthers is a founding member and former Executive Director of BYP100, a Black queer abolitionist youth organization in Chicago. She is also the author of the bestselling 2018 book, Unapologetic: A Black, Queer, and Feminist Mandate for Radical Movements.[1] *In this interview, Mimi Kim explores the influence of Charlene's social work education and experience on her life as a community organizer, abolitionist activist, and movement leader.*

Mimi: With regard to your role as the former executive director of BYP100 and your identification as part of the Black queer feminist movement, we wanted to ask you some questions about social work and the possibilities or impossibilities of social work, the kind of liberation work that we do, and the abolitionist agenda.

You did get a master of social work (MSW) degree at some point in your life. So you spent your two or three years in social work school. I am curious about what drew you to get your MSW?

Charlene: I was an undergraduate student at Illinois Wesleyan University, and my roommate was visiting while she was at Washington University in St. Louis, and she asked, "Will you come with me to visit the school?" And so I looked at the graduate programs and I told myself I couldn't possibly get into the law school. And then I looked at the other graduate programs, and I saw the social work school. I think it was called the George Warren Brown School of Social Work when I first applied but by the time I matriculated, it was called the Brown School of Social Work. I saw information, and they were talking about social justice and working in communities and cities and economic and community development. So I visited the school and visited a class and I was like, Oh, I can do this. I'm familiar with what folks are talking about—the language—and I think I can do this. And so I applied to Wash U and to a few more social work schools too. And I ultimately went to Wash U because I knew I wanted to do macro-level work.

I was interested in policy advocacy at the time, and I was interested in and also having some exposure to clinical practice and clinical work as well. That's how I ended up at Wash U and how I ended up in social work school. While I was there, I studied with Professor Jack Kirkland, who I learned a tremendous amount from and who really shaped how I even look at cities, how cities develop, how they operate. I also learned a lot about the region because he would take us on these tours around St. Louis to East St. Louis and the surrounding St. Louis County area. And it just blew my mind. I took a course called The Revitalization of Economically Depressed Communities. I took a course called Cities: The New Frontier, and I also took more clinical courses. I remember taking this course on juvenile delinquency. That was the stage in my life where I was developing a critical analysis, I would say, of systemic oppression, institutional oppression, all of those things. And I had a number of professors who at that time really helped shape my thinking.

The St. Louis area was also the first time I was ever pulled over by a police officer and was essentially verbally assaulted by the police officer. I went to contest my ticket in that courthouse that is in the Ferguson report that trafficked Black and Brown people. Let me add one more thing. The first time I ever canvased for a political candidate was in St. Louis. I canvased for current mayor, Tishaura Jones, when she was running for the state legislature. I remember volunteering very briefly on the Obama campaign because I was there between 2007 and 2009.

But I was like, I'm going to focus on local races. That's what I'm going to do. So being a social work student was within a broader political development context for me. I had mostly been focused internationally before going to social work school. Going to social work turned my focus more so to what was happening here in the United States and also connecting what was happening here in the United States to the broader world in different ways. And so my social work education was formally within the Brown School, but so much of my education happened because I was in St. Louis and the various political, social, and cultural dynamics in the St. Louis area. And that's when I worked on my first grassroots organizing campaign outside of the university setting.

One day I was sitting in my health-care policy class and a student who I will usually go back and forth with about things in class had something come up on her computer about the Center for Community Change. This is was what actually led me to Washington, DC. I had applied for a presidential management fellowship with the White House or Capitol Hill. But it was really knowing that a social worker could get a field practicum at a national community organizing organization that turned me to DC. The person who I was originally going to work with, Sonah Yun, is an alum of the Brown School and led an entire campaign at the Center for Community Change. And so she was taking in social work students, oh, yes, field and field practicum placements in national community organizing.

And so social work is all I am, and I strongly believe that is because of the type of program that I went to. I had a lot to do with it and where I went to, what city, the location of the school. That's how I ended up in DC. That's how I ended up doing national organizing for health-care reform, national organizing for immigration reform, and it led me to all these various relationships that even allowed me to come into leadership and be with people with a huge network of relationships with people. I can't emphasize enough how critical those connections were as a social work student. And even just the facilitation skills, like when you are trained to do a group as a social worker, a lot of that is transferable to facilitating political education sessions, organizing trainings, all those things. So it was extremely influential in my leadership development, even though I didn't go there to be an organizer.

The Brown School had an emphasis on macro-level social work like the policy and advocacy courses I took. They took us to Jefferson City, the capital of Missouri, the state capital of Missouri. I remember all of that.

What was important was the exposure to those things. Whether I can pinpoint them or not, they stay with me in various ways.

In terms of community organizing, I remember reading some Saul Alinsky, but I don't know how engaged I was with it, to be honest with you, because I had a lot going on at twenty-two years old. I remember a lot more about my field placement with the diversity awareness partnership with Rena. I remember her name as the executive director at the time. This is before the era that we're in now. At that time, they would do these diversity trainings for businesses and organizations. But Rena somehow got us involved in fighting against Ward Connolly's anti-affirmative action legislation in Missouri. That was my first time being in any sort of community organizing setting outside of the university.

Mimi: Shifting gears, I want to ask about the development of BYP100. Do you feel like there was any kind of social work orientation or identification with social work that fed into the development of the organization?

Charlene: I mean, I think for this, for me personally, my understanding or approach to communities, to working in communities, I remember there was this interaction I had with a white woman who was in my class. The question was posed by our professor, named Billy: So there's a community you're going to work in. Should you go into the community with a set plan for what to do? Or should you go into the community and determine the course of action *after* you are there for a while? And I said, after you there for a while, you assess stuff based on what people want, where they are, all of that. She said her position was that you should go in with a plan. And I disagreed, and I know me. I'm born and raised on the South Side of Chicago. I had a sense of how white people could be and particularly how white women could be in disagreement. In class discussions, I had attended a predominately white institution for college. I remember slowing down the tone, the pace, being very intentional about my tone, and she started to cry. She started to cry. And so that was my first experience of a white woman crying because I disagreed with her. I think my experience in the classroom informed who I wanted to work with, how I wanted to work, and also my understanding of how important it was not to go into a community with a plan already set.

So it wasn't necessarily the curriculum but the environment with a bunch of people claiming that they are there to help people in communities, I won't even say "transform" because everybody's not there to transform communities. They're there to help people do something or be of service in communities. And then seeing all these white women who I knew were going to be tasked with making decisions about the lives of Black children, I just knew that there was an issue with that. Even if I couldn't fully articulate it at the time the way I can now, I knew there was a problem.

Mimi: We have people that are already social workers and identify that way, or who are studying to be social workers but who don't want to be part of the problem of the prison industrial complex, surveillance, white supremacy. Social work is becoming more aware of the names for these problems and ways to possibly change, if not transform, the way we do social work or to redefine the good ways people have been doing social work. What do you want to say to people who are looking for a change?

Charlene: I think every social worker who is interested in or has made a commitment to abolition should also be a student of the profession. I think everyone should study the profession, its history both being formally called social work and what we would consider social work today before its formal name, before Jane Addams and during Addams' period, particularly the Progressive Era. In addition to being students of the profession and students of the profession's history, they should also be students of US history and the ways that institutions have been built, the ways that both carceral, particularly explicitly carceral institutions, have been built within institutions that are linked through and still can be understood as carceral institutions. Those that mediate carceral systems, like education, health care, especially mental health care and especially education for people who have been deemed criminal or deemed unfit or undesirable in society. To actually take the time to commit to studying how we got to this place. And the role of people who have charged themselves as social workers, as helpers, as reformers, as advocates, especially so-called child advocates, historically and in our communities. That's the first thing.

The second thing that I think people should know is that no matter what field you study, if you're doing school social work, if you're doing family social work, if you're focusing on health care or mental health or any other specialty within social work, we need abolitionists in every single area, no matter what, across every single terrain.

One thing that Jack Kirkland taught us was that you can take a block that's dealing with all sorts of issues and you can put a social worker in every home—and by the end of the year, he said, they will probably be worse off. They would probably be worse off because we haven't dealt with the systemic issues.

We can't deal with communities just house by house. They have to be dealt with them on a block level, on a community level. Right? Should every family get individual support? Of course. But the strategy has to be at the systems level. It can't just be about individuals. I learned that from Jack Kirkland in social work school. We need people everywhere, and it can't just be on an individual basis.

The third thing I would say is that your clinical skills are valuable. Knowing how to talk with and work with people is, unfortunately, something that a lot of organizers don't know how to do and don't know how to do well. Organizers aren't necessarily trained to the extent to which social workers are trained to work with groups. It's something that you can learn—and really talented and skilled organizers learn and know how to do for sure. You don't have to go to school to learn how to do it. I don't think you have to go to school to learn how to facilitate groups. But you do have to be trained. Even if it's training through doing, you got to learn it somehow. These skills are valuable, but the individual approach has its limits.

You have to be trained in a way that puts people first as opposed to their diagnoses, as opposed to the community they live in, what they don't have, what they do have. And you are actually moving through a people-centered approach and not through an evidence-based approach—because that was the hot thing when I was in school. What evidence? Whose evidence? That was the hot stuff back then, but that was literally over a decade ago.

Challenging how you know what you know and the various frameworks that inform that really, really matters as does always questioning, okay, this is happening to this one person. Why? Because what is happening to this one person has happened before and it is happening in other places. So it is not an individual issue. It is bigger than just the individual. How does your work show up in a way that addresses that?

The other thing I think about is mandated reporting. What are social workers going to do to change who you are mandated to report to and what happens on the other side of that mandated reporting? Of course, we don't want children abused. Of course, we don't want people who say they're going to harm other people or themselves, particularly harming other people, to do it without anyone knowing something, taking some sort of action to prevent it. Of course, we don't want that. But I have seen time and time again when someone is saying they are, for example, having suicidal ideation and the social worker or any other mental health-care worker has to report it. Who shows up first? The police. How is that helpful? I think social workers and other clinicians are really well positioned to organize to change that. And so what are you all going to do to transform it, because that is like the front line? Social workers are on the front line of so much criminalization, and so much of what abolition requires us to transform is happening on the individual level, but it's tied to systemic issues and policies.

Mimi: You were using some of the buzzwords that we use today, and another one is "trauma informed." I look at your work, but also at your book and how you talk about the deep underlying traumas that also lead to the kind of dynamics that we've had in our organizations and our movements. I feel like a lot of your focus has been also on the kinds of dysfunctions we have in with our organizations, that you've all have to deal with so much in BYP100, and that we've all dealt with so much in our personal work. You talk about it a lot in your book, but is there anything that you want to say about that in terms of how we might deal with things like harm?

Charlene: Yeah. This is especially important for social workers, many of whom are trained to diagnose or to look for things like our training in the *Diagnostic and Statistical Manual of Mental Disorders* (DSM), whichever number it's on now. And it's like, what nugget of truth or insight does that provide you? Because a social worker might be able to come into the room and understand that what's happening here is that people are anxious or just have a sense of the dynamic that's at play. What is the shape of this room? What's the energy that's happening in this room right now? And what do you know about people based on your study and also your field placements because you've spent hundreds of hours with people, and what kinds of insights might you be able to use to help better understand that the dynamics of any given group and the dynamics of individuals? Because oftentimes, and I talk about this in the book, but even in the instance of the one transformative justice process that I write about in the book, it is, you know, social work. Many social workers are trained to help two people navigate an issue or listen and get to the heart of the thing that is going on. To me, that's an extremely valuable set of skills to have. But what do you do with that information? I think a lot of times what social work as a profession does with that information is connected to systems that depend on punishment and also depend on violence.

If we are in a community setting and someone has experienced harm or several people have experienced harm, have experienced violence from one another, or if you went to an action and the police beat everybody and that's leading to trauma that folks are now bringing in to the organizing space, how might a social worker facilitate a group conversation about it? How would a social worker potentially debrief that in ways or offer such questions that an organizer could ask who doesn't have a social worker training.

I think that the questions that are less about the political strategy and more about the group dynamics are what someone with a social work background could offer to that sort of situation. And the last thing I'll say is that if you are a community-based social worker or you work in a school or in an organization, you likely know who has the resources and where they are—whether somebody needs housing, the list of people, the list of organizations or whoever provides those things, that kind of stuff is oftentimes in the mind bank of a social worker because that's what they do every single day. They have to navigate these trash systems to help people get what they deserve.

I think that's something that overlaps with really great organizers, too, because they oftentimes know that they'll know who to go to and where to go. And so there's some overlap between trained social workers and organizers. I actually wish that they were in more conversation because there's a lot to learn from both groups.

Mimi: Yeah, I agree. And there all of these overlapping questions. We might ask, what is the liberatory possibility of social work? This is now a big question. Or looking back, what are the liberatory possibilities but also limitations of being in a 501(c)3 structure? A lot of people are trying to deal with whether to go into a formation. Do I start something new? Are we looking at something different?

Charlene: I'll tell you something that you might not expect from me. I don't think the 501(c)3 structure dictates how people actually act and what they do in significant enough ways that are different or significantly different from capitalism itself and any sort of organizational structure. I'm not convinced that there's anything unique to the 501(c)3 that one wouldn't find in a non–legally structured organization. I do think that a board of directors and who those people are and the kind of power that they have and things like that can absolutely impact what happens because of the level of power that a 501(c)3 structure gives to boards of directors in many states. For sure. And I'm not convinced that that can't happen in another setting, either. Then the other thing that oftentimes comes up, which I think is very valid, is the issue of philanthropy and how philanthropic actors leverage things that they don't even own like the program officer. That's not even your money. They replicate predatory and extractive capitalistic practices.

They do that. And I don't know how that is transformed wholly across the system without dismantling capitalism itself. That doesn't mean that we can't do anything. I have seen, over the last decade, shifts in how program officers and foundations show up. But that is a result of a lot of work by probably not a lot of people, a very concerted effort by a number of people to make that happen. That was the result of a lot of hard work. I remember being told years ago when there was a point when foundations wouldn't pay for computers where you can't pay for technology. That was a thing. Some people don't know that. Some people had to organize to get that changed. People had to organize to get general operating funds as opposed to line items, project-based funding. That was work to get there, where people could just do what they needed to do.

Now, of course, people will point to the restrictions on lobbying into 501(c)3 structure. What I would say is that no organization should rely on a legislative strategy or policy-oriented strategy only, particularly if you're going to take up abolitionist politics, because none of these local, state, or federal legislatures or government entities are going to deliver us the goods. So I'm not sure if unlimited lobbying will even get us the thing that we even want. Should it be unrestricted? For sure! I know why they put those restrictions in place. They don't want people to engage with that terrain of political power to the extent that we should be able to without fear, because you should be able to do it for sure. But I'm especially thinking about Black folks and our history, our several centuries in this country, even before it was a country, and the various restrictions that were placed upon people trying to change their lives. There have always been barriers. And the question is, how are we going navigate them? What are we going to do? I'm not cheering the 501(c)3 structure, I just get really tired and bored of the same conversations about what the problem is with them. Because to me, oftentimes the discussion doesn't go deep enough for me because I'm like, OK, so if not this, what do we do? What shall we do? Let's do something else. I'm in. Let's do it. And let's not point to the issues that we have simply with the structure, because that doesn't explain all of the problems that we're having here.

Mimi: This brings us back to some of the dynamics that you were talking about.

Charlene: Yeah. At BYP100 most of our staff were young Black people, many of whom had never had a stable, full-time job with benefits. Or they had lived with economic instability, or if they didn't get a paycheck on time, it could be catastrophic for them. Just one missed paycheck. I don't know a structure that can fully meet that need. I don't know a structure that can meet the economic, social, and mental health needs people have to show up to work as the self that they want to show up as. I don't know a structure that can do that. And I think the issues that arise in those settings, to me, sure, we can do something structurally in an organization, but it's so much bigger than any individual organization. And I saw that firsthand every single day. There were things, of course, that we did that mattered and made a difference, like health-care insurance. And people were paid on time when I was there. We didn't have any unpaid internships. We didn't do that. Everybody had vacation days. You didn't have to earn them. You just got them. Whether you use them or not, you got them. Everybody got the time off. So there are absolutely things that you can do. I don't think that has to do with 501(c)3 structure; I think that has to do with your values.

Mimi: Given that you were an abolitionist organization, identified as an abolitionist organization, looking back now, what would you say were some of the primary things that you were able to do around abolition. How would you define your role in that and what you were able to accomplish?

Charlene: I should note that until 2018, BYP100 was fiscally sponsored. It got its 501(c) status the year I left. And we had a 501(c)4; that was actually the first entity we had. The first one was a 501(c)4. And then later we got the 501(c)3; that was fiscally sponsored. We did that so we could do the lobbying, which for the abolition work wasn't the primary terrain. We could do as much lobbying as we wanted to, but it didn't impact our work like that. Our tax status did not determine what we did and did not do overall. I can remember some moments where it came up from different parts of the leadership in the organization. I will say my position was that I wasn't concerned about a tax status and whatever work we did.

So back to your question. I can't remember exactly what year it was, but membership started develop the Healing and Safety Council. The Healing and Safety Council was tasked with figuring out how we were going to develop abolitionist practices within the organization. That happened within the early years of the organization. It was like, OK, y'all, we said we want to do this thing. How are we going to figure it out? There were convenings. There were trainings. I remember one thing that was developed very specifically was enthusiastic consent training. It wasn't implemented as widely as we would have liked it to have been. There were things that people created. We have a healing and safety manual that membership created for people to use on a chapter and community level. I will say that we did not call the police to deal with anything. And that doesn't mean that when we tried to deal with these things, we dealt with them perfectly, but we knew that the police couldn't deal with it any better than we could. So what was the point of calling them? We endeavored to a great extent to try to figure things out—not just on our own, but also with support from other people outside of the organization. And we didn't get a lot of stuff right, and I hope that's published. We got a lot of stuff wrong. It was not perfect. But I think the Black queer feminist lens is an aspirational thing, you know, an aspirational practice and theory. It is something that you have to work through and toward and be committed to figuring it out. Because if they spent several hundred years building up these institutions, we can not figure it all out in five or ten. They've been doing this for hundreds of years, perfecting their violence, perfecting their punishment, perfecting their harms. But what I can say for sure is that people committed to try to figure it out even with all its imperfections.

Mimi: Do you feel like people who circulated in and out of BYP100 carry those skills with them? Whether they were perfect or not, we have a lot to learn from our failures.

Charlene: I would say that I see people who were members of BYP100 go on to do phenomenal things and still be present and work in various ways. I know what the folks in this organization offered to each other and that it has gone well beyond the organization. And the organization will be ten years old next year. The impact of the work that we did with each other has been exponential for sure.

Mimi: So I want to go back. You identify as a Black queer feminist, or at least those are the three words that come across many, many times. What does that mean to you? And is there a way to practice Black, queer, feminist, social work?

Charlene: I know we don't need that. Yeah, we don't need that. I think Black feminism, there's so much Black feminist thought and practice already, which to me, they have to be together. So for me, it's about the work that people do as social workers. If they want to take up Black feminist thought, Black feminist critical analysis, Black feminist practice, that's about reading, listening, observing, studying Black feminist work. I mean, the vice presidential nominee in Colombia identifies as a Black feminist, and that shapes her politics. It's in all sorts of places,

It's reading the Combahee River Collective Statement and thinking it through: How does this apply to your work? How does it apply to your charge or your purpose in movement? We are fortunate in this day and age to have so many Black feminist texts and examples of Black feminist art. All sorts of things that are out there. And so, get curious. To me, the Black queer feminist lens and taking it up in social work is about cultivating a deep curiosity for what has happened before you came into this and what's happening now. When I talk about the Black queer feminist lens, get curious. Study. Build relationships with people. And know that none of it's going to be perfect, and you might even get your heart broken at some point. This work is about a lifetime commitment.

Mimi: That was just a beautiful, beautiful answer. Is there anything else you want to add to what you already shared?

Charlene: I would say that if you are in a social work program that doesn't have macro-level work, you've got to organize to get it.

13
No Restorative Justice Utopia: Abolition and Working with the State

Tanisha "Wakumi" Douglas

> *Human beings are constantly struggling to make what they believe to be true, right, and just into a reality in their individual and social lives. Progress does not take place like a "shot out of a pistol." It requires the labor, patience, and suffering of the negative. In everything, there is the duality of the positive and the negative. What is important is not any particular idea, but the process of continuing development as the contradictions or limitations inherent in any idea surface and require the leap to a new idea or a new stage of Spirit.*
>
> —Grace Lee Boggs[1]

Introduction and a Note on Language

As a Black, abolitionist social worker rooted deeply in partnerships with Black youth who have been harmed by the legal system, I have found myself searching for tools to "fix" the system, including those also used to abolish it altogether. One such tool that has gotten increased attention in the last decade is *restorative justice* (RJ), or what I will call "what we now call restorative justice" (WWNCRJ). Working with our people already harmed by the state has led us to sticky positions within various state systems (legal, child welfare, mental health, homeless services, etc.) seeking to implement WWNCRJ to reduce systemic harm. As abolitionists, we do not always have the luxury of purity politics but must embrace the contradictions inherent in implementing WWNCRJ to reduce real and everyday harm. We use our understanding of contradictions to sharpen both our politics and our praxis. Through storytelling and lessons from practice wisdom, I will share some observations, insights, and food for thought about tensions in implementing WWNCRJ with state actors as we continue to build an abolitionist future.

The tension many of us feel in working with the state to implement WWNCRJ is at the core of the WWNCRJ movement itself. The reality of this tension was brought straight to the surface during the June 2017 National Association of Community & Restorative Justice conference held in Oakland, California, and hosted by Restorative Justice for Oakland Youth under the leadership of Dr. Fania Davis. Not only did the conference organizers bring spiritual ways, music, dance, art, storytelling, and the healing ways of various Indigenous groups (a rare occurrence during WWNCRJ conferences as per movement lore), they also created an intimate circle space for WWNCRJ practitioners and advocates to literally sit at the feet of Indigenous elders to listen and learn. The session was entitled "Honoring the Indigenous Roots of Restorative Justice"; the classroom was packed, with many of us sitting on the floor. The panel centered five Indigenous elders and included a number of other non-Indigenous elders. During their opening remarks, one Indigenous panelist caught themselves feeling disturbed as they repeatedly used the term "restorative justice" to describe the powerful paradigm and set of experiences it embodies. Even that language, they said, is colonized and violent. How do we talk about a process, a system of being well with one another that is a people's way of being—not a program or solution to a white supremacist problem? What words in the English language can capture this Indigenous relational and spiritual technology? The panelist proposed the phrase "what we now call restorative justice" or WWNCRJ.

In this chapter, I will use "what we now call restorative justice" or WWNCRJ to name what we typically call "restorative justice" or "RJ." I encourage readers to embrace what feels tense and challenging in reading this long, somewhat awkward to the English tongue abbreviation throughout the chapter. If there is discomfort, embrace it. It is our ability to embrace this type of discomfort that will serve us best as we navigate the muddy waters of WWNCRJ and the state. Just like this tension in the language, attempting to integrate an ancient Indigenous practice of being into a culture rooted in colonial violence, erasure, and genocide of those very people is going to come with a myriad of tensions, harms, and contradictions. As social workers, this makes our engagement with WWNCRJ even more crucial as we move toward reclaiming and advocating for the soul of humanity.

WWNCRJ Girls' Diversion Program: Lessons in Working with the State

Overview

To illustrate some of the key tensions in working with the state toward WWNCRJ, I am going to pull back the curtain on the planning and early implementation process of the first-ever WWNCRJ diversion program for Black, Indigenous, and other people of color (BIPOC) girls and transgender and gender nonconforming (TGNC) youth in a local jurisdiction. I was intimately involved in co-leading this process. To allow for a more honest discussion, I will use pseudonyms. This project was a collaboration between Gender Lib (GL), a community-based organization, and the local prosecutor's office. I will provide a brief program overview and then explore three core tensions and three critical lessons from this project, which help to illustrate the very present contradictions and their impact.

GL serves and supports systems-involved girls and TGNC youth. The WWNCRJ diversion program led by GL supports system-involved cis, trans, nonbinary girls under age eighteen in a precharge, postarrest community accountability process. Throughout the WWNCRJ diversion process, GL staff support girls and TGNC youth responsible for causing harm as well as those directly impacted by the harm, by facilitating a face-to-face WWNCRJ process with the responsible youth (the person who caused harm), the person directly impacted (the survivor of harm), as well as with their community, and their caregivers/family. The purpose is to address the impacts of the harm, the root causes of the harm, and collectively create a plan for the young person to repair the harm. At just over 500 girls' arrests for high-level misdemeanor and felony charges

(2019 data), at scale, WWNCRJ diversion had the potential to end girls' criminalization and incarceration in this city altogether.

GL partnered with the Restorative Justice Project, a model WWNCRJ diversion program for young people led by Impact Justice in Oakland, California, to plan and implement this approach. At the time of planning and early implementation, the Restorative Justice Project had successfully implemented WWNCRJ diversion programs in several California jurisdictions, including Alameda County, San Francisco, and Long Beach. Alameda County currently has California's oldest running WWNCRJ diversion program, with a recidivism rate of 18.4% (compared with 32.1% for youth whose cases are processed through the juvenile justice system), a 91% victim satisfaction rate, and a cost of just $4,500 per youth (2019 data).[2]

GL made adaptations to the WWNCRJ model created by the Restorative Justice Project to include youth leadership development programming in organizing, social justice, and healing. Participants would have access to an emotional justice initiative centering peer support through psychoeducation and support groups co-led by a small team of healing artists, including social workers, art therapists, traditional cultural healers and/or yoga and mindfulness instructors, and peer counselors. The initiative also includes social work interns offering supportive counseling sessions, advocacy, and strengths-based case coordination to support youth and families. GL also saw that transformative justice offered a framework for thinking beyond the specific case and for looking at the societal and community conditions that led to the violence. The program builds the skills of youth to address those conditions.

GL collaborated with the local prosecutor's office to offer this WWNCRJ diversion for systems-involved youth. This city has a robust diversion system already in place for citations and misdemeanors (and limited felonies). GL wanted to interrupt harm for youth deeper down the pipeline to prison; those youth were often in the custody of the state. Collaboration with the state toward our ends became our target. The prosecutor's support for WWNCRJ diversion and their agreement to send over precharge referrals that may not have been considered eligible for diversion in the past (due to level of severity and/or prior history of the youth) was a form of systems change toward decarceration and decriminalization of youth. Through WWNCRJ diversion, young people meet with the people directly impacted by harm for a well-prepared, facilitated dialogue during which participants collectively create a plan to repair the harm with the support of family, friends, and community members. This plan supports youth to do right by their (1) victim/survivor, (2) family, (3) community, and (4) themselves. As long as the young person completes the plan (usually within three to six months), no criminal charges are ever filed—avoiding court, probation, and incarceration.

From a community organizing perspective, the prosecutor's office was our target institution. It was our hope that this would create a watershed moment for decarceration that would eventually include boys and youth of all genders. Our strategy for change in our target was to build a sustainable relationship with the prosecutor's office to support pre-WWNCRJ diversion for systems-involved girls and TGNC youth. To create more results, we would serve more youth. GL's broader coalition engaged an inside-out strategy. They were deeply connected to local grassroots organizing and policy advocacy organizations such as Dream Defenders and the Southern Poverty Law Center. These organizers and advocates had been pushing legal and public education institutions to invest in WWNCRJ for over a decade. They would be key players in GL's ecosystem for holding the state accountable.

Tensions and Contradictions

We had a great plan and great minds to support it. We had data proving our theory that WWNCRJ is what girls and TGNC youth needed. We had a track record and working process for engaging young people and families in community. We were passionate and spirited about our purpose. We even had the support of the chief juvenile justice judge—a key bridge-builder between community and the state—in the county. Despite this, we faced numerous tensions and contradictions:

- How do we pivot when the state wants to use WWNCRJ for its own purposes?
- Who should pay for this program: private foundations or the state?
- How do we hold on to the heart and soul of WWNCRJ as we enter sterile, white-dominant, legal spaces?

Each of these questions represents a tension palpably felt by the diversion program organizers and practitioners. In this section, I will present the tensions and contradictions. In the following section, I will present some of the ways we navigated these tensions.

The prosecutor's office's "power over" tactics and habit of centralizing their own needs became clear very early on in our relationship-building with them. In 2018, we cohosted an introductory meeting on WWNCRJ with the chief juvenile judge. Prosecutor's office representatives attended. After the presentation, the judge made sure to get verbal commitments to go forward with WWNCRJ from each department represented at the table. Within days of that meeting, the prosecutor's office contacted me requesting that we take a case. It would "help out" their office for us to take the lead on the case using WWNCRJ. At this time, we had no standing contract with them and no existing organizational infrastructure for taking cases. The case involved a Latinx teen girl who stabbed another Latinx teen girl in a fight related to a love triangle. In making the determination about how to proceed with the state's request, we had to consider: (1) Did we have capacity? And if we did not, could we build programmatic infrastructure quickly?; (2) What would an ideal agreement with the state include that would make us comfortable receiving a referral?; (3) Did the case itself align with the purpose of our program?; and (4) How was this an opportunity for us to strengthen our WWNCRJ practice? After tending to each of these questions (and many more), we ultimately decided to establish a short-term contract with the state and take this as a demonstration case to test our working relationship with the state. For some of us, this was also a chance to prove the efficacy of the approach. For others, that rationale in itself was a tension: Why should we, the harmed, have to continually prove that our ways work to people in systems that perpetually create harm? After several months, we successfully resolved this case using WWNCRJ; all charges were dropped.

This, of course, was not the only time the state made its needs primary in our partnership. Despite their interest in WWNCRJ, the state staunchly maintained their law-and-order focus. During contract negotiations, the state was very clear about its interest in using the content that circle participants share in WWNCRJ processes to prosecute them if they include legal infractions. They repeatedly expressed discomfort with the ironclad confidentiality agreement we presented in our partnership contract. It took several months of negotiation to find a middle ground. This made the tension that we felt as abolitionist social workers and organizers very real. We all questioned if working with this particular state partner (or any) was a good idea. Was it in alignment with our abolitionist aims? Could we actually bring the number of incarcerated girls to zero with a partner that was interested in prosecuting young people based on their heartfelt sharing during circle? It kept us up at night. Ultimately, we were able to come to an agreement on a time-limited memorandum of understanding including circle participant confidentiality (and other critical boundaries with the state) with which we were all comfortable.

Another key tension was around funding. As a common fundraising practice when seeking funding for a new project, organizational leaders may reach out to their "low-hanging fruit" funders. These are the funders with whom trusting relationships have been established and who are more inclined to take a risk on funding an organization's new project. I met with one such funder, Free Fund, as we were getting close to making our first two hires for the diversion program. The program officer was excited to take the call. After we exchanged pleasantries, I shared an overview of the diversion program and how it fit perfectly into Free Fund's priorities. The program officer, who is generally very inquisitive and chatty, was quiet with very few questions. I learned early on in my fundraising experience that radical honesty and transparency are often appreciated by folks who control deep purse strings. I asked her directly about her hesitation. And I'll never forget what she said: "Shouldn't the government be paying for this?" Her question illuminated another tension. It was indeed the government's responsibility to intervene when young people break laws established and enforced by said government. On the books, it is the government's responsibility to take care of children in its jurisdiction. And in white and wealthy communities, they do that quite well—with care and kindness. It is in BIPOC communities where the government behaves with violence. My funder colleague was proposing that part of our organizing intervention should be to push the government in jurisdictions where they have been historically harmful and neglectful to pay for programs to repair that harm and to offer the most innovative and high-quality programs to all young people. And although money certainly reflects priorities, could we really expect a government that was built on exploitation of BIPOC people for its economic benefit to actually invest in quality care for our children? Did we even want this blood money for our abolitionist projects? Is it all blood money? As I approached various funding opportunities, this tension was ever present. In fact, our team spent the first eighteen months after the initial two program hires focused exclusively on creative fundraising with a focus on soliciting funds from community members as well as wealthy individuals in the entertainment industry. The onset of the pandemic halted our plans, and so we were not able to see if this creative fundraising approach would have worked to robustly resource our work.

Lastly, we were confronted regularly with an overall feeling that we had to intentionally hold the "heart and soul" of WWNCRJ or we would lose it. WWNCRJ is rooted firmly in principles that represent the soul of what we are doing and seeking to be. Our team authored these program principles:

- We must honor the dignity, power, and humanity of all people, regardless of whether they caused harm or have been harmed.
- The autonomy, expertise, and consent of directly impacted individuals and communities are at the core of true justice.
- Girls deserve healing and recognition of their trauma and victimization histories that led them into the juvenile legal system.
- No girl wants to be an *offender*. Care and support for perpetrator-survivors break cycles of violence.
- Leadership development of survivors transforms and heals conditions that enable violence in our communities.
- Equitable program design must be responsive to historic and current racial, ethnic, and gender disparities in the juvenile legal system.
- Community-held RJ processes eliminate shame and blame and build capacities that respond to and prevent violence.
- An investment in girls is an investment in families and communities.

NO RESTORATIVE JUSTICE UTOPIA

Keeping these principles alive would be our key task: one that led to confronting numerous contradictions.

One glaring contradiction was how we would ensure racially equitable access to the program. We already noticed in the assignment of the demonstration case that prosecutors might have a tendency to offer the opportunity to white/white-passing Latinx girls and TGNC youth. In this county, white/white-passing Latinx folks hold significant racial and economic privilege despite their immigrant and/or English as a second language status. This is unique to this local context and makes tracking anti-Blackness among immigrant communities even more important. We had to make clear, based on data, that Black youth inclusion is critical to equitable program access. We had numerous internal conversations as we planned and facilitated early program implementation about if we would accept cases that met all of the criteria but the racial equity criteria. These discussions were tense and uncomfortable. None of us wanted to turn away young people in need of an alternative to the legal system because of a racial identity they didn't choose within a white supremacist structure they didn't create. How would we make sure there were enough Black youth in the program in an immigrant/people of color–dominant yet anti-Black context?

Another key tension on maintaining the soul of the approach is about the use of the state as a stick. I would be remiss if I presented WWNCRJ as a process in which all participants joyfully and willingly participate. Practitioners of WWNCRJ share often about the process of navigating participants' resistance and unwillingness to participate. In the backdrop of all diversion programs is what I call "the stick." Either youth who have done harm participate in WWNCRJ or go to jail. Does this really allow for the "power," "autonomy," and "dignity" of youth involved as stated in our principles? Is the very fact of us engaging with the state in conflict with young people's power and dignity? Or do we need the stick? Given that we have all been conditioned in a punishment-based society, do we need a consequence presented to us to do what's right? I don't have a neat and tidy answer to these questions. What is clear is that I absolutely know young people who would not have engaged in WWNCRJ if it had not been for the threat of court and incarceration. Now what, abolitionist social workers, do we do with that? The spirit of WWNCRJ calls us to get into dialogue and exploration about these tensions between theory and praxis.

At this point in the chapter, many readers may be wondering: What do we do with all these tensions? How do we get ourselves out of the mess that white supremacy, patriarchy, capitalism, and colonization have created? Are our adaptations of ancient Indigenous technologies the best tools on the road to abolition? My practice wisdom has taught me that every question, every tension, and every contradiction should be greeted as a welcome gift to our movement for liberation. How can we untangle a knot that we cannot see? It has taken centuries to arrive at this place of entrenched state violence and harm, and it will take time to heal, restore, and transform.

Embodying the Practice: Letting Conflict Make Us Wise

A part of the beauty of opening ourselves to the tensions and contradictions within WWNCRJ is the opportunity to embody the practice. Anyone who has done abolitionist antiviolence, violence interruption, conflict, or harm work knows that this work is messy. To be of use, practitioners must be able to navigate messy humanness, be comfortable being uncomfortable, sit confidently in not knowing the answer to a high-stakes question, and be open to what there is to be learned in it all about oneself, our people, and, yes, even our opposition. In closing, I offer three points of awareness that have served me well on my abolitionist journey in working with state actors and institutions.

1. Be a palm tree—bend so you won't break.

I have the privilege of living on Miccosukee, Seminole, Tequesta land in what we call South Florida. Every day, but particularly during hurricane season when rains are heavy and winds are strong, I notice our palm trees firmly rooted into the earth with trunks flexible enough to bend with the wind. Although I am not an arborist, local lore claims that heavy winds very rarely uproot or break palm trees and that winds even strengthen palm trees' roots. Working with the state taught us the value of flexibility.

For example, when the state asked us to take a case before we were in contract, we saw this as an opportunity to bend to (1) strengthen our own practice and (2) see the state actors more clearly by working with them closely. Our ability to see beyond the "power over" dynamic and find our own power in the partnership was at the root of our flexibility. There was something in this request that served our abolitionist goals; it was our job to find it. And, indeed, we were able to gain invaluable practice in tending to violent harm between girls using WWNCRJ in a case that involved issues of language access, classism, toxic masculinity, and many more dynamics that sharpened us as practitioners. We were also able to see up close and personal how the prosecutor's office operated. We were, on numerous occasions, pleasantly surprised by their hands-off stance and their acceptance of our asserting boundaries when they requested information beyond the scope of what was contractually allowable. We also saw some troubling racial, gender, and power dynamics that we intentionally tracked; doing so helped us be more strategic when it was time to negotiate the five-year contract.

Our ability to be flexible, to sit in the gray area, is deeply connected to decolonization. According to Afrikan-centered psychology, an Afrocentric worldview calls for diunitality, both/and thinking, versus Westerners' dichotomous, either/or thinking.[3] Tensions in implementing WWNCRJ within legal institutions requires we hold our abolitionist visions and the limitations of the state at the same time. Western culture has taught us to limit our sense of what's possible with either/or thinking. Holding a both/and worldview requires us to be more expansive and creative while embracing the limitless possibilities for liberation and beyond.

2. See the humanity in *everyone*.
Dehumanization is a tool of the state. The United States built its global economic and political power by violently stripping African, Indigenous, and migrant people of our most human needs and desires. We have been conditioned to traffic in dehumanization with ease. As we actively built relationships with the people, the human beings, that ran the prosecutor's office, I noticed our team's inclination toward dehumanizing them. With ease, we dismissed and invalidated their feelings and interests. We belittled their concerns. We saw them solely as state actors, denying them the fullness of their human experience, the fullness of their humanity.

That changed for me the more we used WWNCRJ practices during our meetings. I insisted that during every meeting, even the virtual ones, we passed the talking piece to check in before diving into the agenda. In doing so, our team was able to authentically share and hear the authentic sharing of the prosecutor's office staff. We learned about their faith traditions, their families, their fears, and what brings them joy. As we continued to build relationships, I began to see more clearly some of the shared principles and motivations between our team and the people who ran the prosecutor's office. Granted, we had very different beliefs on what it meant to truly transform the lives of young people coming through the juvenile legal system. But the truth was, the people in the prosecutor's office didn't want to see anyone in the community harmed, including the young people. Some of them ascribed to faith traditions that center forgiveness and redemption. They had pride in the number of youth they were able to divert from incarceration. Knowing and seeing this was not just a tool for strategic bargaining in negotiations (although this information was quite useful for that purpose). Seeing this allowed me to soften toward those we would typically call the opposition, toward people who have participated in a system that has done harm. This ultimately is what WWNCRJ invites. It invites us—even in the midst of all the messy contradictions—to open to see full, whole human beings before us—with faults, with fears, with histories of harm and histories of being harmed.

3. Embody. Embody. Embody.

It has become incredibly cliche to say: "be the change." But it is a quintessential truth. Howard Zehr says, "Restorative justice is a compass, not a map."[4] WWNCRJ calls us into a paradigm and invites us to move forward in a good way with other human beings. It calls us into enactment of a set of principles for being. Being requires that we activate these principles with our very bodies, with the words that we say and don't say, with our body language, with our steps toward and away from one another, with how we treat and behave toward friends and foes, with how we treat and behave toward ourselves.

At each meeting with the prosecutor's office, I began to find myself embodying the circle value: "Listen from the heart." With my heart, I could hear the prosecutor's office staff express fear of failure, fear of being responsible for additional harm, and deep motivation to help young people live good lives. If I only listened with my head, I would have heard risk averseness, distrust in community interventions, and paternalism. It is entirely possible that what I heard with my heart and my head were operating at the same time. But if I wanted to open the hearts of the people in the prosecutor's office, then I had to open mine toward them.

Closing Insights

It has been such an honor to share my experiences in this piece. It is my sincerest prayer that these insights are useful as organizers, advocates, practitioners, healers, aunties, movement mamas, community members, and, of course, social workers take steps toward abolition using WWN-CRJ. We must be under no delusion that the state will concede power to us solely because we embody this practice with open hearts, humanity, and flexibility. We need fiery warrior energy and confrontational tactics as we combat the insidious, brutal, and widespread nature of state violence. Our power is in our discernment. It's in our connection to each other and that which is greater than us all, as we decide whether to fight the state or sit in circle (or both!). Each move we make comes with complications, contradictions, and tensions. As we lovingly embrace each challenge, we get closer to freedom.

14

Boycott, Divestment, Sanctions as Abolitionist Praxis for Social Work*

Stéphanie Wahab

Social Work and Palestine

There may be few issues that test social work's stated values of social justice, human dignity, and worth more than the ongoing Israeli occupation of Palestine. Following the razing of 500 Palestinian villages and the displacement of the majority of the Palestinian population in 1948, Israel has engaged in consistent acts of genocide, violence, and oppression against Palestinians through its carceral political and legal systems. The violence of Israel's settler colonialism provides social work with a real-life case study of ongoing genocide, apartheid, dispossession, racism, and carcerality. Although Palestinians are not uniquely defined by their dispossession and suffering, I bring these affective, material, political, social, and economic conditions to bear to shine a light on a system of apartheid, reliant on international support, and a matrix of incarceration. The international community must act now. Furthermore, I call attention to Israel's carceral violence to invite social work colleagues around the world to work in solidarity with Palestinians to hold Israel accountable for its ongoing attempts of erasure of the Indigenous people of Palestine, and to abolish the Israeli occupation of Palestinians and their land.

---

* Though this was written prior to October 7, 2023, the conditions articulated remain, including the Israeli occupation of Palestinian land, liberty, and life, along with intensified ethnic cleansing and genocide. In January 2024, a flagship social work journal published commentary calling voices for Palestinian liberation anti-Semitic.

Social Work Silence and Complicity

Over the course of thirty years in social work, I've noticed that most social work academics, students, and practitioners in the United States (I feel this is different outside of the United States) know very little about the history and present of Palestine. This ignorance runs parallel to a silence about Israeli oppression of Palestinians, a silence often referenced as *progressive except for Palestine*,[1] where social and political groups customarily outraged by racism, apartheid, and human dispossession remain silent. "Too often, social work has chosen professionalization, growth and partnership with harmful state agencies over social justice, solidarity, and self-determination. When it comes to Palestine, there is even more pressure to be quiet."[2] Orientalism, settler colonialism, anti-Arab racism, and taken-for-granted Zionist myths contribute to this ignorance, and readers may find detailed discussions of this issue elsewhere.[3] What is relevant (and connected to this ignorance), however, is the global social work silence in the face of Israeli necropolitics[4] and the necrocapitalism[5] of Zionism. *Necro* comes from the Greek root *nekros*, which means "corpse," hence *necropolitics* refers to the "politics of death." Achille Mbembe defines necropolitics as a framework for understanding "contemporary forms of subjugation of life to the power of death."[6] Necrocapitalism[7] extends Mbembe's theorizing of necropolitics to focus on accumulation through death. More specifically, necrocapitalism speaks to "practices of organizational accumulation that involve violence, dispossession, and death."[8] This silent bystanderism, Palestinian social workers notwithstanding, is deafening in the face of social work's explicit commitments to social justice, human dignity, and human worth. Nevertheless, I remain hopeful in the face of recent shifts in certain spaces toward Palestinian solidarity, especially among abolitionist communities, as evidenced by the inclusion of this chapter in this text.

Apartheid and the Matrix of Incarceration

A robust understanding of the relationship between abolition and Palestinian liberation requires a basic understanding of the settler colonial violence of Zionism,[9] and although a thorough discussion of the racism of Zionism goes beyond the scope of this chapter, I do wish to note some of the linkages for those who are new to understanding Palestinian dispossession and liberation. It is important for readers to understand that the occupation is a structure within Zionism.[10] I lean on understandings of Zionism that frame it as always having been a European colonial project that evolved into an imperial project sustained by the United States.[11] As many have previously argued, Zionism's early writings reveal that the dispossession of the Palestinian people was always at the core of Zionism, hoping to render us as "no people."[12] My colleague and I have argued elsewhere:

> Zionism's domination over Palestinian bodies, land, life, and psyche exists to nurture a binary necropolitics (Mbembe, 2003), where there are those who should be killed, and those who always and forever possess the right to maim, kill, and eliminate (Puar, 2017). Such logic is apparent in Israel's Jewish Nation-State Law as it maintains the exclusivity of the Jewish Israeli state, and the demonization of the disposable other (Jabareen and Bishara, 2019). Framing settlers as always-and-forever victims, rather than as invaders and abusers, ignores Palestinian ordeals, and erases historical memory alongside present narration (Zreik, 2016). Ultimately, the state's brutal attacks, denial of historical and present injustices, coupled with the dismemberment of the Palestinian social, cultural, and spiritual fabric, together constitute intentional national domicide alongside racialized dehumanization.[13]

Beginning in 1948, when Israel established two separate sets of laws—civilian for Jews, and military for Palestinians—Israel has relied on physical and affective[14] containment of Palestinians to fortify its project of erasure and co-optation.[15] One does not need to engage a deep dive inside Israeli laws and policies to see evidence of the carceral blueprint of Zionism and the occupation. Gaza provides the most extreme example of Zionism's carceral backbone, often referred to as the "the world's largest open-air-prison," with 2.2 million people trapped within 138 square miles. The vast majority of Palestinians in Gaza cannot leave as land, sea, and air borders are controlled by Israel, effectively making Israel the warden of the Palestinian prisoners inside Gaza.

Another glaring example of Zionism's carcerality is the apartheid wall, referenced by Zionists as the "security barrier," spanning 472 miles and standing 26 feet high (twice as high as the Berlin wall), and present in Bethlehem, parts of Ramallah, Qalqilya, parts of Tulkarm, and throughout East Jerusalem. The apartheid wall was deemed illegal by the International Court of Justice at The Hague in July 2004, with the court stating that the wall violates international law by restricting Palestinian movement and access throughout the West Bank and is "tantamount to de facto annexation."[16] Despite calls for an immediate stop to construction alongside reparations for the damage caused, Israel ignored the United Nations' decree as it has consistently done since 1948 and continues to build the wall alongside illegal settlements to this day. The conditions containing Gaza coupled with the apartheid wall represent just two glaring examples of Israel's incarceration of Palestinians, where fences, walls, crossing points, and 500 checkpoints and roadblocks are strategically built and maintained to create a sophisticated web of containment, what I refer to as a "matrix of incarceration," with the aim of preventing Palestinian access to their lands, homes, medical care, families, work, water, human dignity, and human rights. Working alongside these physical containment structures are also practices of home arrests, home demolitions, exile, collective punishment, and the criminalization of Palestinian nonprofit human rights organizations. These practices function like a swarm,[17] expanding and entrenching the matrix of incarceration, effectively creating militarized "reservations" or "choking system of Bantustans."[18] Gortler uses the term *Israeli carceral dispositive* to reference the web of government, security, and psychological control holding up and enacting Israel's apartheid state:

> *Israeli carceral dispositive*—a term I use to indicate the assemblage of the Israeli Prison Service, the General Security Services, government officials, and, more importantly, Israeli public opinion and the Zionist psyche—has employed prisoners' self-identification and their collective organization to better control them. It does so by encouraging regional identifications over national ones, by dividing the prisoners, and by encouraging a self-interested comportment.[19]

Reading political prisoner Walid Daka, Gorlter argues that these assemblages are not only meant to erase Palestinians, but also to create particular (obedient and more passive) Palestinian subject positions:

> If the segregated areas Israel demarcated for Palestinians in the occupied territories are akin to bigger prisons, and its practices towards Palestinians in the smaller prisons are a continuation of its policy in the larger ones, then it is useful to first apply theoretical tools to study the smaller prisons. The panopticon is the fundamental form of this control and surveillance that Israel conducts not only to enhance security but to re-shape people.[20]

Consistent with carceral logics and practices, those who resist these forms of containment and dispossession are frequently criminalized, incarcerated, tortured, maimed,[21] and murdered by Israel. Central to this discussion about Zionism's matrix of incarceration is that it has been made possible via international support and complicity, particularly from the United States, such that every US president since Harry Truman has explained that "Israel is our closest strategic ally in the region." The United States alone has historically and consistently given billions ($3.8 most recently and double that for many years) of dollars on a yearly basis, alongside military and construction equipment, to support Zionism's project of erasure.

Boycott, Divestment, Sanctions

Boycotts have long been an element of anticolonial struggles.[22] Inspired by earlier Palestinian boycotts after the *Nakba* of 1948 (what Palestinians refer to as the *catastrophe* when half the population of Palestinians lost their homes and property in addition to becoming stateless in and out of historic Palestine), as well as the South African antiapartheid movement, Boycott, Divestment, Sanctions (BDS) is a Palestinian civil society, nonviolent social movement calling for freedom, justice, and equality. Formed in 2005, BDS is made up of academic associations, unions, refugee and women's organizations, churches, and grassroots liberation organizations. BDS was created explicitly as an organized response to the settler colonial violence of Zionism and its violent and carceral conditions. Its founder Omar Barghouti wrote:

> Faced with overwhelming Israeli oppression, Palestinians under occupation, in refugee camps and in the heart of Israel's distinct form of apartheid have increasingly reached out to the world for understanding,

for compassion, and, more importantly, for solidarity. Palestinians do not beg for sympathy. We deeply resent patronization, for we are no longer a nation of hapless victims. We are resisting racial and colonial oppression, aspiring to attain justice and genuine peace. Above all, we are struggling for the universal principle of equal humanity. But we cannot do it alone.... Given its uncontested military superiority, the unquestioning and all-embracing support it enjoys from the world's only empire and the lack of political will by Arab and European states to hold it in check, Israel has been gravely violating international law, with audacious impunity, showing little if any consideration for the UN or world public opinion.[23]

Hence, the main goal of BDS is to render Israel compliant with international laws that recognize the West Bank, East Jerusalem, and the Syrian Golan Heights as occupied by Israel.[24] Hence, BDS demands an end to the occupation and colonization of all Arab lands and the dismantling of the apartheid wall, recognition of Arab-Palestinians in Israel with full equality, and the promotion and protection of the right of return of Palestinian refugees to their homes as stipulated by United Nations Resolution 194. To better understand what each component of this campaign signifies, I present the definitions for each tactic as articulated by the BDS movement.

BDS articulates three demands in service of the three tactics:[25]

(1) *Ending its occupation and colonization of All Arab lands and dismantling the Wall*: International law recognizes the West Bank (including East Jerusalem), Gaza, and the Syrian Golan Heights as occupied by Israel. As part of its military occupation, Israel steals land and forces Palestinians into ghettos, surrounded by checkpoints, settlements, and watchtowers and an illegal apartheid wall. Israel has imposed a medieval siege on Gaza, turning it into the largest open-air prison in the world. Israel also regularly carries out large-scale assaults on Gaza, which are widely condemned as a constituting war crimes and crimes of humanity.

(2) *Recognizing the fundamental rights of the Arab-Palestinian citizens of Israel to full equality*: One-fifth of Israel's citizens are Palestinians who remained inside the armistice lines after 1948. They are subjected to a system of racial discrimination enshrined in more

than 50 laws that impact every aspect of their lives. The Israeli government continues to forcibly displace Palestinian communities in Israel from their land. Israeli leaders routinely and openly incite racial violence against them.

(3) *Respecting, protecting, and promoting the rights of Palestinian refugees to return to their homes and properties as stipulated in UN Resolution 194*: Since its violent establishment in 1948 through the ethnic cleansing of more than half of the Indigenous people of Palestine, Israel has set out to control as much land and uproot as many Palestinians as it can. As a result of this systematic forced displacement, there are now more than 7.25 million Palestinian refugees. They are denied their right to return to their homes simply because they are not Jewish.

Boycott, Divestment, Sanctions Movement as Abolitionist Praxis

In the same way, solidarity with Palestine has the potential to further transform and render more capacious the political consciousness of our contemporary movements. Black Lives Matter activists and others associated with this very important historical moment of a surging collective consciousness calling for recognition of the persisting structures of racism can play an important role in compelling other areas of social justice activism to take up the cause of Palestine solidarity—specifically, BDS.[26]

As discussed throughout this book, the focus of abolition is both to dismantle police and carceral systems, as well as build liberated societies, free of violence.[27] I lean on Ruth Wilson Gilmore's statement that prison is not a building, "but a set of relationship that undermine rather than stabilize everyday lives everywhere."[28] Placing Wilson's words in conversation with the matrix of incarceration discussed earlier sets the stage for the discussion that follows, that is, one that positions BDS as an abolitionist praxis.

As the daughter of a Palestinian refugee, I am frequently asked, "What can I do?" from those moved to action. My response is that support for BDS represents one action (of many) that enacts solidarity with Palestinians. And although support for BDS may offer an entry point for Palestinian solidarity work, I also believe that abolitionists around the world have something to learn about abolition from Palestinians who have been resisting and subverting police and carceral systems since 1948. Consequently, I position BDS as abolitionist praxis along four rationalities: (1) BDS enacts a praxis of divesting from the carceral state, (2) BDS is a grassroots initiative that relies on civil society; (3) BDS translates dreaming and imagining a different world into action; (4) BDS enacts hope as a discipline.[29]

Divesting from the Carceral State

The three BDS demands articulate a need to divest from the carceral state. Israel is deemed a carceral state by many because of the ways it isolates, controls, and contains Palestinians through a matrix of incarceration. Because the criminalization and occupation of Palestinian land and psyches would not be possible without consistent international financial and material support, BDS aims to disrupt the financing of this system of apartheid. Corporate, individual, and institutional divestment from Zionism's settler colonial project, and the companies that aid and sustain it, aims to dismantle the carceral logics and practices discussed earlier. I argue that this dismantling is consistent with abolitionist practice as discussed by Berger et al.:

> Central to abolitionist work are the many fights for nonreformist reforms—those measures that reduce the power of an oppressive system while illuminating the system's inability to solve the crises it creates.[30]

At my university, Students United for Palestinian Rights led a student campaign in 2016 calling on the university to divest from institutions profiting from human rights violations against Palestinians. Currently, Students United for Palestinian Rights is calling on the university to divest from Boeing. As one of the world's leading defense contractors, Boeing is directly and indirectly involved in many countries that use Boeing weapons against their own people, or people whose lands they are occupying, including in Israel.[31] Al Jazeera reported in 2021 that 260 Palestinians had been killed with thousands more displaced from their homes by Israel.[32] Of note is that Boeing sold $735 million of weaponry to Israel earlier that year. Boycotting and divesting from systems and institutions that support the occupation can take many forms. Those interested in participating can utilize the BDS website to search for the names of companies BDS boycotts,[33] as well as to connect with BDS chapters near them in their own countries.[34]

Reliance on Civil Society

Abolition is a people's movement anchored by a vision to eliminate imprisonment, policing, and surveillance,[35] with a goal to create alternatives to punishment and incarceration. For reasons discussed previously, Palestinians possess tremendous knowledge about imprisonment (in all its forms), as well as the power that resides in the collective to resist and refuse[36] incarceration. Consequently, boycotts as anticolonial praxis represent just one tactic Palestinians have historically engaged to resist the carcerality of Zionism. In fact, BDS was modeled after the Palestinian Campaign for the Academic and Cultural Boycott of Israel of 2004, a response to Israeli academic institutions' complicity with the occupation.[37] The formation of BDS was largely inspired by the antiapartheid South Africa campaigns that played a significant role in garnering international participation in the fight against apartheid. Having witnessed the international community's abject failure at holding Israel accountable to international laws condemning the occupation, Palestinian civil society coalesced (over 170 organizations), representing three sectors (refugees outside the historic homeland, Palestinian citizens of Israel, and Palestinians in the occupied territories) to form BDS.[38] As stateless people, Palestinians do not have the luxury of relying on the state of Israel for help even if they wanted to, particularly since the state in this case is responsible for their oppression and dispossession. Consequently, BDS models the slow, difficult work of organizing people to harness the collective power in service of liberatory change, a type of labor that is also central to abolitionist praxis, particularly feminist abolitionist praxis.[39]

Dreaming and Imagining a Different World Is Action

Because we are all deeply entangled in the oppressive systems that shape our lives, imagining and dreaming different futures is vital to creating new structures and possibilities. Prison and police abolitionist Mariame Kaba suggests we might begin our abolitionist journeys by asking, "What can we imagine for ourselves and the world?"⁴⁰ Hence, if we consider the deeply entrenched Zionist discourses suggesting that Palestinians pose an existential threat to the State of Israel, and that Palestinians are terrorists, less than human, and the aggressors, imagining counternarratives and consequently possibilities constitute important and necessary work. "Theoretically and ideologically, Palestine has also helped us to broaden our vision of abolition, which we have characterized in this era as the abolition of imprisonment and policing. The experience of Palestine pushes us to revisit concepts such as 'the prison nation' or 'the carceral state' in order to seriously understand the quotidian carceralities of the occupation and the ubiquitous policing by not only Israeli forces but also the Palestinian Authority."⁴¹ Creating a future without settler colonial violence (in all its forms) for Palestinians requires imagining a different future as a possibility. BDS was/is a way for Palestinian civil society to "restore public visibility of the nonviolence aspect of Palestinian resistance."⁴²

Hope as a Discipline

Kaba has famously argued that "hope is a discipline."⁴³ By this, she means that hope involves believing that change is always possible. She also discusses that hope isn't just a belief, a thought, a feeling, but also a practice, a doing, an action. Hope as a discipline invites us to consider movement timelines rather than our personal, incidental, brief timelines. Hope as a discipline is radical because it is a move against the status quo. Hope as a discipline moves beyond the imagination into action.

Sumud is a Palestinian term referencing our particular forms of steadfastness. Palestinian feminist Lean Meari⁴⁴ points to the sociopolitical and affective value of *sumud* as a psychological act of both defiance and willful self-affirmation. *Sumud*, she argues, is a healthy attachment to one's inner self and social world. Palestinians have demonstrated persistent *sumud* by continuing to refuse oppression and resist the label of "no people." Consequently, hope as a discipline has been exercised by Palestinians through our *sumud* because Palestinian resistance and survivance is not possible without hope. Take, for example, the six Palestinian political prisoners who escaped Gilboa prison in September 2022 by purportedly digging a tunnel with spoons. The hope that fueled the planning and digging of these tunnels was not contained nor born of this imprisonment, but rather, passed on from generation to generation. When hope is a discipline, an intellectual, spiritual, psychological, and physical practice, time is not linear. Rather, time is a relational and temporal phenomenon constituted of past, present, and future. Boycotts, divestments, and economic sanctions enact practices of hope, hope that a different reality is possible.

Addressing Intimidation Tactics

Given the ongoing Zionist narrative that BDS is anti-Semitic, I offer a few thoughts for those concerned with these claims. First, the accusation that BDS is, at its core, a dog whistle for anti-Semitism, or simply straight-up anti-Semitism, is a tactic intended to intimidate and consequently preclude support for BDS. We must keep in mind that the target of BDS is Israel and Israeli biopolitics and necropolitics impacting Palestinians, not Jews, nor Israelis. Furthermore, we must keep in mind that Israel and its necropolitical policies does not represent all Jewish people, as many Jewish people support and participate in BDS. Although Israel would have the world believe that it represents all Jewish people, for example, through its racist Nation State Law, Jewish people are diverse. Not all Jewish people live in Israel, and even some Jewish people who live in Israel don't feel represented by the state. Jewish anti-Zionism has a long history as articulated by Rabbi Irving F. Reichert (1895–1968), an influential and controversial leader in the Jewish reform movement and the American Council for Judaism. Claims that BDS is anti-Semitic assume that the state of Israel is the same as the Jewish people, or put another way, that Jewish people are homogenous in their identities, beliefs, and politics. The fact that Jewish people make up a demographic majority in Israel, coupled with the fact that Israel has support from Jewish people around the world, does not preclude the existence of critiques of Israel's apartheid and carceral practices from Jewish people inside Israel. In fact, Jewish people in and out of Israel do critique Israel's settler colonial and apartheid violence. I believe, or at least would like to believe, that social workers would agree that a state should make efforts to represent all its people equally, as well as support all its people to have freedom of movement, basic human rights, and access to water, health care, family, and a life free of violence.

A similar argument leveraged against BDS is that anti-Zionism is anti-Semitic, such that BDS critiques of Zionism are labeled as anti-Semitic. A thoughtful discussion of this issue extends beyond the scope of this chapter, in part because it calls on us to work closely with the provenance of the definitions of anti-Semitism, as well as the political move to equate anti-Semitism and anti-Zionism. I stand with the Palestinian Feminist Collective and so many others who reject the conflation of the two.

Resisting Violence = Practicing Hope

Let me be clear that I'm not arguing that BDS offers an endpoint to decolonization nor liberation for Palestinians. BDS has been criticized by some of its staunchest Palestinian advocates for the limitations of its rights-based framework when it comes to addressing and disrupting the violence of settler colonialism.[45] I am suggesting, however, that BDS may serve as an entry point for Palestinian solidarity work, one that offers explicit activities and practices within the context of a broad social movement, led by those most affected by the violence of settler colonialism in Israel. It bears mentioning that although the International Federation of Social Workers voted against supporting BDS in 2021, social work does have a history of engaging in boycotts as evidenced by participation in the "free produce movement" of the Progressive era[46] and the more recent boycotts of Hyatt hotels for workers' rights violations and labor disputes, just to name a few examples. In addition, social work does have a mandate to resist social and racial injustice.[47] This form of civil society solidarity is in service of social work commitments to social justice and human dignity and worth. "BDS is a call to conscience to supporters in civil society around the world to use economic leverage, including lobbying their governments, in order to bring about specific changes in Israeli policies that violate human rights."[48] I encourage all who are concerned with Zionism's carceral violence to join the BDS social movement, in solidarity with Palestinians, as an enactment of abolitionist praxis.

15

Abolitionist and Harm Reduction Praxis for Public Sector Mental Health Services: An Application to Involuntary Hospitalization

Nev Jones and Leah A. Jacobs

Involuntary hospitalization is one of the most overtly carceral yet widely accepted interventions deployed in social work practice. Positioned as an unfortunate but often necessary response to "mental health crises," clinical social workers are unilaterally trained on the criteria and procedures for enacting involuntary holds (also referred to as "petitions" for involuntary commitment or hospitalization). Meanwhile, training on alternative, abolitionist, or harm reduction responses is virtually nonexistent. This chapter aims to describe specific, concrete strategies for preventing and navigating involuntary hospitalization, focusing on the most common arena for their use—public sector mental health service settings. Specifically, we discuss alternative principles and practices for prevention, acute intervention, and postvention. Together, these principles and practices illustrate an abolitionist and harm reduction praxis that emphasizes knowledge and transparency, avoidance of adherence and abstinence-based thinking, acceptance and validation of clients' experiences and frameworks, validation of structural violence, and accompaniment.

Abolition and Harm Reduction: An Orientation to Involuntary Hospitalization

Our vision of a better world is one in which all people have the social and material resources to thrive. Getting there requires the social and economic inequalities that fuel much of what is labeled "crime" or "lethality" (a term commonly used to justify involuntary hospitalization) to be eliminated. Getting there also requires the elimination of carceral responses and their respective institutions, be they prisons or psychiatric hospitals, and their replacement with transformative justice and mad justice approaches. Naturally, this means that in developing a chapter on abolition and involuntary hospitalization, we would write nothing but a proposal for the complete rejection of involuntary hospitalization and refusal to participate in institutions that require the use of involuntary hospitalization, right? Well, not exactly.

We base this chapter on the premise that social workers should simultaneously work toward abolition (e.g., by ensuring the social and economic needs of clients are met, eliminating the involvement of police in involuntary hospitalization, contributing to the development of voluntary and service user-driven alternatives to involuntary hospitalization), while also reducing harms caused by involuntary hospitalization as it continues to be deployed and impact millions of youths and adults in the United States each year. In the words of Mariame Kaba and André Gorz, we therefore include "nonreformist reforms," while keeping "abolition...the horizon."[1]

In our view, both transformative abolitionist and harm reduction approaches are necessary for two primary reasons. First, an increasingly common way for social workers to refuse institutional mandates related to involuntary hospitalization is to move into "private practice." Although understandable (who wants to be part of a broken system?), this trend unfortunately plays directly into neoliberal logics of privatization and results in abandonment of those who arguably require a social worker's support the most—users of public mental health services (i.e., those who experience serious mental illness and are poor and disproportionately Black, Indigenous, and other people of color). Second, integrating abolitionist transformation *and* harm reduction allows us to account for the immediate, urgent needs of those subject to the trauma of involuntary hospitalization. As activist and former political prisoner Anne Hansen reminds us, most imprisoned people need and want help *"now*, not on paper or in their dreams, but right now."[2] As we walk toward the abolitionist horizon, we offer guidance as to what that help might look like for people facing involuntary hospitalization.

In the remainder of the chapter, we lay out a series of practice principles followed by concrete suggestions for both abolitionist transformation and harm reduction that span the crisis continuum (prevention, intervention, postvention). Embedded in our proposed alternative responses is a model for an abolitionist and harm reduction form of social work praxis in community mental health. We see this model, and related elimination of coercive interventions, as fundamental components of the larger project of abolition—one that centrally involves the criminal legal and family policing systems but also public health services.

Overarching Principles

Guided by abolition and harm reduction, as well as mad justice, the approach we articulate here rests on five overarching principles of practice (see Table 1):

(1) Knowledge, openness, and transparency regarding policies and procedures, including providers' own positions, positionalities and power (as distinct from employers')

(2) Shifting away from adherence- and abstinence-based thinking

(3) Acceptance and validation of clients' explanations and frameworks, including of what we might collectively refer to as extreme states and nonconsensual realities

(4) Acknowledgment and validation of structural violence

(5) Accompaniment (during periods of crisis and beyond)

ABOLITION AND HARM REDUCTION FOR MENTAL HEALTH SERVICES

Table 1. Principles of abolitionist and harm reduction mental health praxis

Principle	Brief definition	Specific example
Transparency regarding policies and procedures	Full transparency regarding all crisis-related policies including risk assessment, triage, and any external reporting (e.g., to police departments in state with so-called "red flag" gun laws) Openness about the individual provider's perspective and positionality	Information sheet developed for clients that clearly lays out crisis decision-making protocols, how and when the agency involves police officers, and specific policies regarding involuntary hospitalization
Shifting away from adherence/abstinence thinking	Intentional pivot away from assumptions of the greater expertise of the clinician toward a deeper embrace of client's freedom to make a variety of decisions regarding the use or discontinuation of both prescribed medications and street drugs. Program adoption of systematic harm reduction policies	Conversations about medications and drug use that are value neutral, including balanced acknowledgment of risks and harms (for both prescribed and illegal drugs), and signal strong deference to the client's values and decisions
Validation of client's explanatory frameworks	Program materials and policies avoid privileging any single explanatory frameworks (e.g., serious mental illnesses as chronic brain disorders) Clinical engagement that consistently centers the client's explanatory framework and interpretation	Clinician who deeply engages with a client's experiences of voices and unusual beliefs, asking questions, expressing interest, and resisting the tendency to relabel experiences as pathological and/or decenter or minimize the multivalent (positive and negative) roles they may play in the client's life
Validation of structural violence	Full acknowledgment of the impact of forms of structural violence including racism and harm within mental health and social service systems Collaborative dialogue focused on social change, not (just) individual-level accommodation	Responding to allegations of provider-based racism in a recent inpatient hospitalization by (1) fully validating the reality of this experience; (2) communicating agreement that racist behavior is unacceptable; (3) joining with the client in strategizing direct actions that might be taken (grievances, public letter, etc.)
Accompaniment	To walk beside clients in their journeys, including mental health crises To stand with, witness, and maintain connection before, during, and after involuntary hospitalization	Refusing institutional incentives to reduce contact with clients during involuntary hospitalization and instead increasing time spent with clients during involuntary hospitalization

Although settings vary, it is probably fair to describe an "average" experience among adults labeled with serious mental illness as one in which services revolve around a combination of case management, medication management, and, in better resourced areas, some amount of therapy. Experiences of coercion are virtually ubiquitous, though generally occur more often in inpatient and residential settings than outpatient. Opportunities to engage with experiences of psychosis, mania, and/or dissociation as anything other than epiphenomena of neurobiological disease are rare. And although case management interventions almost universally aspire to meet basic needs in areas such as food, basic income, housing, and transportation, the fixes are generally superficial, resolutely failing to move most clients out of poverty or support true social mobility. Against this backdrop of status quo "care," the principles we emphasize are not meant to be exhaustive, but to help lay the foundation for a harm reduction present and abolitionist future. Although our specific focus is involuntary hospitalization, the substance of these principles is generally broadly applicable to both "ambulatory" and acute public sector mental health services.

Knowledge, Openness, and Transparency Regarding Policies and Procedures

Our message here is relatively simple: replace the paternalism that undergirds numerous aspects of public sector policy and practice with (1) open and transparent communication of policies, including what happens and how decisions are made by clinical teams behind the scenes, and, especially, of internal risk protocols and their rationales and (2) transparency about the clinician's own positions and positionality vis-à-vis these policies. As the trauma and trauma-informed care literatures have long held, loss of narrative control is a hallmark of abusive relationships—the victim is no longer the one telling the story. The normalization of obfuscation in many mental health settings (e.g., absence of any explicit disclosures regarding who has access to a client's electronic health record and what is recorded in it) and resulting guess work imposed by default on clients can be powerfully addressed through more systemic transparency. Concretely, clinicians and programs might routinely share (and make publicly available) internal protocols regarding client disclosure or indications of potential self-harm, harm to others, or self-neglect; what is done with such information; and how decisions are made in relation to information disclosed (i.e., often by a team or with the involvement of a supervisor—not just by the provider to whom the information was disclosed). At a personal level, providers should also be as transparent as possible about their own positions (i.e., differentiating their own values and views from those of the agency or hospital for whom they work; for example, after conveying information about their agency's role in reporting clients to local police departments because of state "red flag" gun laws, they might share that although forced to comply, they personally have serious ethical and political concerns about such laws and their risk of reinforcing and strengthening both racism and mental health stigma).

Questioning and Moving Away from Adherence and Abstinence Thinking

The clinical constructs of adherence and abstinence tend to be premised on beliefs grounded in paternalism and control: providers know better than clients what drugs/medications they should or shouldn't be using and are justified in using coercive tactics (ranging from subtle pressure to judicial force) to bring about the "desired" behavior. Specific instantiations include threats and warnings (e.g., "If you don't start taking your meds you're going to end up in the hospital"; "If you're high, you won't be able to see your therapist") and actual denial or rescission of basic needs (e.g., abstinence- or medication compliance-based subsidized housing). As harm reduction advocates such as Carl Hart have noted, abstinence policies are often undergirded by entrenched racism and classism—a politics of moralization, judgment, and punishment that plays out daily in the US prison and criminal legal system.

We suggest a radical reconsideration of this (albeit very normalized) positionality (power over the "misbehaving" client); as tempting as fantasies of control may be, in reality they embody deep violations of autonomy and personhood and tend to engender disempowerment and resentment rather than self-determined motivation or behavioral change. When we factor in race and class, such relationships, seemingly playing out at an interpersonal level, are further transformed into the everyday machinery of *institutional* racism and discrimination.

Awareness of one's own (provider-side) rationalizations is essential to embracing a different approach, that is, coming to recognize and eventually reflexively challenge one's own sense of unquestioned certainty that one knows what is best for the individual (they should be taking X medications; they should not be using Y drugs). And although pundits and conservative advocacy organizations regularly warn of "letting patients rot with their rights on," the reality of what it means to cultivate a genuinely respectful and deferential relationship is actually quite the opposite: slowing down, not feeling the need to rush to control-based decisions, deeply *investing* in the relationship, in the person, and the inevitably complex choices people make. Redirecting energy to listening and learning and to supporting individuals truly on their own terms.

In general, the reasons clients have for rejecting psychiatric medications are in fact entirely reasonable, and the trade-offs between risks and benefits complicated enough that any belief that a provider can make or knows the "best" decision is at best a kind of grandiose fantasy, at worst a reflection of a lack of deeper knowledge about the state of the science regarding short- and long-term risks and benefits. Antipsychotics with strong anticholinergic properties, for example, are increasingly strongly linked to a substantially higher risk of early-onset dementia, with known biological mechanisms;[3] only hubris could lead a provider to "know" that the short-term benefits of antipsychotics outweigh these risks. For others, long-term side effects may be of less concern than the immediate reality of a profound loss of sense of self due to mental clouding, anhedonia, and loss of interest—again, these are in fact well-established effects of antipsychotics with known biological mechanisms.[4] On the street drug side, the literature on the actual risks and costs of abstinence-based drug policies is already strong enough that harm reduction squarely lands as the "evidence-based" approach to support, even as abstinence-oriented policies persist in real-world practice.[5]

By reorienting from adherence and abstinence to respect for individual choices and (where possible) the cultivation of longer-term relationships characterized by mutual trust, decisions about medication and drug use can be discussed and dialogically worked through, without threats, judgment, or force, reducing the kind of escalating power dynamics that so often lead to involuntary commitment. Providers can also offer education to kin and kith on the more complex realities of both psychiatric medications and street drugs, keeping in mind that many family members will have grown up during the War on Drugs, constantly exposed to fear-based depictions of (illegal) drugs, and, conversely, promedication pharmaceutical drug commercials and oversimplified explanations of how psychiatric medications "work." Education might also include what we know empirically about factors that support or inhibit self-direction (self-determined motivation), as documented in dozens of studies in the self-determination theory literature.[6] Although it might seem like pressure or coercion are the easiest and fastest ways to bring about the "behaviors" one desires in another, a large body of research finds that pressure more often *undermines* the development of autonomous (self-directed) motivation; while under pressure to comply, an individual may comply, but once the pressure is removed (or avoided), the individual returns to their preferred choice or behavior.

Accepting Clients' Explanatory Frameworks and Assigned Meaning

Despite a rapidly growing body of work that speaks to the deep interconnectedness of life events, social and cultural beliefs and practices, and the form and content of what we label psychosis, mania, dissociative experiences and other extreme states,[7] US clinical training and policy tend to continue to default to pharmacotherapy as the primary or only approach to "reducing or ameliorating" symptoms, sometimes alongside management-oriented therapy. Outside of peer-run networks (such as hearing voices groups associated with the international hearing voices movement), meaning-centered approaches are almost nonexistent in public sector mental health.

Prima facie, simply denying the reality of what clients are (actually) experiencing, and reductively reframing experiences as "just symptoms" or "just your disorder," is not an appropriate way to signal respect, interest, and investment in understanding and the rich networks of meaning and identity often bound up with such experiences. Instead, denial and disinterest quickly signal lack of interest or even erasure. Such practices can and should be recognized as forms of relational and symbolic violence—systematically reinscribing clients' experiences as pathological, imagined, and unworthy of serious discussion or attention qua meaning-rich experiences. For some, this symbolic violence may lead to the deep internalization of shame and/or self-rejection; for others, anger, resentment, and disengagement. The alternative we propose, whether in the midst of a crisis, or during or following hospitalization, is to regularly ask clients about their own understanding of their experiences, their connection to cultural context and life events, and the meanings they attribute to them and to collaboratively explore areas of cultural, religious, and/or existential significance.[8] Additional suggestions on "meaning-centered" approaches can be found the Appendix.

Acknowledging and Validating Social and Structural Determinants (Structural Violence)

In the past decade, *social determinants* has become a nearly ubiquitous buzzword in mental health services. In reality, the "casework" or case management functions of social workers (and other community providers) have always included basic needs such as food and shelter. The deeper drivers of health inequalities, however, including social welfare policies, structural racism, and neoliberal economic systems, continue to go more or less unremarked and unaddressed. Connecting an individual with vocational services, for example, is not at all the same as addressing entrenched income inequality and exploitative labor practices; finding subsidized housing in a segregated service ghetto is not the same as acknowledging and working to address redlining, racialized city geopolitics, and geographically distributed environmental racism. Although we of course advise proactively addressing basic needs in the conventional sense, our recommendations here focus more on the importance of providers discussing, acknowledging, and validating, if not actively working to challenge, these deeper sources of inequality: talk about racism, classism, ableism, and other forms of discrimination as *realities*—real sources of structural violence—that impact most public sector mental health clients on a daily basis and are as common within social welfare and health service settings as they are outside. Resist conventional clinical tendencies to focus on "what can be addressed at the level of the individual." Validate the rage clients may feel. Engage in dialogue about what needs to change societally, structurally, and/or within a given mental health agency or health system.

Finally, as the critical American Indian scholar Joseph Gone only quasi-rhetorically asks, referencing legacies of colonial genocide and forced relocation in North America, "[W]hat might self determination in response to [histories of structural violence] resemble if we pursued Justice more so than Healing?"[9] In other words, what if we centered concrete social action, in solidarity with service users, *in the name of justice*, more so than inevitably psychologized mental health supports?

Accompaniment during Periods of Crisis

Despite widespread recognition of the virtues of "continuity in care" and the need for a "continuum of care," mental health, health, and social services are deeply siloed. Even within mental health services, this discontinuity is notable, especially when considering the bureaucratic and physical boundaries between community- and hospital-based services. When a person is involuntarily hospitalized, their community and provider connections are weakened or severed altogether. From the community-based agency or provider perspective, it is logistically and often physically advantageous to think of the client as now under the auspices of hospital clinicians and staff and no longer in need of support from community-based providers. Accompaniment offers an alternative approach, where maintaining connection is prioritized.

Accompaniment is an orientation to practice and a practice itself. In the simplest sense, it means to walk beside someone. As medical anthropologist Paul Farmer explained, one who accompanies says, "I'll go with you and support you on your journey wherever it leads; I'll share your fate for a while. And by 'a while,' I don't mean a little while."[10] Accompaniment involves connection and solidarity and allows the accompanied to decide when the journey is over.

In the context of clinical social work and community mental health, accompaniment would involve really walking beside clients and supporting them. Accompaniment requires moving away from a focus on diagnoses and symptoms, providing care beyond the agency or clinic walls, and intervention that extends beyond time-limited "psychotherapy." Accompaniment instead asks us to see the whole person, to work with them across settings and time, and to intervene to promote social, economic, and mental well-being. In this sense, accompaniment could be viewed as a worthwhile orientation to social work practice in community mental health in general. Here, we name it as an intervention for the acute phase of involuntary hospitalization to emphasize its importance at that time, when standing with, witnessing, and maintaining connection is needed more than ever.

We argue that, during involuntary hospitalization, social workers should accompany clients. Specifically, accompaniment during involuntary hospitalization involves continuing contact with clients (i.e., regularly calling and visiting), witnessing the client's experience, and listening to concerns and fears, sharing information about treatment and interventions, bridging the world of the ward and the community (i.e., facilitating contact with other supports, ensuring financial and other obligations are met on the client's behalf during hospitalization), monitoring treatment of the client by hospital staff, and advocating on the client's behalf in circumstances where treatment is poor or overly coercive.

Areas of Specific Policy or Practice Change across the Crisis Continuum

The principles of practice articulated here generally apply across the crisis continuum of prevention, intervention, and postvention, though in some cases we have chosen to apply them to specific phases in the continuum. In addition to these principles, we want to highlight a set of specific, concrete, anti-carceral policy and practice recommendations applied to each of the above phases—see summary in Table 2.

Addressing Specific Carceral Practices across the Crisis Continuum

Police (or armed security) have become semipermanent fixtures in not only schools, hospitals, and shelters but also a growing number of mental health programs, including crisis stabilization services and outpatient clinics. In many states and jurisdictions, even when police are not involved in the initiation of an involuntary commitment, they are a primary source of transportation (between schools and hospitals, nursing homes and hospitals, from one emergency room ER to a hospital with available psychiatric beds, etc.). In some hospitals, an involuntary admission who

Table 2. Harm reduction policy and practice change across the crisis continuum

	Prevention	Crisis intervention	Postvention
Use of threats	Eliminate use of threats to bring about behavioral compliance, including threats of police involvement, hospitalization, loss of housing or benefits	Eliminate use of threats in inpatient and crisis stabilization settings, including threats of seclusion, restraint, and involuntary injections, police or security officer involvement, longer time in inpatient	Eliminate threats tied to rehospitalization, repeat police involvement, etc.
"Blame and shame" framing	Eliminate comments that attribute mental health and/or substance use challenges to the individual and/or the choices they have made; explicitly emphasize the role of social and structural determinants, including structural racism and structural stigma tied to disability	Eliminate comments that attribute the crisis to the individual (e.g., not taking medications, using street drugs, not listening to clinicians); normalize crisis; accompany by providing as much supportive listening and counseling time as possible	Eliminate comments that attribute the resolved crisis to the individual; emphasize problem-solving focused on social and structural determinants, including structural racism, poverty, and social exclusion; support processing of negative experiences and/or iatrogenic harm (postvention debriefing and processing)
Police involvement	Eliminate/reduce police and security officer presence at or outside outpatient clinics	Eliminate/reduce police officer involvement in crisis response, transportation, and presence in inpatient and crisis stabilization units	Eliminate/reduce police officer involvement in discharge, including discharge transportation
Policies and practices tied to "risk"	Remove signage and policies that imply that clients are a potential threat to clinicians; address structural features that imply or assume risk (e.g., separate bathrooms for clients versus clinicians in an outpatient clinic)	Remove signage and policies that imply that clients are a potential threat to clinicians; address structural features that imply or assume risk (e.g., glassed-in nursing station)	Remove signage and policies that imply that clients are a potential threat to clinicians; eliminate de facto punishments tied to hospitalization (i.e., reduction in benefits or "privileges" because the client was involuntary hospitalized)
Medications	Institute harm reduction–informed deference to clients; eliminate/reduce mandatory drug testing; eliminate/reduce sanctions tied to drug use; support medication discontinuation and tapering	Eliminate punitive uses of medications (forced injection to sedate); eliminate/reduce inappropriate prescribing, polypharmacy and high dosing	Explicit support for safe tapering or discontinuation of excessive psychiatric medications used/prescribed during hospitalization

needs medical testing or care in a nonpsychiatric clinic or unit must be escorted there by a police officer. Even in their physical absence, provider threats of police involvement (e.g., "Comply or I'll call the police," "Agree to involuntary hospitalization or I'll call the police," "Get in the white transport van or I'll call the police") are commonly experienced by service users.

And even when police are not present, punitive logics are generally still firmly entrenched, particularly in crisis response and inpatient contexts. In recent qualitative work with youth and young adults who had been involuntarily hospitalized, for example, there was near universal reporting of "blame and shame" comments—from police, certainly, but equally so social workers, counselors, and nurses.[11] Rather than outliers, such beliefs largely fall in line with the punitive and objectifying practices present in standard inpatient (and often residential) mental health settings: glassed in nurses' stations on inpatient wards, immediate confiscation of cell phones on admission (which happens in no other area of hospital medicine), separate clinician versus patient bathrooms, and the designation of activities such as access to the outdoors as "privileges" that clients must earn through "good behavior." Isolation rooms remain more or less ubiquitous, and seclusion and restraints are universally used "as warranted" across the country. Blood and urine testing (to identify both medication nonadherence and street drug use) in inpatient psychiatry is also generally involuntary in fact—that is, patients cannot refuse testing.

Dismantling—or contributing to the dismantling—of such practices must therefore involve, but go well beyond, simple avoidance of police involvement. Again, see Table 2 for concrete suggestions.

Holistic Discharge Planning

Genuinely holistic discharge planning, whether carried out from the inpatient or outpatient side, is also essential. Specifically, holistic approaches entail decentering conventional provider priorities (e.g., medication management and therapy/case management referrals or abstinence-based support groups like Alcoholics Anonymous), unless they are truly the patient's priorities, and instead discussing and planning supports anchored to (re)integration in schools, workplaces, and faith-based communities; addressing complex family or kinship dynamics; providing access to legal advocacy (as relevant) and resources for safely tapering or discontinuing unnecessary and/or potentially harmful medications prescribed in inpatient or crisis residential settings (see more on the latter in the "Postvention Medication Tapering and Discontinuation" section). As noted previously, discussion of structural violence and related change-oriented resources or avenues for action should also be a part of holistic planning unless truly irrelevant or inapplicable. (For example, referral to community resources and grassroots initiatives focused on combating the structural violence clients more or less automatically face in returning to shelters or the streets [if unhoused] or to overpoliced, segregated neighborhoods.)

Postvention Debriefing

As is true for any other difficult (or potentially traumatic) event, opportunities to debrief and process experiences of crisis intervention, police involvement, and/or involuntary hospitalization can be both deeply validating and healing. Depending on the client in question, providers might proactively suggest progressive, antioppressive external resources for processing and/or dialogue (e.g., national mutual aid initiatives run by abolitionist groups like Project Let's and the Fireweed Collective—see Appendix for list), as well as clearly conveying their own willingness to talk through what happened and ownership of the provider's role in initiation or execution of an involuntary hold (as applicable). It is important that such conversations not shy away from or avoid the carceral aspects of what may have happened (e.g., racism, dehumanizing treatment, violence) but acknowledge, and where applicable "own," these practices: accept and affirm that provider-initiated discrimination and violence are an everyday reality in psychiatric hospitals; that power hierarchies are pervasive, and basic rights and dignities are routinely violated. If a client wants to file a grievance or take legal action, assist with this. If other colleagues were directly involved (and/or have become sources of anger, betrayal, or fear due to their role), offer to facilitate a conversation (if desired), to mediate or advocate. Subtler negative experiences should also be acknowledged, validated, and unpacked—for example, paternalistic treatment, overmedication, less overt but still inappropriately moralizing interactions with hospital staff, and violence witnessed rather than directly experienced. (If this sounds like common sense, consider that in extended direct service work and qualitative research on involuntary commitment, it has been a rare outlier to encounter someone who reports ever having had such a conversation—in some cases across decades of treatment and dozens of providers.)

Postvention Medication Tapering and Discontinuation

Inpatient and crisis residential settings often function as de facto "medication stabilization" units, and many inpatient psychiatrists primarily focus on rapid amelioration of symptoms and/or outright tranquilization. It's not uncommon for clients to emerge from an involuntary hospitalization with twice the number of psychiatric medications they were originally on and/or having been prescribed (and compelled to take) substantially higher doses. In many cases, these medications then need to be tapered down or discontinued. Depending on the medications in question—some pose more risks of acute withdrawal symptoms and sequelae than others—providers should help connect clients with prescribers who are willing and prepared to support this process (for a primer, see Gupna and colleagues' *Deprescribing in Psychiatry*[12]) as well as with more grassroots, freely accessible mutual support resources, such as *The Harm Reduction Guide to Coming off Psychiatric Drugs*[13] and *The Withdrawal Project* at Inner Compass.[14]

Discussion

In the chapter, we sketch a form of abolitionist and harm reduction praxis for social work in community mental health. This praxis emphasizes knowledge and transparency, avoidance of adherence and abstinence-based thinking, acceptance and validation of clients' experiences and frameworks, validation of structural violence, and accompaniment. We recognize that, like other social service systems, entrenched carceral practices in mental health settings will not change overnight. Simply recognizing that mental health services regularly default to force and coercion, rather than assuming they are benign services that should be funded in place of the police, is a first step toward change. Shifting principles of practice and making high-impact changes to status quo policy and practice are next steps.

In the sphere of social work, one essential locus of such change is training and pedagogy. The status quo practices critiqued in the body of this chapter are unfortunately widely taught (and performatively enacted) in master of social work programs across the country. Oversimplified "evidence-based practice" frameworks are often uncritically supported, and clinical paternalism endorsed (i.e., social workers are the experts and need to "protect" clients/service recipients through involuntary and, more generally, top-down interventions). Particularly when it comes to "addictions" and "serious mental illness," biomedical reductionism is widespread. For example, clinical social work frameworks often hold that serious mental illness and addiction should be understood as primarily biological diseases or disorders, albeit influenced by social and structural determinants, and present symptoms of these disorders reductively as socially undesired psychopathology. Complex identity claims tied to drug use and psychiatric disability are rarely featured in the social work curricula we are aware of. For example, little to no attention is afforded the neurodiversity and mad pride/mad justice movements and contemporary attempts to reframe psychiatrized experiences as religious, spiritual, aesthetic, or philosophical in nature rather than narrowly psychiatric or psychological. Likewise, non-Anglo-US cultural healing frameworks (e.g., South African *Sangoma* and Japanese *Morita* and *Naikan* approaches) are rarely even introduced to students in the context of mental illness, much less seriously engaged with.

An abolitionist pedagogy must break out of this narrow framework, capacitating a far more expansive, and pluralistic, set of ways of understanding and engaging with experiences that have historically been labeled "abnormal," "pathological," or "deviant." And, in keeping with the disability justice principle of "leadership by the most impacted," service users, activists, and activist-scholars who identify as (or have been labeled) disabled or mad should be integral to efforts to transform curricula and training.

Second, the widespread tendency to present social work (and social workers) as a benign and benevolent alternative to overt carceral agents (such as police officers) not only conflicts with the reality of implicit and explicit coercion within mental health systems, but also serves to strengthen and uphold what are in fact often deeply oppressive structures and practices. Here not only more mainstream social workers but also many (prison industrial complex) abolitionists have fallen short in naming and challenging damaging practices reproduced and enacted *in* clinical social work. Shifts in language and framing regarding the child welfare system—renamed and reframed as the "family policing system"—have helped reposition social workers in child welfare as agents of family policing rather than well-intentioned bystanders (or child protectors). Similar reframing on the mental health side may help render carceral mental health practices more visible and their departure from transformative social justice more apparent. Similarly, the powerfully synergistic functions of racism, classism, and ableism need to be made explicit: perhaps nowhere do paternalism and stigma align with consequences as devastating and often fatal as they do for Black men simultaneously labeled with "serious mental illness" and/or "addictions"—invoking entrenched and mutually reinforcing stereotypes regarding "dangerousness" and "threat" that all but guarantee more overtly coercive responses and excess use of force.[15] Antiracism without attention to the historical, legal, and sociostructural intersections of race, disability, "insanity" and "mental defect," and the manifestations of these linked constructs in dominant approaches to "serious mental illness" and "addictions" must be understood as a very incomplete form of antiracism (or antioppression).

Abolitionists and abolitionist social workers in other focus areas thus have a critical role to play by actively joining in critique of public sector mental health services and allying with service user/survivor critics. Left unspoken and unsaid, harm will persist, and that harm will not end with the more limited abolition of prisons, jails, and family policing. To quote Martin Luther King Jr., "[I]njustice anywhere is a threat to justice everywhere. We are caught in an inescapable network of mutuality."[16]

Conclusion

Our application of an abolitionist and harm reduction praxis for social work in community mental health in this chapter is not meant to be exhaustive, but rather a planting of seeds, an invitation for critical reflection, some starting place for taking action. Policing is surely a visible problem in public sector mental health services, but the many subtler ways in which carceral practices and relational and symbolic violence play out are no less harmful. An abolitionist future requires that social workers and other providers sensitize themselves to current harms, including those that tend to intensify around mental health crises, often culminating in involuntary commitment. Let us begin by reducing the harms surrounding such interventions, while moving toward more fundamental changes in system responses to disability, madness, and drug use.

Appendix

Meaning Center Praxis and Alternative Narratives

Project LETS Psychiatric Survivor Clinic: www.projectlets.org/ps-clinic

The Voice Collective (UK): www.voicecollective.co.uk

Durham University, Understanding Voices Project: www.understandingvoices.com

Rethink Psychosis: www.rethinkpsychosis.weebly.com

British Psychological Association, *Understanding Psychosis*: www.bps.org.uk/guideline/understanding-psychosis-and-schizophrenia

Fireweed Collective: https://fireweedcollective.org

Wildflower Alliance, including Alternatives to Suicide: www.wildfloweralliance.org

Institute for the Development of Human Arts (IDHA): www.idha-nyc.org/about-idha

Medication Deprescribing and Discontinuation

Gupta, S., John Cahill, and Rebecca Miller. *Deprescribing in Psychiatry*. Oxford University Press; 2019.

Harm Reduction Guide to Coming off Psychiatric Drugs: www.fireweedcollective.org/publication/harm-reduction-guide-to-coming-off-psychiatric-drugs/

The Withdrawal Project, Inner Compass: www.withdrawal.theinnercompass.org

Rethinking Crisis Response

Interrupting Criminalization, Defund the Police—Invest in Community Care: A Guide to Alternative Mental Health Crisis Responses: www.interruptingcriminalization.com/non-police-crisis-response-guide

Project LETS Crisis Support Resource List: www.projectlets.org/crisis-support

Kaufman-Mthumkhulu, Stefanie Lyn. "We Don't Need Cops to Become Social Workers: We Need Peer Support + Community Response

Networks." Medium. www.medium.com/@stefkaufman/we-dont-need
-cops-to-become-social-workers-we-need-peer-support-b8e6c4ffe87a

Videos and Documentaries Focused on Sociocultural Diversity in the Context of "Serious Mental Illness"

Healing Voices. Directed by P.J. Moynihan. Digital Eyes Film, 2016.

Crazywise. Directed by Phil Borges and Kevin Tomlinson. Phil Borges Productions, 2016.

Madness: A Meaningful Journey. Produced by Voices Vic. https://youtu.be/ffNy2zfkjnk.

Afflictions: Culture & Mental Illness in Indonesia. Directed by Robert Lemelson. Elemental Productions, 2011.

What Matters Most video series. Directed by Oscar Jimenez-Solomon. New York State Psychiatric Institute, Center for Excellence in Cultural Competency, 2020. www.nyculturalcompetence.org/what-matters-most.

Acknowledgments

The coeditors of *Abolition and Social Work: Possibilities, Paradoxes, and the Practice of Community Care* would first like to thank our colleagues and comrades at the Network for Advancing Abolitionist Social Work (NAASW) for being the catalyst of this book and its many offerings. A big shout out to past and present NAASW Collaborators including Ben Sadoff, Brianna Suslovic, Caitlin Becker, Christina Roe, Michelle Grier, Nikita Shaman, Ravita Choudhury, Rosie Rios, Sarah Knight, Sheila Vakaria, Tiffany McFadden, and Vivianne Guevarra. We are immensely appreciative to all the contributors in this book for their generosity, experience, and willingness to share in this project. A huge thank you to Mariame Kaba for taking the time to read the book and offer an incredible foreword and thank you to all our colleagues and comrades who read and supported this book. Special thanks to everyone at Haymarket Books who are always there to open their political space whether through webinars or encouragement to create this book. Lastly, we co-editors thank Kill Joy (@kill.joy.land), the book cover artist whose bold creative work connects the power of words to visual images grounded in land, labor, and ancestors.

Mimi sends special words of gratitude to her heart and political homies from Incite!, Just Practice/Interrupting Criminalization friends and comrades, and pod family gathering strong in Tongva land.

Cameron would like to thank the countless teachers, mentors, and collaborators who he has learned from, both in deep relationship and from afar. There are too many to name, but he must acknowledge the late great Kathy Boudin with whom he worked closely for more than a decade, and whose lifeway was to lean into paradox, possibility, and practice. He would also like to thank Cheryl Wilkins who has continuously taught him about the centrality of people and community to the experience of justice. Lastly, he would like to thank his family, friends, his partner

Nadia, and his baby Najwa, for being sources of love, support and all the things that make life beautiful.

Durrell would like to thank all those who have invested their time and hearts and have invested in his development over the years. The list is too long to name everyone individually. He would also like to thank all his former students whom he's had not only the pleasure to teach but to learn from. He'd like to thank his immediate family, extended family and chosen family for the countless and unwavering support. And finally, but certainly not least he would like to thank his wife Nicole and son DJ who are the driving force and motivation to all that he does and aspires to do.

Notes

Foreword

1. Mariame Kaba, "Why I'm Raising Money To Build An Ida B. Wells Monument," *HuffPost* (May 2, 2018). www.huffpost.com/entry/opinion-kaba-ida-wells-lynching_n_5ae9bfc6e4b022f71a03e4bc.
2. Megan McKinney, "Ida B. Wells: The 'Drive' in Her Name," *Classic Chicago Magazine*, (August 19, 2018), classicchicagomagazine.com/ida-b-wells-the-drive-in-her-name/.
3. Mariame Kaba and Andrea J. Ritchie, *No More Police: A Case for Abolition* (New York: The New Press, 2022).
4. Kaba and Richie, *No More Police*.
5. Mia Bay, *To Tell the Truth Freely: The Life of Ida B. Wells*, 2009, p. 286.)
6. Bay, *To Tell the Truth Freely*, 292.
7. Prison Culture, "Ida B Wells and Solitary Confinement," *US Prison Culture*, https://www.usprisonculture.com/blog/2015/07/03/ida-b-wells-and-solitary-confinement/

Introduction

1. Mariame Kaba and Andrea Ritchie, *No More Police: The Case for Police Abolition* (New York: The New Press, 2023).
2. NASW Code of Ethics and the Value of Social Justice: "Social workers pursue social change, particularly with and on behalf of vulnerable and oppressed individuals and groups of people. Social workers' social change efforts are focused primarily on issues of poverty, unemployment, discrimination, and other forms of social injustice. These activities seek to promote sensitivity to and knowledge about oppression and cultural and ethnic diversity. Social workers strive to ensure access to needed information, services, and resources; equality of opportunity; and meaningful participation in decision making for all people." Association of Social Workers, "Code of Ethics." NASW, National Association of Social Workers, 2021, www.socialworkers.org/About/Ethics/Code-of-Ethics/Code-of-Ethics-English.
3. This book features many of those who have long been contributing to abolition within and at the margins of social work. The scholarship and thinking of Beth E. Richie, Mimi E. Kim, Leah Jacobs, Dorothy Roberts, Alan Detlaff, and Kirk "Jae" James have been particularly influential to our own work.
4. Laura Abrams and Alan Dettlaff, "An Open Letter to NASW and Allied Organizations on Social Work's Relationship with Law Enforcement," *Medium* (June 23, 2020).
5. These rich debates were informed by social work abolitionists in our social work community.

2 Conceptualizing Abolitionist Social Work

1. From this quote: "PIC abolition is a vision of a restructured society in a world where we have everything we need: food, shelter, education, health, art, beauty, clean water, and more. Things that are foundational to our personal and community safety," from Mariame Kaba, *We Do This 'Til We Free Us: Abolitionist Organizing and Transforming Justice* (Chicago, IL: Haymarket Books, 2021).
2. Social Work Helper, "Social Workers Against Criminalization Launch New Initiative in the Wake of Protests—SWHELPER," *SWHelper*, 2015, www.swhelper.org/2015/01/21/social-workers-criminalization-launch-new-initiative-wake-protests/.
3. Cameron Rasmussen and Kirk "Jae" James, "Trading Cops for Social Workers Isn't the Solution to Police Violence," *Truthout*, July 17, 2020, https://truthout.org/articles/trading-cops-for-social-workers-isnt-the-solution-to-police-violence/
4. Rasmussen and James, "Trading Cops."
5. Leah A. Jacobs, Mimi E. Kim, Darren L. Whitfield, Rachel E. Gartner, Meg Panichelli, et al., "Defund the Police: Moving towards an Anti-Carceral Social Work," *Journal of Progressive Human Services* 32, no. 1 (August 2020): 37–62, https://doi.org/10.1080/10428232.2020.1852865.
6. Ruth Wilson Gilmore, *Abolition Geography: Essays towards Liberation* (London: Verso Books, 2023).
7. Kristen Brock-Petroshius, Dominique Mikell, Durrell Malik Washington Sr., and Kirk James, "From Social Justice to Abolition: Living Up to Social Work's Grand Challenge of Eliminating Racism," *Journal of Ethnic & Cultural Diversity in Social Work* 31 (2022): 3–5, 225–39, doi: 10.1080/15313204.2022.2070891.
8. Craig Fortier and Edward Hon-Sing Wong, "The Settler Colonialism of Social Work and the Social Work of Settler Colonialism," *Settler Colonial Studies* 9, no. 4 (2018): 437–56, www.doi.org/10.1080/2201473x.2018.1519962; also see chapters in this volume from Beltran et al. and Harty et al.
9. Fortier and Hon-Sing Wong, "The Settler Colonialism."
10. Dean Spade, *Mutual Aid: Building Solidarity During This Crisis (and the next)* (London: Verso, 2020).
11. Ruth Wilson Gilmore and Mariame Kaba have helped us to understand this phrase as the presencing work of abolition, to create institutions and practices that make us whole, healthy, and safe.
12. See Interrupting Criminalization, "Abolition and the State." www.interruptingcriminalization.com/abolition-and-the-state; see Mi Jente, "Sin El Qué," www.mijente.net/2020/03/sin-el-que/; and see Cameron Rasmussen, "Towards Abolitionist Social Work," in *Abolition Social Work and Social Work Abolition*, Craig Fortier, Edward Hong Sing, Nicole Penak, et al., eds. (MN: Between the Lines, Forthcoming 2024).
13. Cameron Rasmussen, "Towards Abolitionist Social Work."
14. See the work of Mia Mingus, Bay Area Transformative Justice Collective and Creative Interventions, as well as Spade, *Mutual Aid*.
15. See Interrupting Criminalization, "So Is This Actually an Abolitionist Proposal or Strategy?" www.interruptingcriminalization.com/binder.
16. Rasmussen and James, "Trading Cops."

3 Abolitionist Reform for Social Workers

1. Jane Addams, "Respect for Law," *The Independent*, January 3, 1901: 18–20.

2. Although Addams was focused on lynching in the Southern United States, white mobs lynched Black, Indigenous, and people of color across the North as well. For a comprehensive study on the history of lynching in the United States, see the third edition of Lynching in America: *Confronting the Legacy of Racial Terror* published in 2017 by the Equal Justice Initiative: www.lynchinginamerica.eji.org/report/.
3. Ida Barnett-Wells, "Lynching Our National Crime," transcript of speech delivered at the National Negro Conference, New York, June 1, 1909, 174, www.hdl.handle.net/2027/coo.31924067126858?urlappend=%3Bseq=182%3Bownerid=13510798903027939-198.
4. Ida Barnett-Wells, "Lynching and the Excuse for It," *The Independent*, May 16, 1901: 1133–6.
5. At this time, "progressive punishment" advocated by northerners included innovations such as the indeterminate sentence, parole, probation, specialized prisons and courts for specific populations, and an emphasis on moral and vocational (re)education.
6. Tony Platt, *Beyond These Walls: Rethinking Crime and Punishment in the United States* (New York: St. Martin's Press, 2019), 23.
7. Critical Resistance, "What Is the PIC? What Is Abolition?" www.criticalresistance.org/mission-vision/not-so-common-language/.
8. Leah A. Jacobs, et al., "Defund the Police: Moving Towards an Anti-Carceral Social Work," *Journal of Progressive Human Services* 32, no. 1 (2021): 37–62.
9. Harsha Walia and Andrew Dilts, "Dismantle and Transform: On Abolition, Decolonization, and Insurgent Politics," in *Abolishing Carceral Society*, Abolition Collective, ed. (New York, Common Notions, 2018), 29.
10. Dana Green, "Abolition," in *Encyclopedia of Prisons and Correctional Facilities*, Vol. 1, Mary Bosworth, ed. (Thousand Oaks, CA: Sage Publications, 2005), 2–5.
11. André Gorz, *Strategy for Labor: A Radical Proposal* (Boston, MA: Beacon Press, 1967), 7.
12. Maya Schenwar and Victoria Law, *Prison by Any Other Name: The Harmful Consequences of Popular Reforms* (New York, The New Press, 2020), 27.
13. Beth E. Richie, *Arrested Justice: Black Women, Violence, and America's Prison Nation* (New York, New York University Press, 2012).
14. For comprehensive investigations of this "reach," see Tony Platt's *Beyond These Walls*, as well as Maya Schenwar and Victoria Law's *Prison by Any Other Name*.
15. These three examples all affect the size, scope, and power of the prison industrial complex but are broken down here for simplicity to highlight specific consequences of carceral reform.
16. See Emi Koyama and Lauren Martin, "Abusive Power and Control within the Domestic Violence Shelter," *Eminism*, 2002, www.eminism.org/readings/pdf-rdg/wheel-sheet.pdf.
17. See Abolition Research Group, "The Problem with Community Policing," *A World without Police*, October 8, 2017, www.aworldwithoutpolice.org/2017/10/08/the-problem-with-community-policing/; Kristian Williams, "Your Friendly Neighborhood Police State," in *Our Enemies in Blue: Police and Power in America* (Chico, CA: AK Press, 2015).
18. Dan Berger, Mariame Kaba, and David Stein, "What Abolitionists Do," *Jacobin*, August 24 (2017), para 3.
19. Mohamed Shehk, "Abolitionist Reforms," in *The Routledge International Handbook Of Penal Abolition*, Michael J. Coyle and David Scott, eds. (New York: Routledge, 2021).
20. See Mariame Kaba's interview with Josie Duffy Rice and Clint Smith on episode

20. "Mariame Kaba and Prison Abolition" *Justice in America*, www.theappeal.org/justice-in-america-episode-20-mariame-kaba-and-prison-abolition/.
21. Gorz, *Strategy for Labor*, 7.
22. Critical Resistance, "Abolition Is Essential in 2021: Annual Report," 2022, www.criticalresistance.org/annual-reports/2021-annual-report/.
23. Descriptions from Critical Resistance, "Abolition Is Essential," 2.
24. At the time, this included the Creative Interventions Toolkit (creative-interventions.org), Generation Five's Transformative Justice guide (generationfive.org), and various curricula published by Project Nia (project-nia.org).
25. An invaluable resource for this curriculum was the Washington State Coalition Against Domestic Violence's resource, "How's Your Relationship? Conversations with Someone about Their Abusive Behavior," 2015, www.wscadv.org/wp-content/uploads/2015/06/Hows-Your-Relationship-Abusive-Behavior-Cards.pdf.
26. Audre Lorde, "Learning from the 60s," in *Sister Outsider: Essays and Speeches* (Berkely, CA: Crossing Press, 2012).
27. Roelsgaard, Natascha Toft, "'The Offense of Blackness': Race Women's Counter Storytelling and Exposé of the Southern Convict Leasing Regime" (PhD diss., Ohio University, 2022), 245, www.etd.ohiolink.edu/apexprod/rws_etd/send_file/send?accession=ohiou1642160688722517&disposition=inline.
28. Roelsgaard, "The Offense of Blackness," 24.
29. Eve L. Ewing, "Mariame Kaba: Everything Worthwhile Is Done with Other People," interview, *Adi Magazine: Rehumanizing Policy* (Fall 2019), www.adimagazine.com/articles/mariame-kaba-everything-worthwhile-is-done-with-other-people.

4 Indigenist Abolition

1. M. S. Gali, "Stolen Freedom: The Ongoing Incarceration of California's Indigenous Peoples," 2020, *Medium*, www.level.medium.com/stolen-freedom-the-ongoing-incarceration-of-californias-indigenous-peoples-a5f55eba2765#:~:text=Abolition%20is%20decolonization; beginning section.
2. Andrew Curley, Pallavi Gupta, Lara Lookabaugh, Christopher Neubert, and Sara Smith, "Decolonisation Is a Political Project: Overcoming Impasses between Indigenous Sovereignty and Abolition," *Antipode* 54, no. 4 (July 2022): 1046, https://doi.org/10.1111/anti.12830.
3. Curley et al., "Decolonization Is a Political Product," 1047.
4. Curley et al., "Decolonization Is a Political Product,"; Gali, "Stolen Freedom".
5. As cited in Curley et al., "Decolonization Is a Political Product," 1052.
6. Krista L. Benson, "Carrying Stories of Incarcerated Indigenous Women as Tools for Prison Abolition," *Frontiers: A Journal of Women Studies* 41, no. 2 (2020): 143, https://doi.org/10.5250/fronjwomestud.41.2.0143; Mimi E. Kim, "Anti-Carceral Feminism: The Contradictions of Progress and the Possibilities of Counter-Hegemonic Struggle," *Affilia* 35, no. 3 (August 2020): 309–26, www.doi.org/10.1177/0886109919878276.
7. Crimethinc, "To Change Everything: An Anarchist Appeal" (2018), www.crimethinc.com/tce.
8. Crimethinc, "To Change Everything."
9. Stephanie Lumsden, "Reproductive Justice, Sovereignty, and Incarceration: Prison Abolition Politics and California Indians," *American Indian Culture and Research Journal* 40, no. 1 (January 1, 2016): 40, www.doi.org/10.17953/aicrj.40.1.lumsden.
10. Stephen L. Pevar, *The Rights of Indians and Tribes*, Oxford: Oxford University Press, 2012.

11. Stephanie Lumsden, "Reproductive Justice."
12. Wallace Coffey and Rebecca Tsosie. "Rethinking the Tribal Sovereignty Doctrine: Cultural Sovereignty and the Collective Future of Indian Nations," *Stanford Law & Policy Review* 12 (2001): 191.
13. Miller as quoted in Lumsden, Stephanie, "Reproductive justice, sovereignty, and incarceration: Prison abolition politics and California Indians." *American Indian Culture and Research Journal* 40.1 (2016): 33-46.
14. Ramona Beltrán and Gita Mehrotra. "Honoring Our Intellectual Ancestors: A Feminist of Color Treaty for Creating Allied Collaboration," *Affilia* 30.1 (2015): 106–16.
15. Jo-Ann Archibald, *Indigenous Storywork: Educating the Heart, Mind, Body, and Spirit* (Vancouver: UBC Press, 2008), 76.
16. Archibald, *Indigenous Storywork*.
17. Christine T. Lowery, "A Qualitative Model of Long-Term Recovery for American Indian Women," *Journal of Human Behavior in the Social Environment* 2, no. 1–2 (1999): 35–50; Christine T. Lowery and Mark A. Mattaini, "The Science of Sharing Power: Native American Thought and Behavior Analysis," *Behavior and Social Issues* 9 (1999): 3–23.
18. R. Beltran and S. Begun, "'It Is Medicine': Narratives of Healing from the Aotearoa Digital Storytelling as Indigenous Media Project (ADSIMP)," *Psychology & Developing Societies* 26, no. 2 (September 1, 2014): 155–79. www.doi.org/10.1177/0971333614549137; Beltrán et al. 2014; Danica Brown, "Our Vision of Health for Future Generations: An Exploration of Proximal and Intermediary Motivations with Women of the Choctaw Nation of Oklahoma," January 1, 2000, www.doi.org/10.15760/etd.6687; Aman Sium and Eric Ritskes, "Speaking Truth to Power: Indigenous Storytelling as an Act of Living Resistance," Decolonization: *Indigeneity, Education & Society* 2, no. 1 (2013); Christine T Lowery, "American Indian Narratives" . . . My Spirit Is Starting to Come Back," *Reflections: Narratives of Professional Helping* 4, no. 3 (1998): 26–35.
19. Emily Willard, "Beyond Transitional Justice: Learning from Indigenous Maya Mam Resistance in Guatemala," *International Journal of Transitional Justice* 15, no. 3 (March 2, 2022): 490–509, www.doi.org/10.1093/ijtj/ijab021; Baumann, 2019 as cited by Emily Willard, "Beyond Transitional Justice: Learning from Indigenous Maya Mam Resistance in Guatemala," *International Journal of Transitional Justice* 15, no. 33 (2021): 503.
20. Margaret Kovach, *Indigenous Methodologies: Characteristics, Conversations, and Contexts* (Toronto, Canada: University of Toronto Press, 2021).
21. Jamie Simpson Steele, "Talk-Story: A Quest for New Research Methodology in Neocolonial Hawai'i," *Youth Theatre Journal* 26, no. 1 (January 2012): 38–49, www.doi.org/10.1080/08929092.2012.678213.
22. Paulo Freire, Donaldo P. Macedo, and Ira Shor, *Pedagogy of the Oppressed*, Myra Bergman Ramos, transl., 50th anniversary ed. (New York: Bloomsbury Academic, 2018), 109.
23. Raul Alberto Mora, "Counter-Narrative. *Qualitative Inquiry* 8, no.1 (2014): 23–44.
24. Eve Tuck, "Suspending Damage: A Letter to Communities," *Harvard Educational Review* 79, no. 3 (September 1, 2009): 409, www.doi.org/10.17763/haer.79.3.n0016675661t3n15.
25. Eve Tuck, "Suspending Damage," 416.
26. Samantha Matters, "Strategic Foresight in Métis Communities: Lessons from Indigenous Futurism" (2019).
27. Grace L. Dillon, ed., *Walking the Clouds: An Anthology of Indigenous Science Fiction*,

Sun Tracks: An American Indian Literary Series, Vol. 69 (Tucson, AZ: University of Arizona Press, 2012); Samantha Matters, "Strategic Foresight in Métis Communities: Lessons from Indigenous Futurism" (2019).
28. Toronto Abolition Convergence, "An Indigenous Abolitionist Study Guide," *Yellowhead Institute*, 10 (August 2020), www.yellowheadinstitute.org/2020/08/10/an-indigenous-abolitionist-study-group-guide/.
29. Beth E. Richie and Kayla M. Martensen, "Resisting Carcerality, Embracing Abolition: Implications for Feminist Social Work Practice," *Affilia* 35, no. 1 (February 2020): 12–6, www.doi.org/10.1177/0886109919897576, p 14.

5   Abolition: The Missing Link

1. National Association of Social Workers, "Ethics," 2021, www.www.socialworkers.org/About/Ethics/Code-of-Ethics/Code-of-Ethics-English.
2. Candice C. Beasley, Melissa I. Singh, and Katherine Drechsler, "Anti-Racism and Equity-Mindedness in Social Work Field Education: A Systematic Review," *Journal of Ethnic & Cultural Diversity in Social Work* 31, no. 3–5 (September 3, 2022): 173–85, www.doi.org/10.1080/15313204.2021.1991868.
3. National Association of Social Workers, "Institutional Racism and the Social Work Profession: A Call to Action," Report by the Presidential Task Force Subcommittee on Institutional Racism, NASW, Washington, DC, (2007), 23, www.socialworkers.org/LinkClick.aspx?fileticket=SWK1aR53FAk%3D&portalid=0.
4. National Association of Social Workers, "Social Work History," www.socialworkers.org/News/Facts/Social-Work-History#:~:text=Since%20the%20first%20social%20work,problems%20to%20the%20public's%20attention.
5. Candice C. Beasley et al., "Anti-Racism and Equity-Mindedness;" Barbara W. White, ed. *Color in a White Society: Selected Papers from the NASW Conference--Color in a White Society, Los Angeles, California, June 1982*. Washington, DC: NASW Press, 1984.
6. NASW, "Institutional Racism and the Social Work Profession," 4
7. NASW, "Institutional Racism and the Social Work Profession."
8. NASW, "Institutional Racism and the Social Work Profession."
9. Candice C. Beasley, Melissa I. Singh, and Katherine Drechsler, "Anti-Racism and Equity-Mindedness in Social Work Field Education: A Systematic Review," *Journal of Ethnic & Cultural Diversity in Social Work* 31, no. 3–5 (2022): 173–85, www.doi.org/10.1080/15313204.2021.1991868; Martell L. Teasley, Susan McCarter, Bongki Woo, Laneshia R. Conner, Michael S. Spencer, and Tatyana Green, "Eliminate Racism," Grand Challenges for Social Work Initiative Working Paper No. 26 (Cleveland, OH: American Academy of Social Work & Social Welfare, 2021), www.grandchallengesforsocialwork.org/wp-content/uploads/2021/05/Eliminate-Racism-Concept-Paper.pdf.
10. Candice C. Beasley et al., "Anti-Racism and Equity-Mindedness," 2.
11. Gwendolyn C. Gilbert, "The Role of Social Work in Black Liberation," *The Black Scholar* 6, no. 4 (1974): 16–23, www.jstor.org/stable/41065785; Sheliza Ladhani and Kathleen C. Sitter, "The Revival of Anti-Racism: Considerations for Social Work Education," *Critical Social Work* 21, no. 1 (2020): 54–65, www.doi.org/10.22329/csw.v21i1.6227; Judith Ann Trolander, "Fighting Racism and Sexism: The Council on Social Work Education," *Social Service Review* 71, no. 1 (1997): 110–34, www.doi.org/.10.1086/604233.
12. Mekada Graham. "Reframing Black Perspectives in Social Work: New Directions?" *Social Work Education* 28, no. 3 (2009): 268–80, www.doi.org/10.1080

/02615470802659431.
13. Lena Dominelli and Jo Campling, "Anti-Oppressive Practice in Action: Working with Individuals," *Anti-Oppressive Social Work Theory and Practice* (2002): 85–108, www.doi.org/10.1007/978-1-4039-1400-2_5.
14. Gordon Pon, "A Labour of Love or of Response? Anti-Racism Education and Responsibility," *Canadian Social Work Review / Revue Canadienne de Service Social* 24, no. 2 (2007): 141–53, www.jstor.org/stable/41669871..
15. Bonita Lawrence and Enakshi Dua, "Decolonizing Antiracism," *Social Justice* 32, no. 4 (102) (2005): 120–43, http://www.jstor.org/stable/29768340; Henry Miller. "Social Work in the Black Ghetto: The New Colonialism." *Social Work* 14, no. 3 (1969): 65–76. www.jstor.org/stable/23709910.
16. Rhea V. Almeida, Lisa Marie Werkmeister Rozas, Bronwyn Cross-Denny, Karen Kyeunghae Lee, and Ann-Marie Yamada, "Coloniality and Intersectionality in Social Work Education and Practice," *Journal of Progressive Human Services* 30, no. 2 (May 4, 2019): 148–64, www.doi.org/10.1080/10428232.2019.1574195.
17. Jennifer Maree Stanley, "Intersectional and Relational Frameworks: Confronting Anti-Blackness, Settler Colonialism, and Neoliberalism in U.S. Social Work," *Journal of Progressive Human Services* 31, no. 3 (September 1, 2020): 210–25, www.doi.org/10.1080/10428232.2019.1703246.
18. Henry Miller, "Social Work in the Black Ghetto," 68.
19. Rhea V. Almeida et al., "Coloniality and Intersectionality."
20. Rhea V. Almeida et al., "Coloniality and Intersectionality."
21. Rhea V. Almeida et al., "Coloniality and Intersectionality."
22. Autumn Asher BlackDeer and Maria Gandarilla Ocampo, "#SocialWorkSoWhite: A Critical Perspective on Settler Colonialism, White Supremacy, and Social Justice in Social Work," *Advances in Social Work* 22, no. 2 (November 8, 2022): 720–40, www.doi.org/10.18060/24986.
23. Jennifer Maree Stanley, "Intersectional and Relational Frameworks."
24. National Association of Social Workers, "Sovereignty and the Health of Indigenous Peoples," *Social Work Speaks* (2002), www.socialworkers.org/DesktopModules/DnnSharp/SearchBoost/FileDownload.ashx?file=26435&sb-bhvr=1
25. National Association of Social Workers, "Ethics."
26. Hilary N. Weaver, Lacey M. Sloan, Carenlee Barkdull, and Pālama Lee, "CSWE Statement of Accountability and Reconciliation for Harms Done to Indigenous and Tribal Peoples," Council on Social Work Education (2021), www.cswe.org/getattachment/Education-Resources/Indigenous-and-Tribal-Content/CSWE-Statement-of-Accountability-and-Reconciliation-for-Harms-Done-to-Indigenous-and-Tribal-Peoples.pdf.
27. Giovanni Hernandez-Carranza, Mirna Carranza, and Elizabeth Grigg, "Using Auto-Ethnography to Bring Visibility to Coloniality," *Qualitative Social Work* 20, no. 6 (November 2021): 1517–35, www.doi.org/10.1177/14733250211039514.
28. Patricia Reid-Merritt, *Righteous Self Determination: The Black Social Work Movement in America*. (Baltimore, MD: Black Classic Press, Imprint Editions, 2010); Barbara Bryant Solomon, *Black Empowerment: Social Work in Oppressed Communities* (New York: Columbia University Press, 1976).
29. Jerome H. Schiele, *Human Services and the Afrocentric Paradigm* (New York: Routledge, 2013): 218, www.doi.org/10.4324/9781315043500
30. Leah A. Jacobs, et al., "Defund the Police: Moving Towards an Anti-Carceral Social Work," *Journal of Progressive Human Services* 32, no. 1 (January 2, 2021):

37–62, www.doi.org/10.1080/10428232.2020.1852865.
31. Alan Dettlaff, Kristen Weber, Maya Pendleton, Bill Bettencourt, and Leonard Burton, *How We endUP: A Future without Family Policing*, upEnd (2021), www.upendmovement.org/wp-content/uploads/2021/06/How-We-endUP-6.18.21.pdf; Dorothy E. Roberts, *Torn Apart: How the Child Welfare System Destroys Black Families—and How Abolition Can Build a Safer World*, 1st ed. (New York: Basic Books, 2022).
32. Paul Michael, "'A World to Win': In Defence of (Dissenting) Social Work—A Response to Chris Maylea," *The British Journal of Social Work* 51, no. 4 (June 28, 2021): 1131–49, www.doi.org/10.1093/bjsw/bcab009; Chris Maylea, "The End of Social Work," *The British Journal of Social Work* 51, no. 2 (April 3, 2021): 772–89, www.doi.org/10.1093/bjsw/bcaa203; Joe Whelan, "On Your Marx . . . ? A World to Win or the Dismantlement of a Profession? On Why We Need a Reckoning," *The British Journal of Social Work* 52, no. 2 (March 17, 2022): 1168–81, www.doi.org/10.1093/bjsw/bcab132.
33. Leonel Castillo, *Chicano Task Force Report*, Council on Social Work Education (1973); Genevieve T. Hill, *Black Task Force Report: Suggested Guides for the Integration of Black Content Into the Social Work Curriculum*, Council on Social Work Education (1973); Faye U. Munoz, *Asian American Task Force Report: Problems and Issues in Social Work Education*, Council on Social Work Education (1973); John E. Mackey, *American Indian Task Force Report*, Council on Social Work Education (1973); José Morales, *Puerto Rican Task Force Report*; Council on Social Work Education (1973).
34. Leonel Castillo, *Chicano Task Force Report*; Genevieve T. Hill, *Black Task Force Report*, iii.
35. Faye U. Munoz, *Asian American Task Force Report*, 6–7.
36. John E. Mackey, *American Indian Task Force Report*, 8.
37. José Morales, *Puerto Rican Task Force Report*, 3
38. John E. Mackey, *American Indian Task Force Report*, 14.
39. Faye U. Munoz, *Asian American Task Force Report*, 2.
40. John E. Mackey, *American Indian Task Force Report*, 13.
41. Nancy Shoemaker, "A Typology of Colonialism," *The Newsmagazine of the American Historical Association: Perspectives on History* (2015), www.historians.org/research-and-publications/perspectives-on-history/october-2015/a-typology-of-colonialism.
42. Nancy Shoemaker, "A Typology of Colonialism," 2015.

6 Is Social Work Obsolete?

1. See Jane Lewis, "Women and Late-Nineteenth-Century Social Work," in *Regulating Womanhood*, 1st ed., edited by Carol Smart (London: Routledge, 1992).
2. Ruth Wilson Gilmore, *Golden Gulag: Prisons, Surplus, Crisis, and Opposition in Globalizing California*, 2nd ed. (Oakland, CA: University of California Press, 2018).
3. See "Mayor Adams Announces $15 Million Revolving Fund for Nonprofit Homeless Service Providers to Build, Own, and Operate Shelters" (press release), www.nyc.gov/office-of-the-mayor/news/161-23/mayor-adams-15-million-revolving-fund-nonprofit-homeless-service-providers-build-
4. See NASW, "Social Workers Ethical Responsibility to the Broader Society," www.socialworkers.org/About/Ethics/Code-of-Ethics/Code-of-Ethics-English/Social-Workers-Ethical-Responsibilities-to-the-Broader-Society.
5. See Neil Gale, "The Life and Times of Jane Addams" (Chicago, IL: Digital Research Library of Illinois History, Chicago, 2019), www.drloihjournal.blogspot.com/2019/03/the-life-and-times-of-jane-addams.html

6. Rosemary Rees, *Poverty and Public Health, 1815-1948* (Oxford: Heinemann, 2001), 193.
7. See NAASW and Haymarket Webinar, "Is Social Work Obsolete?" www.haymarketbooks.org/blogs/432-is-social-work-obsolete.
8. See "NASW Responds to Negative Column on Social Work and Policing" (statement from former NASW CEO Angelo McClain), www.socialworkersspeak.org/media/nasw-responds-to-negative-column-on-social-work-and-policing.html.
9. Merriam-Webster, "Help," www.merriam-webster.com/dictionary/help.
10. Angela Y. Davis, *Are Prisons Obsolete?* (Seven Stories Press, New York, 2003).
11. Desmond Tutu, Forward, in *Dignity: In Honor of the Rights of Indigenous Peoples* by Dana Gluckstein (powerHouse Books, Brooklyn, 2010).
12. Merriam-Webster, "Support," www.merriam-webster.com/dictionary/support.

7 Abolition and the Welfare State

1. Ruth Wilson Gilmore, "Making Abolition Geography in California's Central Valley with Ruth Wilson Gilmore," *The Funambulist*, December 20, 2018, https://thefunambulist.net/magazine/21-space-activism/interview-making-abolition-geography-california-central-valley-ruth-wilson-gilmore.
2. See Ruth Wilson Gilmore, *Abolition Geography: Essays Toward Liberation* (London: Verso Press, 2022); Mariame Kaba and Andrea Ritchie, *No More Police: The Case for Police Abolition* (New York: The New Press, 2023); Dean Spade, *Mutual Aid: Building Solidarity During This Crisis (and the Next)* (Oakland: AK Press, 2020).
3. See André Gorz, *Strategy for Labor: A Radical Proposal* (Boston: Beacon Press, 1967).
4. See Mimi Abramovitz, "From the Welfare State to the Carceral State: Whither Social Reproduction?" *Affilia: Feminist Inquiry in Social Work* 38, no. 1 (2023); David Garland, "The Birth of the Welfare Sanction," *Journal of Law and Society* 8, no. 1 (1981); Frances Fox Piven and Richard Cloward, *Regulating the Poor* (New York: Vintage/Random, 1971).
5. Mariame Kaba, *We Do This 'Til We Free Us: Abolitionist Organizing and Transforming Justice* (Chicago, IL: Haymarket Books, 2021), 72.
6. Asa Briggs, "The Welfare State in Historical Perspective," *European Journal of Sociology* 2, no. 2, 221 (1961).
7. Gøsta Esping-Anderson, *The Three Worlds of Welfare Capitalism* (Princeton: Princeton University Press, 1990).
8. Ira Katznelson, *When Affirmative Action Was White: The Untold History of Racial Inequality in Twentieth-Century America* (New York: W. W. Norton, 2005).
9. David Garland, *The Welfare State: A Very Brief Introduction* (London: Oxford University Press, 2016), 46.
10. David Garland, *The Welfare State*, 50.
11. Frances Fox Piven and Richard Cloward, *Regulating the Poor* (New York: Penguin, 1971).
12. David Garland, "The Birth."
13. David Garland, *The Culture of Control: Crime and Social Order in Contemporary Society* (Chicago: University of Chicago Press, 2002).
14. Loïc Wacquant, *Punishing the Poor: The Neoliberal Government of Social Insecurity* (Durham: Duke University Press, 2009).
15. Mimi Abramovitz, "From the Welfare State."
16. Mimi Abramovitz, "From the Welfare State," 25.
17. Mimi E. Kim, "Challenging the Pursuit of Criminalisation in an Era of Mass Incarceration: The Limitations of Social Work Responses to Domestic Violence in

the USA," *British Journal of Social Work* 43, no. 7 (2013); Beth E. Richie, *Arrested Justice: Black Women, Violence, and America's Prison Nation* (New York: New York University Press, 2012).
18. David Garland, *The Welfare State*.
19. Pierre Bourdieu, "The Left Hand and the Right Hand of the State," in *Acts of Resistance* (Cambridge: Polity, 1999),
20. Mariame Kaba and Andrea Ritchie, *No More Police*, 208.
21. Ruth Wilson Gilmore and Craig Gilmore, "Restating the Obvious," in *Abolition Geography* (London: Verso Books, 2022).
22. Dean Spade, *Mutual Aid*.
23. William C. Anderson, *The Nation on No Map: Black Anarchism and Abolition* (Oakland, CA: AK Press, 2021).
24. Mariame Kaba and Andrea Ritchie, *No More Police*, 213.
25. W. E. B. Du Bois, *Black Reconstruction in America* (New Brunswick: Transaction Publishers, 1935).
26. Angela Y. Davis, *Abolition Democracy: Beyond Empire, Prisons, and Torture* (Oakland: AK Press, 2005).
27. "Ruth Wilson Gilmore w/ Alberto Toscano and Brenna Bhandar," *The Dig*, May 28, 2022, www.thedigradio.com/podcast/ruth-wilson-gilmore-w-alberto-toscano-and-brenna-bhandar/.
28. David Garland, *The Welfare State*.
29. Ruth Wilson Gilmore and Craig Gilmore, 2022.
30. Dean Spade, *Mutual Aid*.
31. William C. Anderson, *The Nation on No Map: Black Anarchism and Abolition* (Oakland: AK Press, 2021).
32. David Garland, *The Welfare State*.

8 Ending Carceral Social Work

1. National Association of Social Workers, "Read the Code of Ethics," 2021, www.socialworkers.org/About/Ethics/Code-of-Ethics/Code-of-Ethics-English.
2. US Department of Health and Human Services, Administration for Children and Families, Administration on Children, Youth and Families, Children's Bureau, "The AFCARS Report: Preliminary FY2021 Estimates as of June 28, 2022," June 2022, www.acf.hhs.gov/sites/default/files/documents/cb/afcars-report-29.pdf.
3. Child Welfare Information Gateway, "Definitions of Child Abuse and Neglect," US Department of Health and Human Services, Administration for Children and Families, Children's Bureau, May 2022, www.childwelfare.gov/pubPDFs/define.pdf.
4. Shanta Trivedi, "The Harm of Child Removal," *New York University Review of Law and Social Change* 43 (February 2019): 523–580. www.doi.org/10.2139/ssrn.3341033.
5. Kristina Lovato, Corina Lopez, Leyla Karimli, and Laura S. Abrams, "The Impact of Deportation-Related Family Separations on the Well-Being of Latinx Children and Youth: A Review of the Literature," *Children and Youth Services Review* 95 (December 2018): 109–16; Christopher Wildeman, Alyssa W. Goldman, and Kristin Turney., "Parental Incarceration and Child Health in the United States," *Epidemiologic Reviews* 40, no. 1 (June 1, 2018): 146–56. www.doi.org/10.1093/epirev/mxx013.
6. Joseph J. Doyle and Anna Aizer, "Economics of Child Protection: Maltreatment, Foster Care, and Intimate Partner Violence," *Annual Review of Economics* 10, no. 1 (August 2, 2018): 87–108, www.doi.org/10.1146/annurev-economics-080217-053237; Sue D.

Hobbs, Daniel Bederian-Gardner, Christin M. Ogle, Sarah Bakanosky, Rachel Narr, and Gail S. Goodman, "Foster Youth and at-Risk non-Foster Youth: A Propensity Score and Structural Equation Modeling Analysis," *Children and Youth Services Review* 126 (July 2021): 106034, www.doi.org/10.1016/j.childyouth.2021.106034; Peter J. Pecora, Jason Williams, Ronald C. Kessler, A. Chris Downs, Kirk O'Brien, Eva Hiripi, and Sarah Morello, "Assessing the Effects of Foster Care: Early Results from the Casey National Alumni Study," Seattle, WA: *Casey Family Programs* 28 (2003), www.casey.org/national-alumni-study/.

7. Hyunil Kim, Christopher Wildeman, Melissa Jonson-Reid, and Brett Drake, "Lifetime Prevalence of Investigating Child Maltreatment among US Children," *American Journal of Public Health* 107, no. 2 (February 2017): 274–80. www.doi.org/10.2105/AJPH.2016.303545.

8. Youngmin Yi, Frank R. Edwards, and Christopher Wildeman, "Cumulative Prevalence of Confirmed Maltreatment and Foster Care Placement for US Children by Race/Ethnicity, 2011–2016," *American Journal of Public Health* 110, no. 5 (May 2020): 704–9, www.doi.org/10.2105/AJPH.2019.305554.

9. Emily Putnam-Hornstein, Eunhye Ahn, John Prindle, Joseph Magruder, Daniel Webster, and Christopher Wildeman, "Cumulative Rates of Child Protection Involvement and Terminations of Parental Rights in a California Birth Cohort, 1999–2017," *American Journal of Public Health* 111, no. 6 (June 2021): 1157–63, www.doi.org/10.2105/AJPH.2021.306214.

10. Greg Abbott, Letter to the Honorable Jamie Masters, Commissioner, Texas Department of Family and Protective Services, February 2022, www.gov.texas.gov/uploads/files/press/O-MastersJaime202202221358.pdf.

11. Mical Raz, *Abusive Policies: How the American Child Welfare System Lost Its Way*, Studies in Social Medicine (Chapel Hill: The University of North Carolina Press, 2020).

12. Angelo McClain. "Social Workers Cooperate with Police Forces," *The Wall Street Journal*, 2020, www.wsj.com/articles/social-workers-cooperate-with-police-forces-11592255480.

13. National Association of Social Workers, "Undoing Racism through Social Work: NASW Report to the Profession on Racial Justice Priorities and Action," 2021, www.socialworkers.org/LinkClick.aspx?fileticket=29AYH9qAdXc%3D&portalid=0.

14. *Social Work Speaks: National Association of Social Workers Policy Statements 2021-2023*, 12th ed, Washington, DC: NASW Press, 2021.

10 Reaching for an Abolitionist Horizon within Professionalized Social-Change Work

1. Ruth Wilson Gilmore, *Golden Gulag: Prisons, Surplus, Crisis, and Opposition in Globalizing California* (Berkeley: University of California Press, 2007), 11.

2. The use of the word *professionalized* is to specify the form of social-change work I'm focusing on in this chapter and to acknowledge that there are many forms of social-change work (e.g., organizing done within communities and in direct opposition to state agencies/institutions and the nonprofit industrial complex, by people who do not have social work degrees). The injection of the word *change* in between *social* and *work* is to signify that what I believe we all should be laboring toward is transformation. It's not enough to merely "work" within the "social" realm; we must be committed to changing the social landscape to one where everyone is cared for and has what they need to thrive.

3. For work critically analyzing the "do good" part, please see the following texts: Joyce Bell, *The Black Power Movement and American Social Work* (New York:

Columbia University Press, 2014); Chris Chapman and A. J. Withers, *A Violent History of Benevolence: Interlocking Oppression in the Moral Economies of Social Working* (Toronto: University of Toronto Press, 2019); Leslie Margolin, *Under the Cover of Kindness: The Invention of Social Work* (Charlottesville, VA: University of Virginia Press, 1997); Yoosun Park, "Facilitating Injustice: The Complicity of Social Workers in the Forced Removal and Incarceration of Japanese Americans, 1941–1946," *Social Service Review* 82, no.3 (2008): 447–83.

4. I first began to understand this while working overseas in my early 20s. During that time, I was mentored by a woman who labored within professionalized social-change work and was committed to a politic of solidarity. When the formal structure and resources of her agency or other social-service organizations could be tapped without causing harm to community members in need, she would do so, and when they couldn't, she would find alternative routes of support that oftentimes went against the profession's and agency's stated codes of conduct. While navigating complex structures and finding ways to make the present more survivable for people, she was also contributing to leftist movements for large-scale social change because she knew collective action was the only way to make the needle move. My understanding of the limitations of paid work has only deepened since this experience two decades ago. A long line of generous, critical mentors; organizers; radical professionalized social-change workers; and texts like *Normal Life: Administrative Violence, Critical Trans Politics, & the Limits of Law* and *The Revolution Will Not Be Funded: Beyond the Non-Profit Industrial Complex* have been instrumental in the development of my learning, analysis, and political commitments.
5. Mariame Kaba (@Prisonculture), 2022, "We're going to continue to do what we can, with the resources at our disposal, within our capacity, to lessen suffering where we are, for as many people as we can. That's really it," Twitter, April 14, 2022, 7:12 PM, www.twitter.com/prisonculture/status/1514773638955732994.
6. Ruth Wilson Gilmore, *Abolition Geography: Essays Toward Liberation* (London: Verso Press, 2022), 79.
7. Joyce Bell, *The Black Power Movement and American Social Work* (New York: Columbia University Press, 2014), 135.
8. Ruth Wilson Gilmore, *Abolition Geography*, 79.
9. Ruth Wilson Gilmore, interviewed by Joshua Briond and Jared Ware, "Millennials Are Killing Capitalism," podcast audio, August 5, 2022, www.millennialsarekillingcapitalism.libsyn.com/everybody-changes-in-the-process-of-building-a-movement-ruth-wilson-gilmore-on-abolition-geography.
10. Solana Rice and Mariame Kaba, "Practicing Imagination," *The Forge: Organizing Strategy and Practice*, May 20, 2021, https://forgeorganizing.org/article/practicing-imagination.
11. Ruth Wilson Gilmore, *Abolition Geography*, 79.
12. AWKWORD, "Awkword Interviews: Dylan Rodriguez, Author, Professor, & Critical Resistance Founding Member," YouTube video, 1:17:06, August 13, 2021, www.youtube.com/watch?v=Y4EbO5xFHdU.
13. Mariame Kaba (@Prisonculture), "Better to be antagonistic to oppression than to be proximate to power. A number of organizations need to internalize this." Twitter, March 15, 2022, 10:44 AM, www.twitter.com/prisonculture/status/1503774070604713984.
14. Toni Cade Bambara, *Deep Sightings and Rescue Missions: Fiction, Essays, and Conversations* (New York: Vintage Books, 1996), 246–7.
15. Toni Cade Bambara, *Deep Sightings*, 246.

16. Namrata Verghese, "What Is Necropolitics? The Political Calculation of Life and Death," *Teen Vogue*, March 10, 2021, www.teenvogue.com/story/what-is-necropolitics.
17. "2022 Police Violence Report," Mapping Police Violence, www.policeviolencereport.org/.
18. Austin C. McCoy, "When Biden Says 'Fund the Police,' It Should Spur Our Efforts to Defund Them," Truthout, March 19, 2022, www.truthout.org/articles/when-biden-says-fund-the-police-it-should-spur-our-efforts-to-defund-them/.
19. Naomi Klein, *This Changes Everything: Capitalism vs The Climate* (New York: Simon & Schuster, 2015).
20. For a strong mix of historical and present-day critical analyses of white professionalized social-change work, please explore the special double issue of *Advances in Social Work*, which can be fully accessed here: www.journals.iupui.edu/index.php/advancesinsocialwork/issue/view/1521.
21. James and Grace Lee Boggs, *Revolution and Evolution in the Twentieth Century* (New York: Monthly Review Press, 2008).
22. Kelly M. Hayes (@MsKellyMHayes), "If you ask someone to prove they need accommodations, that's not accessibility," Twitter, April 1, 2022, 9:30 AM, www.twitter.com/MsKellyMHayes/status/1509916041475993602?s=20&t=YsN4Og8d.
23. Beth E. Richie and Kayla M. Martensen, "Resisting Carcerality, Embracing Abolition: Implications for Feminist Social Work Practice," *Affilia* 35, no. 1 (2020): 13.
24. Mariame Kaba, Tamara K. Nopper, and Naomi Murakawa, *We Do This 'Til We Free Us: Abolitionist Organizing and Transforming Justice* (Chicago, IL: Haymarket Books, 2021), 181.
25. Mariame Kaba, Tamara K. Nopper, and Naomi Murakawa, *We Do This*, 181.
26. Once again uplifting the text *The Revolution Will Not Be Funded*, which provides a clear-eyed analysis of how troubling nonprofit structures are and how they undermine collective social change.
27. Erica Meiners, "Our Academic Penalscape: Slow Work in Always Urgent Times," *The Journal of Culture and Education* 17, no. 1 (2018): 15–23.
28. H. Rap Brown quotes Bobby Seale at the Free Huey Rally in Oakland, which took place on February 17, 1968. Audio of this speech can be found here: www.americanarchive.org/catalog/cpb-aacip-28-4m91834b8n.

11 Staying in Love with Each Other's Survival

1. Young Women's Empowerment Project (YWEP) was led by and for young people of color in the sex trade and street economy in Chicago, Illinois, from 2002 to 2014.
2. For more about this lifesaving concept, please see Shira Hassan, *Saving Our Own Lives: A Liberatory Practice of Harm Reduction* (Chicago, IL: Haymarket Books, 2022).
3. Hassan, *Saving Our Own Lives*.
4. The first syringe distribution venture is often attributed to Jon Stuen-Parker in 1983, a heroin user and medical student at Yale. However, my own QTBIPOC lineage puts him among many other radical activists who were operating clandestine projects all over the country in the early 1980s.
5. The Color of Violence is an anthology edited by INCITE!, published in 2006 by South End Press and republished by Duke University Press in 2016.
6. Young Women's Empowerment Project. It has been on our website but also in our leaflets and zines since 2009
7. Zachary Drucker, "Trans Icon Miss Major: 'We've Got to Reclaim Who the Fuck We Are,'" *Vice Magazine*, www.vice.com/en/article/j5z58d/miss-major-griffin-

gracy-transgender-survival-guide.
8. Emi Koyama, "Disloyal to Feminism," in *Color of Violence* (2003): 208-222, www.doi.org/10.1215/9780822373445-025.
9. See the *Revolution Will Not Be Funded: Beyond the Non-Profit Industrial Complex* by Incite! See *Women of Color and Trans People of Color Against Violence*, published by South End Press in 2007 and republished by Duke University Press in 2017, for more history about the term *nonprofit industrial complex* and how nonprofits were created and used to subvert the people's power and revolution.
10. Shira Hassan, *Saving Our Own Lives: A Liberatory Practice of Harm Reduction* (Chicago, IL: Haymarket Books, 2022).

12 A Conversation with Charlene A. Carruthers about Social Work and Abolition

1. Charlene A. Carruthers, *Unapologetic: A Black, Queer, and Feminist Mandate for Radical Movements*, Boston MA: Beacon Press, 2019.

13 No Restorative Justice Utopia

1. Grace Lee Boggs, *Living for Change: An Autobiography* (Minneapolis: University of Minnesota Press, 2016).
2. See Impact Justice, "Restorative Community Conferencing: A Study of Community Works West's Restorative Justice Youth Diversion Program in Alameda County," 2017, www.impactjustice.org/wp-content/uploads/CWW_RJreport.pdf.
3. See Edward Burce Bynum, *The African Unconscious: Roots of Ancient Mysticism and Modern Psychology* (Teachers College Press, 1999).
4. Howard Zehr, *The Little Book of Restorative Justice* (Intercourse, PA: Good Books, 2002), 10.

14 Boycott, Divestment, Sanctions as Abolitionist Praxis for Social Work

1. Nadera Shalhoub-Kevorkian, Stéphanie Wahab, and Ferdoos Abed-Rabo Al-Issa, "Feminist Except for Palestine: Where Are Feminist Social Workers on Palestine?" *Affilia* 37, no. 2 (May 2022): 204–14, www.doi.org/10.1177/08861099221079381; Marc Lamont Hill and Mitchell Plitnick, *Except for Palestine: The Limits of Progressive Politics* (New York: The New Press, 2022).
2. Zeena Aljiwad and Cameron Rasmussen, "Social Workers Can No Longer Remain Silent on Oppression of Palestinians," Truthout, November 2021, www.truthout.org/articles/social-workers-can-no-longer-remain-silent-on-oppression-of-palestinians/.
3. Ilan Pappé, *The Ethnic Cleansing of Palestine* (Oxford: Oneworld, 2007); Patrick Wolfe, "Settler Colonialism and the Elimination of the Native," *Journal of Genocide Research* 8, no. 4 (December 2006): 387–409, www.doi.org/10.1080/14623520601056240; Rashid Khalidi, *The Hundred Years' War on Palestine: A History of Settler Colonialism and Resistance, 1917–2017* (New York: Metropolitan).
4. Achille Mbembe, "Necropolitics," *Public Culture* 15, no. 1 (January 1, 2003): 11–40, www.doi.org/10.1215/08992363-15-1-11.
5. Nadera Shalhoub-Kevorkian and Stéphanie Wahab, "Colonial Necrocapitalism, State Secrecy and the Palestinian Freedom Tunnel," *Social and Health Sciences* 19, no. 2 (December 21, 2021), www.doi.org/10.25159/2957-3645/10488.
6. Achille Mbembe, "Necropolitics," 39.
7. Subrahbata Bobby Banerjee, "Necrocapitalism," *Organization Studies* 29 (2008):

1541–63.
8. Subrahbata Bobby Bannerjee, "Necrocapitalism," 1543.
9. See Ilhan Pappé, *The Ethnic Cleansing of Palestine*; Rashid Khalidi, *The Hundred Years' War on Palestine*; Patrick Wolfe, "Settler Colonialism."
10. See Patrick Wolfe, "Settler Colonialism."
11. Nada Elia, *Greater than the Sum of Our Parts: Feminism, Inter/Nationalism, and Palestine* (London, Las Vegas, NV: Pluto Press New Wing, 2023).
12. Denise Ferreira da Silva, "No-Bodies: Law, Raciality and Violence," *Griffith Law Review* 18, no. 2 (January 2009): 212–36, www.doi.org/10.1080/10383441.2009.10854638.
13. Nadera Shalhoub-Kevorkian and Stephanie Wahab, "Colonial Necrocapitalism."
14. Mikko Joronen and Mark Griffiths, "The Affective Politics of Precarity: Home Demolitions in Occupied Palestine," Environment and Planning D: *Society and Space* 37, no. 3 (June 2019): 561–76, www.doi.org/10.1177/0263775818824341; Samah Jabr, 2007, "Occupation of the Mind," *The New Internationalist*, May 1, 2007, www.newint.org/features/special/2007/05/01/emotionalhealth.
15. Glen Sean Coulthard, *Red Skin, White Masks: Rejecting the Colonial Politics of Recognition* (Minneapolis: University of Minnesota Press, 2014).
16. United Nations, Meetings Coverage and Press Release: "International Court of Justice Advisory Opinion Finds Israel's Construction of the Wall 'Contrary to International Law,'" July 9, 2004, www.press.un.org/en/2004/icj616.doc.htm
17. Yarimar Bonilla, "The Swarm of Disaster," *Political Geography* 78 (April 2020): 102182, www.doi.org/10.1016/j.polgeo.2020.102182.
18. Omar Barghouti, "Boycott as an Act of Moral Resistance: The Case for Boycotting Israel," *Indybay*, December 2004, www.indybay.org/newsitems/2004/12/25/17113381.php.
19. Shai Gortler, "The Sumud Within: Walid Daka's Abolitionist Decolonization," *Contemporary Political Theory* 21, no. 4 (2022), 502, www.doi.org/10.1057/s41296-021-00537-2.
20. Shai Gortler, "The Sumud Within," 503 (referencing his Anthology of Walid Daka's writings translated, 10).
21. Jasbir K. Puar, "The 'Right' to Maim: Disablement and Inhumanist Biopolitics in Palestine," *Borderlands* 14 (1) (2015): 1–27.
22. Abdel Razzaq Takriti, "Before BDS: Lineages of Boycott in Palestine," *Radical History Review* 2019, no. 134 (May 1, 2019): 58–95, www.doi.org/10.1215/01636545-7323408.
23. Omar Barghouti, "Boycott as an Act."
24. United Nations, "Commission of Inquiry Finds That the Israeli Occupation Is Unlawful Under International Law," United Nations Human Rights Office of the High Commissioner, Media Center, October 22, 2022, www.ohchr.org/en/press-releases/2022/10/commission-inquiry-finds-israeli-occupation-unlawful-under-international-law.
25. See BDS, "What Is BDS," www.bdsmovement.net/what-is-bds.
26. Angela Y. Davis and Frank Barat, *Freedom Is a Constant Struggle: Ferguson, Palestine, and the Foundations of a Movement* (Chicago, IL: Haymarket Books, 2016).
27. Shana Agid, "'Dismantle, Change, Build': Designing Abolition at the Intersections of Local, Large-Scale, and Imagined Infrastructures," *Design Studies* 59 (November 2018): 95–116, www.doi.org/10.1016/j.destud.2018.05.006.
28. Ruth Wilson Gilmore, *Golden Gulag: Prisons, Surplus, Crisis, and Opposition in Globalizing California*, American Crossroads 21 (Berkeley, CA: University of

California Press, 2007), 242.
29. Mariame Kaba, Tamara K. Nopper, and Naomi Murakawa, *We Do This 'Til We Free Us: Abolitionist Organizing and Transforming Justice*, Abolitionist Papers (Chicago, IL: Haymarket Books, 2021).
30. Dan Berger, Mariame Kaba, and David Stein, 2017, "What Abolitionists Do," *Jacobin Magazine*, August 2017, www.jacobinmag.com/2017/08/prison-abolition-reform-mass-incarceration.
31. Boeing, "Built to Endure," *Boeing Frontiers*, Feature Story, May 2008.
32. Maram Humaid, "In Gaza, Young Victims of Israeli Bombing Recount a Brutal 2021," *Al Jazeera*, December 2021, www.aljazeera.com/news/2021/12/31/palestine-gaza-young-victims-israel-bombardment-may.
33. BDS, "Know What to Boycott," www.bdsmovement.net/get-involved/what-to-boycott.
34. BDS, "Join a BDS Campaign," www.bdsmovement.net/get-involved/join-a-bds-campaign.
35. Critical Resistance, "What Is the PIC? What Is Abolition?" 2023, www.criticalresistance.org/mission-vision/not-so-common-language/.
36. Audra Simpson, "On Ethnographic Refusal: Indigeneity, 'Voice' and Colonial Citizenship," *Junctures: The journal for thematic dialogue*, 9, 67-80, www.junctures.org/index.php/junctures/article/view/66.
37. Omar Barghouti, "Boycott, Academic Freedom and the Moral Responsibility to Uphold Human Rights." AAUP Journal of Academic Freedom, 2013, Vol. 4, www.aaup.org/JAF4/boycott-academic-freedom-and-moral-responsibility-.V8ciOfkrJQI.
38. Barghouti, "Boycott."
39. Angela Y. Davis, Gina Dent, Erica R. Meiners, and Beth Richie, *Abolition. Feminism. Now*, Abolitionist Papers Series (Chicago, IL: Haymarket Books, 2022).
40. Mariame Kaba, Tamara K. Nopper, and Naomi Murakawa, *We Do This*, 5.
41. Angela Y. Davis, "Angela Davis on Black Lives Matter, Palestine, and the Future of Radicalism," in *Futures of Black Radicalism*, Chapter 15, Gaye Theresa Johnson and Alex Lubin eds. (London: Verso Books, 2017), www.lithub.com/angela-davis-on-black-lives-matter-palestine-and-the-future-of-radicalism/.
42. Marc Lamont Hill and Mitchell Plitnick, *Except for Palestine*, 56.
43. Mariame Kaba, *We Do This 'til We Free Us* (Chicago, IL: Haymarket Books, 2021).
44. Lena Meari, "*Sumud*: A Palestinian Philosophy of Confrontation in Colonial Prisons," *South Atlantic Quarterly* 113, no. 3 (July 1, 2014): 547–78, www.doi.org/10.1215/00382876-2692182.
45. Nada Elia, *Greater than the Sum*; Noura Erakat, "What Role for Law in the Role of Palestinian Struggle for Liberation?" *Al-Shabaka Briefs*, March 2014, www.al-shabaka.org/op-eds/what-role-for-law-in-the-palestinian-struggle-for-liberation/.
46. Elizabeth Bradford Lightfoot, "Consumer Activism for Social Change," *Social Work* 64, no. 4 (October 31, 2019): 301–9, www.doi.org/10.1093/sw/swz035.
47. Bethany Jo Murray, Victoria Copeland, and Alan J. Dettlaff, "Reflections on the Ethical Possibilities and Limitations of Abolitionist Praxis in Social Work," *Affilia* February 12, 2023, www.doi.org/10.1177/08861099221114615.
48. Marc Lamont Hill and Mitchell Plitnick, *Except for Palestine*, 76.

15 Abolitionist and Harm Reduction Praxis for Public Sector Mental Health Services

1. Mariame Kaba, "Toward the Horizon of Abolition," in *We Do This 'Til We Free Us* (Chicago, IL: Haymarket Books, 2021), 96.

2. "Harm Reduction Guided by the Goal of Abolition of Prisons and Capitalism: An Interview with Former Direct Action Member Ann Hansen," *kersplebedeb* (blog), August 24, 2021, www.kersplebedeb.com/posts/harm-reduction-guided-by-the-goal-of-the-abolition-of-prisons-and-capitalism-an-interview-with-former-direct-action-member-and-ex-prisoner-ann-hansen/.
3. K. Jonas, A. Abi-Dargham, and R. Kotov, "Two Hypotheses on the High Incidence of Dementia in Psychotic Disorders," *JAMA Psychiatry* 78, no. 12 (2021): 1305–6.
4. L. Voruganti and A. G. Awad, "Neuroleptic Dysphoria: Towards a New Synthesis," *Psychopharmacology* 171, no. 2 (2004): 121–32.
5. "Harm Reduction Guided by the Goal," *kersplebedeb*.
6. R. M. Ryan and E. L. Deci, *Self-Determination Theory: Basic Psychological Needs in Motivation, Development, and Wellness* (New York: Guilford Publications, 2017).
7. M. Brown and R. S. Brown, eds., *Emancipatory Perspectives on Madness: Psychological, Social, and Spiritual Dimensions* (London: Routledge, 2020).
8. N. Jones and M. Shattell, "Engaging with Voices: Rethinking the Clinical Treatment of Psychosis," *Issues in Mental Health Nursing* 34, no. 7 (2013): 562–3; D. Corstens, E. Longden, S. McCarthy-Jones, R. Waddingham, and N. Thomas, "Emerging Perspectives from the Hearing Voices Movement: Implications for Research and Practice," *Schizophrenia Bulletin* 40 (2014): S285–94.
9. J. P. Gone, "Historical Trauma, Therapy Culture, and the Indigenous Boarding School Legacy," Presentation at the 2014 Annual Meeting of the Network for Aboriginal Mental Health Research, McGill University, Montreal, QC, June 2014.
10. P. Farmer, "Partners in Help: Assisting the Poor for the Long Term," *Foreign Affairs* (2011); see also M. Watkins, M. "Psychosocial Accompaniment," *Journal of Social and Political Psychology* 3, no. 1 (2015): 324–41.
11. N. Jones, B. K. Gius, M. Shields, S. Collings, C. Rosen, and M. Munson, "Investigating the Impact of Involuntary Psychiatric Hospitalization on Youth and Young Adult Trust and Help-Seeking in Pathways to Care," *Social Psychiatry and Psychiatric Epidemiology* 56, no. 11 (2021): 2017–27.
12. S. Gupta, John Cahill, and Rebecca Miller, *Deprescribing in Psychiatry* (Oxford: Oxford University Press, 2019).
13. "Harm Reduction Guide to Coming off Psychiatric Drugs," Fireweed Collective 2019, www.fireweedcollective.org/publication/harm-reduction-guide-to-coming-off-psychiatric-drugs/.
14. "The Withdrawal Project," Inner Compass, https://withdrawal.theinnercompass.org/.
15. A. Dilts, "Incurable Blackness: Criminal Disenfranchisement, Mental Disability, and the White Citizen," *Disability Studies Quarterly* 32, no. 3 (2012); S. Meerai, I. Abdillahi, and J. Poole, "An Introduction to anti-Black Sanism," *Intersectionalities: A Global Journal of Social Work Analysis, Research, Polity, and Practice* 5, no. 3 (2016): 18–35; J. M. Metzl, and K. T. MacLeish, "Mental Illness, Mass Shootings, and the Politics of American Firearms," *American Journal of Public Health* 105, no. 2 (2015): 240–9; J. M. Metzl, "Structural Health and the Politics of African American Masculinity," *American Journal of Men's Health* 7, no. 4 supplement (2013): 68S–72S; J. M. Metzl, "The Protest Psychosis: How Schizophrenia Became a Black Disease" (Beacon Press, 2010); Z. Stuckey, "Race, Apology, and Public Memory at Maryland's Hospital for the 'Negro' Insane," *Disability Studies Quarterly* 37, no. 1 (2017).
16. Martin Luther King Jr., *Letter from Birmingham Jail*, London: Penguin Classics (2018).

Index

Page numbers in italics refer to images.

2020 uprisings, 1–2, 21, 85–86, 92
Abbott, Greg, 111
abolition. *See also* prison-industrial complex
   Boycott, Divestment, Sanctions (BDS) movement as, 190–91
   commodification of, 139
   dismantle-change-build framework for, 40
   and history of social work, 65–66, 69, 73–74
   imagination and, 46, 52, 62, 63–64, 84–85, 90
   Liberatory Harm Reduction and, 146, 152–56
   paid work and, 130–32
   as practice, 89, 134–35
   as presence, 92
   vs. racial capitalism, 103, 105, 106
   as repairing harm, 55
   of social work, 80, 83, 85, 86, 89–91
   social workers opposed to, 126
   and the state, 93–94, 102–3, 106
   truth telling central to, 52–53
   as universally applicable, 162–63
abolition democracy, 103
abolition feminism, 7, 16
"abolitionist horizon," 134, 135–39
abolitionist organizations, 31–32, 93, 128, 168
abolitionist social work, 3–4, 23
   accountability of, 30
   boundaries for, 155–56
   CHAAAF on, 75–76
   changing roles in, 60
   cognitive dissonance in, 59–61
   as community-centered, 61–62, 93–94, 101, 105, 149–50
   emergence of, 2–3, 6, 21–22
   inviting others into, 135
   and Liberatory Harm Reduction, 152–57
   as practice vs. identity, 29, 134–35, 139
   practicing, 27–31, 51
   principles of, 23–27, 103, 136–39, 178–79, 182–83, 198–200
   as relational, 40, 88
   transparency in, 48, 55, 56, 58–59
abolitionist state, welfare in, 104–5
abolition of slavery, 16, 36
abortion, privacy framing of, 14–15
Abramovitz, Mimi, 100
abuse. *See also* child welfare system; survivors
   in abolitionist future, 105
   and loss of narrative control, 200
   of survivors, 27, 37, 151
academia, hierarchies of, 60
accountability
   to community, 56, 57–58, 61–62, 64, 139
   for harm, 41
   transformative justice and, 148
activists, x, 11–13, 17–18, 60–61
   antipolicing, 92–93
   assassination of, 17
   disabled, 211
   harm reduction promoted by, 143–44, 147, 152, 154
   housing rights, 124–25
   individual vs. collective, 131–32
   pro-Palestine, 190–91
   transformative justice and, 149–50
Adalah Justice Project, 31

Adams, Eric, 81
Addams, Jane, vii, viii, 33–35, 82, 162
Administration for Children's Services (ACS), 120, 121–23, 125
Adoption and Safe Families Act, 129
Afrocentrism, 69, 181
Alameda County, 174
anarchism, 106
Anderson, William, 103, 106
anger, validating, 204
anti-Blackness, 67–68, 96, 179
anti-capitalism, 25, 57
anti-carceral social work. *See* abolitionist social work
anti-colonialism, 75–76
   as anti-racism, 74
   boycotts and, 188, 192
   historical efforts in, 67–69
antipsychotics, 202
anti-racism, 75–76
   as anti-colonialism, 74
   anti-Semitism and, 18
   disability and, 212
   historical efforts in, 66–67
   as systemic struggle, 151
antirape movement, 11–12
anti-Semitism, 18, 194–95
anti-violence movement, 7, 180
   carceral, 101, 150–51
   harm reduction and, 149, 152
   periodizing, 11
anti-Zionism, Jewish, 194
apartheid, 184, 185–88, 191–92
Archibald, Joanne, 50
authority vs. power, 47–48, 53, 54. *See also* power
Baker, Ella, 139
Bambara, Toni Cade, 135
Barghouti, Omar, 188–89
Barnett, Ferdinand Lee, x, xi
Bauman, Dianne, 50
Becker, Caitlin, 116, 126, 128
behavior, pathologizing, 26
Bell, Joyce, 133
Beltrán, Ramona, 49, 52–53, 56–57, 63
Bender, John, 87
Bennetch, Jennifer, 124–25
Berger, Dan, 191
Biden, Joe, 136

BIPOC women, 14–15. *See also* Black women
Birmingham Civil Rights Institute, 17
Black children, 110–11, 112, 113, 116–17, 118–19
Black community
   double regulation and, 100
   institutional racism and, 72, 73, 167
   mutual aid in, x
   self-determination of, 73
Black families
   child welfare system harming, 110–11, 112, 113, 116–18
   white women's power over, 162
Black feminists, 7, 42, 158, 169
Black liberation work, 21, 76
Black Lives Matter, 13, 21
Black men
   lynching of, vii–viii, 11, 12, 33–34
   Negro Fellowship League supporting, x–xi
   stigmatization of, 212
Blackness, criminalization of, vii, 22, 33–34, 44, 116–17, 137–38
Black Panthers, 147
Black queer feminism, 158, 168–70
Black women
   child welfare system and, 116–18, 122, 199
   devaluing of, 16
   sexual violence against, 10, 11
   transgender, 14
   white solidarity with, 12, 13
   work available to, 10
Black Women's Club movement, 34
bodies
   Black, policing of, 119
   and bodily autonomy, 154
   honoring, 156
   searching, 36–37, 127, 145
Boeing, 191–92
Boggs, Grace Lee, 136, 171
Bonsanquet, Helen, 80
both/and thinking, 181
Bourdieu, Pierre, 102
Boycott, Divestment, Sanctions (BDS) movement, 188–90
   as abolitionist praxis, xii, 190–95
   as anti-Semitic, 194–95
   demands of, 189–90

INDEX

and divesting from carceral state, 191–92
imagination of, 191, 192–94
limitations of, 195
origins of, 192
and reliance on civil society, 191, 192
Braden, Anne, 12
Brown, Danica, 49, 51–52, 53, 56, 59–60
Bureau of Indian Affairs, 60–61
Burke, Tarana, 13
BYP100, 158, 161, 167–68, 169
Campbell, "Chicken" Joe, x–xi
capitalism
  and carceral systems, 93
  and necrocapitalism, 185
  nonprofit-industrial complex and, 166
  poverty caused by, 95, 98
  punishment and, 99–100
  racial, 25, 102–3, 136
  welfare benefiting, 93, 95–96, 99, 102–4, 107–8
carceral feminism, 15, 16, 101, 151–52
carceral social work, 22, 24, 59, 85–86
carceral systems, 26–27, 31. *See also* involuntary hospitalizations; mandatory reporting; prison industrial complex
  capitalism and, 93
  civil society vs., 192
  dismantling, 40–41
  disposability under, 61, 62
  divesting from, 191–92
  ending partnerships with, 29, 114
  imagining future beyond, 64
  of Israel, 184, 193
  practicums in, 114
  protest against, 92–93
  racism and, 96
  in shelters, viii, 36–37, 150–52
  social work education about, 113–14
  survivors in, 145–46, 150–51
  welfare state and, viii, 5, 96, 99–102, 103, 107
  working against, 28, 113, 114
  working inside and around, 28–30, 35, 101
care. *See also* support
  conditions on, 150–51, 208
  discipline and, 98
  mandatory reporting vs., 137

in nonwhite communities, 28, 61–62, 90–91
policing opposed to, ix
sex work and, 148
sharing resources as, 138
welfare state and, relationship between, 106–7
Caruthers, Charlene A., 158
caseworkers, 124, 125–26
Casey Foundation, 120–21
Center for Community Change, 160
Center for NuLeadership on Human Justice and Healing, 31
ceremonies, 56, 57–58
charity. *See* help
Charity Organization Society, 80, 83
Child Abuse Prevention and Treatment Act (CAPTA), 111
children
  gender-affirming care for, 111
  "residential therapeutic centers" for, viii, 119
  rights of, 117
  separated from families, 110–11, 120, 124
child welfare system, 2, 87, 212
  abolition of, 121, 128–29
  aging out of, 118
  anonymous reporting and, 124–25, 127
  Black children suffering under, 110–11, 112, 113, 116–17, 118–19
  Black mothers' experience of, 116–18, 122, 199
  caseworkers, 124, 125–26
  documented harms of, 118–19, 121
  justice system and, 123–24
  kidnapping children, 118, 122, 124
  legal defense in, 123, 128
  malicious use of, 124–25, 127
  people invested in, 120–25
  policy changes to, 126–29
  poverty and, 110, 118–19, 121
  as slavery, 117–18
  social control through, 109–10, 112, 119
Chunn, Jay, 133
cities, 159
Civil Rights Movement, 11, 12, 69, 70, 96
civil society, reliance on, 191, 192
climate change, 136
clinical skills, 163

Clinton, Bill, 96
Cloward, Richard, 99
Coffey, Wallace, 48
collective care, 4. *See also* community
colonialism
   BIPOC communities harmed by, 72, 73–74
   vs. coloniality, 25, 68
   and racism, as inextricable, 71–72, 73–76
   in social work, 65–66, 67–69, 74
   typologies of, 74–75
coloniality, 25, 65, 67–69
"Color in a White Society," 66–67
Combahee River Collective Statement, 169
Committee for Equal Justice, 12
communication, 42, 43, 163, 164–65, 199, 200
community
   carcerality opposed to, 64
   conflict in, 55, 61, 105
   group dynamics of, 164–65
   interventions, 155
   investment in, 128
   involuntary hospitalizations and, 205, 206
   life stages in, 56, 57–58
   love for, 62–63
   needs and wants of, 161
   roles in, 61–62
   sharing resources within, 138
   state's relation to, 88–89
   support within, 88–91, 146
   transformative justice and, 150, 173, 174, 175, 178
conflict, approaches to, 61
conscientization, 54
convict leasing, 44
corporate welfare, 99
Council on Social Work Education Multicultural Task Forces (MCTFs), 65, 70
   on abolition, 72–73
   Asian American, 71, 72–73
   Black, 72, 73
   on colonialism and racism, 69, 71–72
   historical critical analysis of, 70–71
   Native American, 71
   Puerto Rican, 72
counternarratives, 54–55
COVID-19, 134, 136
"crack babies," 111

Creative Interventions, 31, 148
crime, inequalities leading to, 197
criminalization. *See also* WWNCRJ girls' diversion program
   of Blackness, vii, 22, 33–34, 44, 116–17, 137–38
   as impediment to ending violence, 15
   of Indigeneity, 47, 64, 137–38
   interrupting, 173–75
   of Palestinians, 188, 191, 193
   vs. recriminalization, 137–38
   social workers on front line of, 164
   of survivors, 41–42, 145, 150–51, 153, 155, 156
crisis continuum, 206–8
crisis intervention, 42, 61, 207, 209. *See also* involuntary hospitalizations; mental health services
critical consciousness, 54
Critical Historical Antiracism, Anticolonialism, and Abolitionism Framework (CHAAAF), 65–66, 74–76
Critical Resistance, 26, 30, 40, 43, 93
cross-system coordination, 43
cultural belonging, 56–58
Curley, Andrew, 47
Daka, Walid, 187
Dannhouser, Jess, 121
Daoud, Sarah, 154
data collection, 43
Davis, Angela Y., 7, 10, 17, 87, 103, 148
Davis, Sallye Bell, 9–10, 12
decolonization, 25, 47, 64. *See also* Palestine
   and both/and thinking, 181
   story work and, 50
Deer, Ada, 60–61
"defund the police" movement, 1, 38
dehumanization, 181
DeRogatis, Jim, 16
deservedness, 59, 80–81, 82–83, 87
desire vs. damage-centered research, 63
"deviance," 1
diagnosis, 61, 163, 205
Diagnostic Statistical Manual (DSM), 61, 164
Dillon, Grace, 63–64
disability, 137, 211
disabled women, 13
discipline, mechanisms of, 2, 5

dismantle-change-build framework, 40
disposability, 61, 62
dissent, record of, 43–44
Dixon, Ejeris, 148
domestic violence. *See* gender-based violence
domestic violence shelters, 37, 150–52
double regulation, 100
Douglas, Wakumi, 32
"downtown resource officer" (DRO), 38
drug use, 145–48, 211
Du Bois, W. E. B., 16, 103
Dunbar, Annie Zean, 49, 55, 56, 60
economy, government of, 98
education, social work
    Caruthers on, 158–61, 170
    cities as locus of, 159–60
    communication in, 163
    on history of social work, 162
    macro-level, 159, 160–61, 170
    on nonprofit industrial systems, 139
    practicums, 114, 160, 161
    on racist carceral systems, 113–14, 134
Esping-Andersen, Gøsta, 95
ethics, 81, 109, 113–14, 115
everywoman, 13
families
    ending violence within, 8
    money helping, 126
    rights of, 122–25, 127
    "training," 119–20
family separation. *See* child welfare system
Farmer, Paul, 205
feminism
    abolition, 7, 16
    Black, 7, 42, 158, 169
    carceral, 15, 16, 101, 151–52
    white, 7, 151
Fernandez, Angela, 50, 55–56, 60–61, 62–63
Floyd, George, 1, 52, 86, 112
Fortier, Craig, 25
foster system, 9, 110, 117, 118–19, 121. *See also* child welfare system
Fourth Amendment, 122, 123–25
Franco, Marielle, 17
Freedom Community Center, 31
free market, 95–96, 100, 106
Freire, Paolo, 54
Fullwood, Catlin, 148

funding, xi, 29, 35, 39, 166, 177–78
futurisms and speculative fiction, 52, 63–64
Gali, Morning Star, 47
Garland, David, 97–98, 99–100, 101, 104–5, 107
gaslighting, 87
Gaza, 186, 189
gender-affirming care for children, 111–12
gender-based violence, 8, 13, 15, 16–17
gender binary, prisons reproducing, 14
Gender Lib (GL), 173, 174, 175
Gilboa Prison break, 193–94
Gilmore, Craig, 103, 106
Gilmore, Ruth Wilson, 26, 92, 130
    on the master's tools, 132, 133
    on prisons, 80, 190
    on the state, 103, 106
    on violence of capitalism, 25
Gone, Joseph, 205
Gortler, Shai, 187–88
Gorz, André, 40, 93, 197
gradualism, 36
Great Depression, 80, 95
Great Migration, x
Grier, Michelle, 84
Griffin-Gracy, Miss Major, 149
group work, 42
Güven, Leyla, 17
Hampton, Dream, 15–16
Hansen, Anne, 198
harm reduction, 143–44. *See also* Liberatory Harm Reduction
    and anti-violence work, 149, 152
    co-opted by public health, 144, 148, 152, 154–55, 156–57
    defining, 144–45
    and medication tapering, 209, 210
    in mental health services, 196, 197–98, 201–3, 210, 212–13
    naming structural violence in, 149
    origins of, 147–48
    sex workers central to, 148
Harrell, Sam, vii
Hart, Carl, 201
Hassan, Shira, ix
Hayes, Kelly, 137
healing, 55–56
    non-Anglo approaches to, 211
    prioritizing justice over, 205, 209

sobriety disconnected from, 146–47
help, 107
   deservedness as basis for, 82–83
   giving and receiving, 59
   vs. solidarity, 26
   vs. support, 86–89, 107
hierarchies
   in academia, 60
   vs. community, 58, 62
   of deservedness, 82–83
   racist, 13, 48, 68
   in social work, dismantling, 138
   subservience and, 83–84
Hill, Octavia, 80
homeless shelters, 36–37, 81
Hon-Sing Wong, Edward, 25
hope, 140, 191, 193–94, 195
housing, 81, 82, 124
imagination
   in BDS movement, 191, 192–93
   Indigenous, 63–64
   role of, in abolition, 46, 52, 62, 63–64, 84–85, 90
immigration, 16–17, 76
Incite!, 93, 148
Indigenist abolition, 46, 47, 48
Indigenous cultures
   imagination in, 63–64
   introductions in, 48, 57, 58
   justice in, 61, 62–63
   and restorative justice language, 172
   social work's harm to, 68–69
   story work in, 50–51, 59, 64
   value systems of, 53
Indigenous futurism, 63–64
Indigenous land reclamation, 76
Indigenous sovereignty, 25, 48, 54, 60
informed consent, 127
institutions, life-affirming, 26, 40
institutions of social work, 26, 81, 107–8, 138–39. *See also* child welfare system; welfare state
   access to, 25
   attachment to, 80
   carceral, ix–x, 28–29, 85–86, 87, 100–101
   coloniality of, 60, 64, 68–69
   replacing, 51–52, 85, 90–91
intergenerational wisdom, 52

International Federation of Social Workers, 195
Interrupting Criminalization, 27, 30, 31
intersectionality, 24, 46, 55
introductions, 48, 57, 58, 171–72
involuntary hospitalizations, 155, 196, 213
   accompaniment during, 205–6, 207
   alternatives to, 196
   community ties and, 205, 206
   and holistic discharge planning, 208–9
   orientation to, 197–98
   police and, 206–8
   and postvention debriefing, xi–xii, 209–10
Israel. *See also* Boycott, Divestment, Sanctions (BDS) movement; Palestine
   carcerality of, 186–88
   Nation-State Law of, 186, 194
   occupation by, 17, 184, 186, 189, 191–92, 193
   silence concerning, 185
Jacobs, Leah, xi–xii, 24
James, Kirk "Jae," 24, 30
Jefferson City, 160
Jewish anti-Zionism, 194
Jim Crow, x, 44
JMACforFamilies, 32, 128
Johnson, Lyndon B., 96
Jones, Nev, xi–xii
justice. *See* social justice
Justice Committee, 31
Kaba, Mariame, 26, 45, 130, 148, 197
   on abolition and stateness, 102–3
   on accountability, 139
   on defunding police, 93
   on hope, 193
   on imagination, 192–93
   Interrupting Criminalization co-founded by, 31
   on questioning, 133
Kelly, R., 15–16
Kim, Mimi E., viii, 22, 24, 31, 148
King, Martin Luther, 12, 212
Kirkland, Jack, 159, 163
Kovach, Margaret, 50
Koyama, Emi, 151, 152, *153*
Kurdish women's movement, 17
Law, Victoria, 36
Law for Black Lives, 128
legitimization of social work, 5

INDEX

"lethality," 197
liability laws, 25, 37, 154, 155, 156
liberalism, free-market, 95–96
liberation, 26–27
   abolition as, 70–71, 72–73, 74, 135
   as collective struggle, 132
   framed as futile, 131
   hope for, 140
   paid work vs., 131–32, 138–39
   realism as enemy of, 90
   social work's potential for, 166–67
Liberatory Harm Reduction, 144–45. *See also* harm reduction
   defining, 146–47
   as nonbinary, 150
   principles of, 152, 153
   vs. public health harm reduction, 144, 148, 152, 154–55, 156–57
   recommendations for practicing, 155–56
   as resilience strategy, 156–57
   sex workers central to, 148
   tensions in practice of, 152–55
   and transformative justice, 148–52
lobbying, 166–67, 168
Lorde, Audre, 132
Lumsden, Stephanie, 48
lynching, vii–viii, 11, 12, 33–34
macro-level work, 159, 160–61, 170
mad justice, 197, 198–99, 211
"mandated support," 2
mandatory reporting, 110, 111–12, 155
   abolishing, 127–28, 136–37
   strategies for changing, 164
   transparency about, 199, 201
mass incarceration, 22, 100, 151
Mbembe, Achille, 185
McClain, Angelo, 112
McMillan, Joyce, viii, 2, 32
   on Dorothy Roberts, 116, 117
   personal experiences of, 117, 118, 121, 122
   on training to police families, 119–20
means testing, 95, 98
Meari, Lean, 193
medication, 154, 203, 208–9, 210
mental health services. *See also* crisis continuum; involuntary hospitalizations
   and accepting clients' meaning, 203–4
   and accompaniment in times of crisis, 205–6, 207
   acknowledging structural violence in, 204–5, 209
   adherence and abstinence thinking in, 201–3
   building relationships in, 202–3
   coercion and carcerality in, 200, 201, 203, 206–8, 210, 211–13
   education in, 202–3
   ethical, principles of, 198–200
   harm reduction in, 196, 197–98, 201–3, 210, 212–13
   and holistic discharge planning, 208–9
   medications in, 202, 209
   and postvention debriefing, 209–10
   transparency about, 198–99, 200–201
   violence in, 203–4, 209–10
middle class, 93, 98–99
Mi Gente, 27
Miller, Henry, 68
modeling, 55–56, 57, 58
Movement for Family Power, 32
movements, periodizing, 11
multi-issue struggle, 42
mutual aid, ix, 6, 28, 52, 106–7
the Nakba, 188
naming ceremonies, 57–58
National Association for the Advancement of Colored People (NAACP), 11–12
National Association of Black Social Workers, 69, 133
National Association of Colored Women (NACW), 44
National Association of Community & Restorative Justice, 172
National Association of Social Work (NASW)
   2020 uprisings and, 85–86, 112
   anti-racist efforts in, 66–67
   Code of Ethics of, 66, 81, 109, 115
   on coloniality, 68–69
   critique of, 2–3
   liberation from, 115
   "social justice" in, 5, 66, 81, 109, 115
   on social worker bias, 113
National Harm Reduction Coalition, 152
National Organization for Women (NOW), 11
national organizing, 160
necrocapitalism, 185
necropolitics, 185, 186

needs assessment, 43
Negro Fellowship League (NFL), vii, x–xi
neoliberalism, 38, 96, 99, 100–102
networking, 160
Network to Advance Abolitionist Social Work (NAASW), 2–3, 21–22, 23, 116
neurodiversity, 211
New York, child welfare system in, 118, 120, 122–23, 127
New York City, 81
nonprofit industrial complex, ix, 139, 154–55, 166–67
objectification, 47
Öcalan, Abdullah, 17
Odeh, Rasmea, 17
Office of Children and Family Services (OCFS), 122–23
Ohlone people, 7–8
paid work, limitations of, 130–32
Palestine. *See also* Boycott, Divestment, Sanctions (BDS) movement
  history of violence against, 184, 186
  ignorance about, 185
  occupation of, 17, 184, 186, 189, 191–92, 193
  right to return to, 190
  "security barrier" against, 186–87, 188
Palestinian Authority, 193
Palestinians
  criminalization of, 188
  as existential threat to Israel, 193
  hope of, 193–94
  killed by Boeing weapons, 191–92
  learning from, 190–91
  nonviolent resistance of, 193
  solidarity with, xii, 6, 17–18, 190, 195
  as stateless, 192
paradoxes of abolition and social work, 5
parental registries, 120
Parks, Rosa, 11–12
paternalism, 87, 200, 201, 211, 212
pathologizing behavior, 26
Philadelphia, family policing in, 124–25
Piepzna-Samarasinha, Leah Lakshmi, 148
Piven, Frances Fox, 99
police
  abolishing, ix, 52
  in child welfare system, 123–24
  defunding, 1, 38
  DROs, 38
  increased funding for, 136
  mandatory reporting and, 164
  in mental health services, 206–8
  obsolescence of, 93, 168
  vs. policing, ix
  social workers aiding, viii–x, 1–3, 85–86, 112–13, 122–25
police violence, 38, 52, 134, 150, 165
  as aberration, 86
  organizations fighting, 22, 31
  protests against, 1, 2, 21, 85, 92
  social work complicit in, 1, 85–86, 112–13
  in St. Louis, 159
policing the family. *See* child welfare system
policy, 43, 154, 166–67, 168
political organizing, 159–60, 166–67
poor people, 99, 167–68
poor relief, 94
possibilities of abolition and social work, 4
possibility of freedom, 35, 40, 44
poverty
  abolition of, 94
  abortion access and, 14–15
  capitalist development causing, 95, 98
  child welfare system and, 110, 118–19, 121
  permanence of, 83
  pimping, 118–19
  structural origins of, 82, 119, 207
power
  vs. authority, 47–48, 53, 54
  building, 31, 154
  discerning, 181
  story work and, 50
power dynamics, 84
praxis of abolition and social work, 5–6, 30–31
prefigurative politics, 105–7, 132
presencing of abolition, 92
principles of abolitionist social work, 23–31
prisoners
  Negro Fellowship League supporting, x–xi
  reentry programs for, 37–38
  transgender, 14
  urgent need of, 198
prisonfare, 100
prison industrial complex, 4, 80

abolitionist reform of, 16, 28, 35, 39–43, 130
  growth of, 37–39, 96, 100–101, 102, 136, 137
  power and size of, 36–38
  "reforming," 35
  signs of collaboration with, 39
  "prison nation," 36
prisons
  children in, viii, 119
  as gendering apparatuses, 14
  as ideological apparatuses, 15
  order ensured by, 87
  as relational, 190
  slavery and, 44
privacy, right to, 14–15
private practice, 197
private property, 95
privatization of resources, 81, 82
problems
  changing approaches to, 41
  individuals seen as, 15, 26, 80, 86–87, 107, 120, 136–38
  state's definition of, 40
  systems as, 26, 31, 137–38, 149–50
Progressive Era, 162, 195
Project Nia, 30
protests against police violence, 1, 2, 21, 85, 92
public health, 144, 148, 152, 154–55, 156–57
publicly funded social services, 98, 104–5
punishment
  framed as help, 59
  repudiation of, 27, 64
queer liberation, 158, 168–69
racial capitalism, 25, 102–3, 136
racial zoning laws, 10
racism. *See also* child welfare system
  and colonialism, as inextricable, 71–72, 73–76
  education about, 113–14
  in mental health services, 201
  naming, 66
  in social work, 65, 66–67
  in welfare, 96, 98, 102
  Zionist, 185, 189–90
racist hierarchies, 13, 48
racist violence, vii–viii, 10, 11, 12, 33–34
Rasmussen, Cameron W., viii, 24, 27, 30

Reagan, Ronald, 96
red flag laws, 199, 201
reductionism, 211
reform, 39–43, 84–85, 93, 154, 191, 197
rehabilitation, 100
Reichert, Irving F., 194
reparations, 56
restorative justice, 27. *See also* WWNCRJ girls' diversion program
  colonization and, 172–73
  contradictions in, 172, 180
  embodying, 182–83
  flexibility in, 180–81
  humanity of everyone in, 181–82
  terminology of, 171–72
Restorative Justice Project, 174
Richie, Beth, 13, 14, 22, 36
rights, 82
  of children, 117
  as "earned," 83
  of families, 122–25, 127
  Fourth Amendment, 122, 123–25
  involuntary hospitalization and, 209
  of Palestinians, 187–88, 189–90, 191, 196
risk, 145–46, 154
risk reduction, 144
Ritchie, Andrea, viii, ix, 31, 102–3
Roberts, Dorothy, viii, 2
  on abolition, 118, 119
  on Black family separation, 116–17
  on residential therapeutic centers, 119
Roelsgaard, Natascha Toft, 43–44
Roe v. Wade, 14
Sand Creek Massacre, 52
Schenwar, Maya, 36
Schultz, Katie, 49, 52, 53, 56, 57–58, 60, 63
Scottsboro Nine, 11
Seale, Bobby, 140
segregation, 9
self-deception, 135–36
self-determination, 26–27, 63, 154
  of Black communities, 73
  Indigenous, 48, 54
  justice and, 205
self-injury, 145, 154, 201
self-transformation, 136
services. *See* child welfare system; welfare state
settlement houses, 5, 82, 87

settler colonialism, 4, 67–69, 74–75, 130.
    See also colonialism; coloniality
  vs. community, 58
  continuation of, 7–8, 54
  deservedness and, 59
  values of, 53
  Zionist, 184, 185, 188–89, 191, 193, 195
settler-enslaver epistemologies, 47
sexual violence
  Black feminist responses to, 7
  in Black women's workplaces, 10
  against disabled women, 13
  police, 150
  in Southern Black Freedom Movement, 11
  against trans women, 13–14
  women blamed for, 11
sex workers, 144, 145, 147–48, 149, 152, 156
shame, 156, 204, 208
Shoemaker, Nancy, 74
Shuttlesworth, Fred, 17
Siraj, Matin Shahawar, 40–41
slavery, 16, 36, 44, 118
Smith, Frank, 149
sobriety, 146–47
social insurance, 97, 104, 106
socialism, 94, 106
social justice, 17, 195, 205, 209, 212
  as draw to social work, 159
  inadequate definitions of, 2, 5, 101
  social work opposed to, 81–82, 109
  and solidarity with Palestine, 184, 185, 190
social reproduction, 100
social services, publicly funded, 98, 104–5
social work. *See also* abolitionist social work; child welfare system
  abolition of, 80, 83, 85, 86, 89–91
  vs. care work, 90–91
  coloniality of, 65–66, 67–69, 74
  as damage-centered, 63, 81–82, 83–84
  degrees, burning, 79–80
  deprofessionalization of, 25
  domination reinforced by, 5, 21–22
  funding for, xi, 29, 35, 39, 166, 177–78
  history of, 65–66, 73–74, 80, 82
  language of, 53, 211–12
  liberatory potential of, 166–67
  and the master's tools, 132–34

  power dynamics of, 84
  public perception of, 81–82
  questioning, 133–34
  racism in, 65, 66–67
  as "solution" to policing, 21, 22
  transforming, 24, 133–34
social workers
  bias of, 113
  as gatekeepers, 38, 86, 91
  harm to families caused by, 126
  limits of paid work of, 130–32
  personal histories of, 56
  police aided by, viii–x, 1–3, 85–86, 112–13, 122–25
  record of dissent of, 43–44
  skills of, 42–43
  as state agents, xii, 29, 39, 51, 53, 135, 137
Social Workers Against Criminalization (SWAC), 22
Society for Social Work and Research (SSWR), 7
"soft policing," viii–x, 1–2, 21, 22
  defining, viii
  policing made more palatable by, ix, xii, 85–86, 211–12
  social workers protesting, 2–3
solidarity
  accompaniment as, 205
  with Black women, 12, 13
  vs. charity, 26
  with Palestinians, xii, 6, 17–18, 190, 195
Solomon, Art, 64
S.O.U.L. Sisters Leadership Collective, 32
Spade, Dean, 26, 30, 103, 106
speculative fiction and futurisms, 52, 63–64
the state. *See also* carceral systems; state violence
  abolition and, 93–94, 102–3, 106
  alienation caused by, 46
  Black families subjugated by, 111
  communities' relationship to, 88–89
  dehumanization as tool of, 181
  equality before, 194–95
  funding social work, 29, 35
  "hands" of, 102
  humanity of those representing, 181–82
  noncarceral, possibility of, 102–3
  restorative justice and, 172

social work's relationship to, 27–30, 35–39, 59–61, 155
working against, 28, 156
working around, 29–30
working inside, 28–29, 35, 155, 156
working outside of, 28
state violence, 1–2, 8, 28, 101, 103
confronting, 149
social work covering for, 38, 81, 90
white ignorance of, 44
stigmatization, 93, 95, 98
St. Louis, 159
structural inequalities, 5, 73, 89, 137
acknowledging, 204–5, 209
blaming people for, 120
charity maintaining, 26
structural violence, 15–16, 149, 155, 198–99, 204–5, 209
Students United for Palestinian Rights, 191
subservience, 83–84
success, divestment from, 40, 43–44
suicidal ideation, reporting, 164
sumud (steadfastness), 193–94
support, 2, 138–39, 178
accompaniment as, 205–6, 207
community, 88–91, 146
conservatives dismantling, 96
deservedness and, 59, 80–81, 82–83, 87
of families, 122, 127–28
groups, 117–18, 174
vs. help, 86–89, 107
in Liberatory Harm Reduction, 146
of prisoners, x–xi, 29–30, 40–42
surveillance, viii–ix, 39
anti-Muslim, 40–41
by DROs, 38
in mental health services, 208
at shelters, 36–37
Survived & Punished, 41, 42
Surviving R. Kelly, 15–16
survivors, 150–52
boundaries of, 155
in carceral systems, 145–46, 150–51
criminalization of, 41–42, 145, 150–51, 153, 155, 156
identities of, 151–52
and risk, 145–46
strategies of, 146–47, 153
systems. *See also* carceral systems
challenging thinking about, 163–64

critical consciousness of, 54
divesting from, 128
enmeshment in, 131
as problems, 26, 81, 115, 149, 163
working within, 36, 59, 113–15, 139, 171, 173–76, 204
talk story, 46–47, 51–53. *See also* Indigenous cultures
Taylor, Recy, 12
Terrell, Mary Church, 44
thrivance, 50, 55
Till, Emmett, 11
Title IV-E programs, 114
transformative justice, 3, 6, 27, 28
community role in, 150, 173, 174, 175, 178
defining, 149–50
harm reduction and, 143–44, 148–52
transparency, 48, 55, 56, 58–59
trans women
activism of, 7, 8, 147, 149
violence against, 13–14
trauma
diagnosis and, 164
family separation as, 110, 120
girls' experience of, 178
in group settings, 164–65
of involuntary hospitalization, 197–98, 200–201
and loss of narrative control, 200
mutual aid and, 144
risk and, 145–46
transparency about, 55, 56
trauma-centered practice, 145–46, 152, 155, 156
truth telling, 52–53, 54, 55
Tsosie, Rebecca, 48
Tuck, Eve, 63
Tutu, Desmond, 87
United Kingdom, 94
United States
borders of, 16–17
deservedness in, 83
genocide and displacement in, 52–53
history of, 162
Israel supported by, 188
private property in, 95
racial capitalism of, 25, 102–3, 136
racism of institutions of, 72, 167, 169
slavery and, 16, 36, 44

upEND Movement, 32
violence. *See also* gender-based violence; state violence
  in abolitionist future, 42, 61, 105
  accountability for, 41
  Blackness associated with, 34, 44
  criminalization of survivors of, 41–42, 145, 150–51, 155, 156
  debriefing about, 165
  ending, 8, 10, 15
  family, 8
  as individual problem, 15
  interconnectedness of forms of, 8
  in mental health services, 203–4, 209–10
  nonstate interventions in, 3, 148
  resisting, hope as, 195
  structural basis of, 15–16, 149, 155, 198–99, 204–5, 209
Wacquant, Loïc, 100
Wahab, Stéphanie, xii
Walia, Harsha, 35
Walmsley, Thomas, 12–13
War on Drugs, 145
Washington, DC, 160
"welfare," 95, 97–98
welfare state, viii–ix, 93, 107–8. *See also* child welfare system
  abolitionist approaches to, 104–5, 106–7
  beneficiaries of, 93, 98–99, 102, 107–8
  capitalism benefiting from, 93, 95–96, 99, 102–4, 107–8
  carceral nature of, viii, 5, 96, 99–102, 103, 107
  and care, relationship between, 106–7
  discipline of, 99–102
  free market and, 95–96, 100, 106
  functions of, 97–98, 101–2, 104
  history of, 94–96
  as non-emancipatory, 103
  privatization of, 99
Wells, Anthony, 125
Wells-Barnett, Ida B., vii–viii, x–xi, xii, 33–35, 44
"what we now call restorative justice" (WWNCRJ). *See* restorative justice; WWNCRJ girls' diversion program
white feminism, 7, 151
whiteness, 47, 48, 56–57, 58, 68
white social work, 133

white supremacy, lynching and, vii–viii, 11, 12, 33–34
white supremacy in social work, 1, 130
  and carceral solutions, 24, 136
  colonialism and, 67–69, 74
  professionalization and, 25, 132–34
white women
  crying over disagreements, 161
  everywoman racialized as, 13, 151
  lynching and, vii, 11, 12, 33–34
  power of, over Black children, 162
women's movement, 12
Women with a Vision, 148
Woolfolk, Odessa, 17
workfare, 100
workplaces, sexual violence in, 10
WWNCRJ girls' diversion program. *See also* restorative justice
  funding for, 177–78
  overview of, 173–75
  principles of, 178–79
  racially equitable access to, 179
  state's role in, 174–75, 176–78, 180–81
  tensions in, 175–80
  willingness to participate in, 179–80
Young Lords, 147
Young Women's Christian Association (YWCA), 9–10
Young Women's Empowerment Project, 149
Yun, Sonah, 160
Zehr, Howard, 182
Zionism, 184, 185–86, 188–89, 191, 193, 195

Contributor Biographies

Dr. Ramona Beltrán is Associate Professor of social work at the University of Denver. Academic Director. Producer. Dancer. Mother. An award-winning public intellectual with global initiatives in historical trauma and healing and storytelling methodologies that have been cited by researchers and practitioners alike. In her 20 years of professional experience, spanning the United States to New Zealand, she has worked alongside institutions and Indigenous and Latinx communities, spotlighting solutions that are present in our creative and cultural-driven modalities. Her contributions have been invited by distinguished institutions including the Centers for Disease Control and Prevention and Harvard University as well as prominent cultural institutions including the Denver Art Museum, History Colorado, and the Latino Cultural Arts Center. Dr. Beltran is a fiercely loving mother of three and is a multiracial Chicana of Indigenous descent. She acknowledges that all the earth has an Indigenous name, and a community meant to steward it.

Dr. Autumn Asher BlackDeer is a queer anti-colonial scholar-activist from the Southern Cheyenne Nation and serves as an assistant professor in the Graduate School of Social Work at the University of Denver. Her scholarship illuminates the impact of structural violence on American Indian and Alaska Native communities. Dr. BlackDeer centers Indigenous voices throughout her research by using quantitative approaches and big data as tools for responsible storytelling. Dr. BlackDeer is a racial equity scholar with an emphasis on Indigenous tribal sovereignty and is deeply committed to furthering anti-colonial abolitionist work.

Danica Love Brown, MSW, CACIII, PhD, is a citizen of the Choctaw Nation of Oklahoma born and raised in Northern New Mexico. Danica is the Behavioral Health Director at the Northwest Portland Area Indian Health Board and has worked as a mental health and substance use counselor, social worker, and youth advocate for over 20 years. Danica is an Indigenous Wellness Research Institute ISMART fellow alumni, Council of Social Work Education, Minority Fellowship Program fellow alumni, and Northwest Native American Research Center for Health fellow alumni. Her research has focused on Indigenous Ways of Knowing and decolonizing methodologies to address historical trauma and health disparities in Tribal communities.

Charlene A. Carruthers (she/her) is a writer, filmmaker, community organizer, and Black Studies PhD candidate at Northwestern University. A practitioner of telling more complete stories, her work interrogates historical conjunctures of Black freedom-making post-emancipation and decolonial revolution, Black governance, and Black feminist abolitionist geographies. Her work spans more than 15 years of community organizing across racial, gender and economic justice movements. Charlene wrote and directed *The Funnel*, a short film, which received the Queer Black Voices Award at the 35th Annual aGLIFF Prism Film Festival. She received a Master of Social Work from the Brown School at Washington University in St. Louis. Charlene is author of *Unapologetic: A Black, Queer and Feminist Mandate for Radical Movements* (Beacon Press, 2018).

Angela Y. Davis is a political activist, scholar, author, and speaker. She is an outspoken advocate for the oppressed and exploited, writing on Black liberation, prison abolition, the intersections of race, gender, and class, and international solidarity with Palestine. She is the author of several books, including *Freedom is a Constant Struggle*, *Women, Race, and Class*, and *Are Prisons Obsolete?* She is the subject of the acclaimed documentary *Free Angela and All Political Prisoners* and is Distinguished Professor Emerita at the University of California, Santa Cruz.

Alan Dettlaff is a professor at the University of Houston Graduate College of Social Work, where he also served as Dean from 2015 to 2022. Alan began his career as a social worker in the family policing system, where he worked as an investigative caseworker and administrator. Today his work focuses on ending the harm that results from this system. In 2020, he helped to create and launch the upEND movement, a collaborative effort dedicated to abolishing the family policing system and building alternatives that focus on healing and liberation. Alan is author of *Confronting the Racist Legacy of the American Child Welfare System: The Case for Abolition*, published by Oxford University Press in 2023. He is also co-founding editor of *Abolitionist Perspectives in Social Work*, a peer-reviewed scholarly journal dedicated to developing and disseminating an abolitionist praxis in social work.

Tanisha "Wakumi" Douglas is a creator, mother, survivor, social justice leader, curator, ritualist and iyanifa. Her people are Jamaican with legacies of enslavement and maroonage. Her ancestors include spiritual seers, farmers, entrepreneurs, and herbalists. Wakumi is the daughter of a father who served 33 years in prison and a servant-leader, God-fearing mother. This fueled her 20-year dedication to organizing to end mass incarceration. She founded and raised over $8 million for a youth-led abolitionist non-profit. She is a 2020 Soros Justice fellow and a 2018 Move to End Violence fellow. She has worked as a circle keeper, social worker, organizer, trainer, and popular educator for many movement organizations. Wakumi attended Georgetown University and Columbia University, where she founded the first "Beyond the Bars" conference in 2010 as a student organizer. She is featured in *PUSHOUT: Criminalization of Black Girls in Schools*, *Huffington Post*, NPR and others. She is currently writing, curating healing and spiritual experiences for movements through The Givers Revival and living a joy-filled life.

Annie Zean Dunbar is a Liberian American junior scholar, writer, educator, and social worker. She is a doctoral candidate and adjunct instructor at the University of Denver Graduate School of Social Work. Zean's research and artistic practice foreground Black feminist traditions and epistemes to examine the interstitial experiences of displaced peoples in the United States. Her research interests include racialization and identity, organizational theory, mutual aid and community care, and long-term newcomer belonging in the US. Zean's creative writing centers conceptions of truth and omission, liminality, temporality, memory, and the effusive nature of healing.

Dr. Angela Fernandez/Kenyukīw (Eagle Woman) (she/her) is a member of the Awāēsāēh (Bear) clan and citizen of the Menominee Nation where she was born and raised. Her social work and public health roles have included clinical and community practice, academic teaching and research, and administration. She has worked in inpatient, outpatient, community, academic, non-profit, and government settings. Her interests lie at the intersections of Indigenous intergenerational and planetary health.

Kassandra Frederique is a social worker, organizer, and nonprofit executive. She believes in people and their ability to create their own change.

Claudette Grinnell-Davis is an assistant professor of social work in the American South who emphasizes in the classroom the necessity of being self-critical about one's practice in the classroom, emphasizing that the line between facilitating liberation and being an oppressor in systems practice is razor thin. When not thinking about how to make the classroom a place of healing while deconstructing colonizing learning patterns, Claudette likes to bring light to the world by making art out of broken glass.

Sam Harrell (they/them) is an assistant professor of Social Work at Seattle University, a doctoral candidate in Social Work and Social Research at Portland State University, the Editorial Assistant for Affilia: Feminist Inquiry in Social Work, and an Editorial Board member for Abolitionist Perspectives in Social Work. Sam has a BSW and MSW from Indiana University. They have worked in social welfare areas including child welfare, prison and jail re-entry, emergency shelters, LGBTQ+ youth services, violence prevention, and crisis intervention. Sam's current research explores the role of social workers as prison wardens and police officers in the Progressive Era United States.

Dr. Justin S. Harty is an Assistant Professor at Arizona State University's School of Social Work. Dr. Harty's research centers on the experiences of young Black fathers exiting foster care, father involvement in child welfare, and the historical aspects of father-related services in social work. His interdisciplinary approach aims to improve services for fathers and families of color in home visiting, child welfare, and foster care. Fundamental to Dr. Harty's social justice work is his commitment to dismantling racism and colonialism within the social work profession.

Dr. Harty mobilizes social change by using Black social work history to directly address white supremacy, racism, and colonialism while leveraging long-standing African traditions of self-help and mutual aid to help social workers and Black communities continue our resistance against oppression and inequality.

Shira Hassan has been working in her own community and speaking nationally on the sex trade, liberatory harm reduction, self-injury, healing justice and transformative justice for nearly thirty years. Currently working as a fellow at Interrupting Criminalization, Shira runs the Transformative Justice Help Desk. Along with Mariame Kaba, she is the coauthor of *Fumbling Towards Repair: A Workbook for Community Accountability Facilitators* and the author of *Saving Our Own Lives: A Liberatory Practice of Harm Reduction*.

Leah Jacobs is a critical social work scholar. She uses social science to understand social problems and their potential solutions. Her work rests on two premises; social welfare and public safety re inextricably connected, and a world without carceral social work or prisons is possible. She is faculty at the University of Pittsburgh School of Social Work.

Nev Jones is a critical activist-scholar and assistant professor in the School of Social Work at the University of Pittsburgh. Her work takes up meaning-centered, anti-carceral approaches to policy and practice within the public mental health system in the United States, with a strong focus on experiences and interventions associated with long-term psychiatric disability.

Mariame Kaba is an organizer, educator, librarian/archivist, and prison industrial complex (PIC) abolitionist who is active in movements for racial, gender, and transformative justice. Kaba co-leads Interrupting Criminalization, an organization she co-founded with Andrea Ritchie in 2018. She is the author of the *New York Times* Bestseller *We Do This 'Til We Free Us: Abolitionist Organizing and Transforming Justice* (Haymarket Books, 2021) & most recently *Let This Radicalize You: Organizing and the Revolution of Reciprocal Care* with Kelly Hayes (Haymarket, May 2023) among several other titles that offer support and tools for repair, transformation, and moving toward a future without incarceration and policing.

Mimi E. Kim is associate professor of social work at California State University, Long Beach, and founder of Creative Interventions. Kim continues her political work through promotion of transformative justice and abolitionist visions and practices of community care and safety.

Joyce McMillan is a thought leader, advocate, activist, community organizer, and educator. Her mission is to remove systemic barriers in communities of color by bringing awareness to the racial disparities in systems where people of color are disproportionately affected. Joyce believes the conversation about systemic oppression must happen on all levels consistently before meaningful change can occur. She completed a restorative certificate program at the New School and believes change will not happen independently of healing. Her goal is to abolish systems of harm while creating concrete community resources. Joyce led child welfare family engagement and advocacy efforts at Sinergia Inc. Prior, she was the Program Director at Child Welfare Organizing Project (CWOP) where she created a community space, to educate the community about restorative practices to empower, affirm, transform, and heal communities of color that have been traumatized by systemic injustices.

Network to Advance Abolitionist Social Work (NAASW) is a national collective of abolitionist social work practitioners and activist scholars striving to amplify a practice of social work aimed at dismantling the prison industrial complex (PIC) and building the life-affirming horizon to which abolition aspires. NAASW's efforts include ongoing political education, research, and knowledge generation around carceral and abolitionist social work, development of an online hub of abolitionist social work resources, and broader organizing and advocacy efforts to integrate and center abolitionist ideas and practices into social work.

María Gandarilla Ocampo, MSW, is a social work doctoral candidate at the Brown School, Washington University in St. Louis. Her research centers on child maltreatment mandated reporting policies and community-based prevention efforts. María is specifically dedicated to exploring the implementation and effects of mandated reporting policies on children, families, and systems, which is the core of her dissertation. Currently, María employs mixed methods research to generate evidence and shape policy for universal and community-based prevention initiatives supporting children and families. María is strongly committed to fostering a society where Black and Brown families are liberated and flourishing.

Cameron W. Rasmussen is a social worker, educator, researcher, and facilitator and an associate director at the Center for Justice at Columbia University who lives with his partner and child in New York City.

Dorothy Roberts is a distinguished professor of Africana Studies, Law, and Sociology at the University of Pennsylvania and an internationally acclaimed reproductive justice scholar and activist. Her major works include the award-winning *Killing the Black Body: Race, Reproduction, and the Meaning of Liberty*; *Shattered Bonds: The Color of Child Welfare*; and *Torn Apart: How the Child Welfare System Destroys Black Families—and How Abolition Can Build a Safer World*, as well as more than 100 articles and essays. A member of the American Academy of Arts and Sciences, American Philosophical Society, and National Academy of Medicine, she is the recipient of the Bronx Defenders Ally in the Pursuit of Justice Award; Juvenile Law Center Leadership Prize; Abortion Liberation

Fund of PA Rosie Jimenez Award; New Voices for Reproductive Justice Voice of Vision Award; Society of Family Planning Lifetime Achievement Award; and American Psychiatric Association Solomon Carter Fuller Award.

Dr. Sophia Sarantakos is an educator, writer, and community organizer. They are a faculty member at the University of Denver Graduate School of Social Work, and their research, writing, and organizing are focused on how the workers and resources of professionalized social-change work can be coordinated in service to an abolitionist horizon. As part of their building work, Dr. Sarantakos co-created the Abolitionist Social Change Collective (ASCC), a virtual space for all paid and unpaid social-change workers to convene and strengthen their ability to engage in an abolitionist praxis. Prior to entering academia, Dr. Sarantakos was a social work practitioner for ten years.

Katie Schultz is an Assistant Professor of Social Work at the University of Michigan and a citizen of the Choctaw Nation of Oklahoma. Her research focuses primarily on responding to violence and associated outcomes and understanding community and cultural connectedness in American Indian and Alaska Native communities. Her current studies focus on the use of culturally honoring services among tribal advocacy programs; risk and protective factors related to involvement in criminal legal systems among a Native population; and investigating social networks and associations with substance use, violence, and suicide among American Indian adolescents.

Stéphanie Wahab PhD., MSW is a Professor at Portland State University's School of Social Work. She is a Palestinian-Québécoise, feminist, activist scholar. Her research and scholarship tend to occur at the intersections of individual and state sanctioned violence including but not limited to intimate partner violence, sex trades, systemic racism, militarization, and occupation. She is a member of the Palestinian Feminist Collective, and co-editor of *Feminisms in Social Work Research: Promise and Possibilities for Justice Based Knowledge*.

Durrell M. Washington Sr. is a social worker, educator, facilitator, and researcher from the Bronx, New York.

Printed in the USA
CPSIA information can be obtained
at www.ICGtesting.com
JSHW020528130624
64685JS00001B/2